Learning in Cultural Context
Family, Peers, and School

International and Cultural Psychology Series

Series Editor: **Anthony Marsella,** *University of Hawai`i, Honolulu, Hawai`i*

A continuation Order Plan is available for this series. A continuation order will bring delivery of each
new volume immediately upon publication. Volumes are billed only upon actual shipment. For further
information please contact the publisher.

Learning in Cultural Context
Family, Peers, and School

Ashley E. Maynard
University of Hawai`i, Honolulu, Hawai`i

Mary I. Martini
University of Hawai`i, Honolulu, Hawai`i

Kluwer Academic / Plenum Publishers
New York, Boston, Dordrecht, London, Moscow

Library of Congress Cataloging-in-Publication Data

Learning in cultural context : family, peers, and school / [edited by] Ashley E. Maynard,
   Mary I. Martini.
      p.   cm. — (International and cultural psychology series)
   Includes bibliographical references and index.
   ISBN 0-306-48683-0 (hardbound) — ISBN 0-306-48684-9 (e-book)
      1. Learning—Social aspects—Cross-cultural studies.   2. Learning, Psychology
   of—Cross-cultural studies.   I. Maynard, Ashley E.   II. Martini, Mary I.   III. Series.

LB1060.L3825 2005
370.15′23–dc22
                                                                    2004054840

ISBN 0-306-48683-0

© 2005 by Kluwer Academic/Plenum Publishers, New York
233 Spring Street, New York, New York 10013

http://www.kluweronline.com

10 9 8 7 6 5 4 3 2 1

A C.I.P. record for this book is available from the Library of Congress.

Permissions for books published in Europe: permissions@wkap.nl
Permissions for books published in the United States of America: permissions@wkap.com

Printed in the United States of America

Contributors

Lucinda P. Bernheimer, Department of Psychiatry, NPI Center for Culture and Health, University of California, Los Angeles, *USA*

Nina K. Buchanan, Education Department, University of Hawai`i Charter School Resource Center, University of Hawai`i at Hilo, 200 W. Kawili Street, Hilo, Hawai`i 96720-4091, *USA*, ninab@hawaii.edu

Jacquelin H. Carroll, University of Hawai`i and the Center for Research on Education, Diversity, and Excellence (CREDE), 1776 University Avenue, Honolulu, Hawai`i 96822, *USA*

Jennifer Coots, Department of Educational Psychology, Administration, & Counseling, California State University, Long Beach

Helen M. Davis, Dept. of Psychiatry and Biobehavioral Sciences, Neuropsychiatric Institute, Center for Culture and Health, University of California, Los Angeles, 760 Westwood, Plaza, Box 62, Los Angeles, California 90024-1759, USA, Hmdavis@ucla.edu

Barbara D. DeBaryshe, University of Hawai`i Center on the Family, 2515 Campus Road, Honolulu, Hawai`i, 96822 USA, debarysh@hawaii.edu

Iwalani Else, University of Hawai`i School of Medicine, 1356 Lusitana Street, UH Tower, 4th floor, Honolulu, Hawai`i 968813 USA, elsei@dop.hawaii.edu

Mary Gauvain, University of California at Riverside, Olmsted Hall 2319, University of California, Riverside, California 92521, USA Mary.Gauvain@ucr.edu

Patricia M. Greenfield, FPR-UCLA, Center for Culture, Brain, and Development, 1282A Franz Hall, 405 Hilgard Avenue, Los Angeles, California 90095 USA

Dana M. Gorecki, University of Hawai`i Center on the Family 2515 Campus Road, Honolulu, Hawai`i 96822, USA

Shawn Malia Kana'iaupuni, Kamehameha Schools, 567 S. King Street, Ste 400, Honolulu, Hawai`i 96813, USA, shkanaia@ksbe.edu

Mary I. Martini, *Department of Family and Consumer Science, 2515 Campus Road*, University of Hawai`i at Manoa, Honolulu, Hawai`i 96822, USA, mmartini@lava.net

Catherine Matheson, Department of Psychiatry, NPI Center for Culture and Health, University of California, Los Angeles

Ashley E. Maynard, Department of Psychology, University of Hawai`i, 2430 Campus Road, Gartley #110, Honolulu, Hawai`i 96822, amaynard@hawaii.edu

Laurie Schick, Department of Applied Linguistics & TESL, University of California, Los Angeles, Los Angeles, California 90095-1531, schick@humnet.ucla.edu

Thomas S. Weisner, Departments of Psychiatry (NPI Center for Culture and Health) & Anthropology, University of California, Los Angeles, Box 62, Los Angeles, CA 90024-1759, tweisner@ucla.edu

Tasha R. Wyatt, University of Hawai`i and the Center for Research on Education, Diversity, and Excellence (CREDE), 1776 University Avenue, Honolulu, Hawai`i 96822, USA

Lois A. Yamauchi, University of Hawai`i and the Center for Research on Education, Diversity, and Excellence (CREDE), 1776 University Avenue, Honolulu, Hawai`i 96822, USA Yamauchi@hawaii.edu

Contents

III. APPROACHES TO SUPPORTING LEARNING IN
MIDDLE- AND HIGH-SCHOOL SETTINGS

Introduction: Cultural Learning in Context

Ashley E. Maynard

This book is the product of a series of workshops, focused on sociocultural theory and its applications to learning, funded by the National Science Foundation, and organized by Ashley Maynard and Mary Martini. The workshops focused primarily on three related questions of shared interest: What are the best conditions for learning? How can we use sociocultural theory to understand children's learning in context? How can we transfer what we know about learning in informal contexts to formal education? Related questions pertained to the learning opportunities afforded by cultural models and tools, families, peers, and schools. An additional interest was the ways that learning opportunities, particularly those in school settings, could be increased or enhanced by a better understanding of culture more generally, including cultural practices. This book attempts to answer these questions from a variety of perspectives, including psychology, anthropology, linguistics, and education. We use a multi-method approach to consider what happens in the child's environment to make cultural learning possible (Maynard, 2002; Tomasello, Kruger, & Ratner, 1993; Kruger & Tomasello, 1996).

LEARNING IN CONTEXTS

This volume explores the ways that teaching and learning are central to the capacity to transmit culture. The chapters are informed by sociocultural

1

theory, stemming from Vygotsky (1978), which emphasizes the role of social interaction, cultural tools, and history in children's development. The chapters are based on the premise that learning is a cultural process that happens through participation in cultural activities (Rogoff, 1990, 2003). Children rely on information, in the form of both nonverbal actions and the direct provision of information, from various people, such as parents, siblings, teachers, and peers, and other sources in order to participate in activities (Valsiner, 1989).

The following chapters focus on physical, social, and linguistic contexts of learning. Physical and social contexts include family interactions at home and interactions with peers and teachers at school. The linguistic context is directly examined in Laurie Schick's chapter on the socialization of morality in adolescent dance classes.

All the chapters review or report research programs that center around some kind of learning, most in a particular context. Furthermore, the authors take seriously the notion that contexts are influenced by cultural goals and models for behavior, and that there may be interrelationships among the learning contexts in which people find themselves.

Framing the Study of Learning in Context

The authors of the chapters in this volume have benefited from more than 30 years of research on culture and cognitive development, which has become more focused on an understanding of the surrounding, interpersonal contexts that support cognitive growth (Butterworth, 1993). Beginning with a pioneering book, *The Cultural Context of Learning and Thinking*, Cole, Gay, Glick, and Sharp (1971) expressed the importance of understanding children's development within cultural context. Cole and colleagues aimed to improve the education of Kpelle children in Liberia, where their studies were conducted, by exploring the cognitive abilities that children brought with them to school. The premise was that people would be good at doing activities, including using particular modes of thought, that they found important and which they had the opportunity to practice often. In the first chapter, Mary Gauvain reviews the everyday contexts of children's learning, noting also the centrality of informal contexts in children's lives and the important learning that happens in seemingly mundane interactions.

Two other paradigms have emerged from the notion that context is important for learning: socially distributed cognition and situated learning. These paradigms center around the notion that cognition exists not only in the minds of individuals but in the contexts of activities, the tools used, and *among* the participants of activities (Hutchins, 1993; Vygotsky, 1978). Research on socially distributed cognition (e.g., Resnick, Levine, & Teasley, 1991) attempts to study the *"division of cognitive labor"* (Hutchins, 1991, p. 284, his emphasis) in adult activities. The study of the division of cognitive labor is concerned with what part each person plays in the conduct of an activity. How do people use what they know to do a group task when they may not all have the same information? Though there has been much research into the ways that cognition is socially distributed in adult interactions, very few studies have examined the socially distributed nature of cognition in childhood.

Socially Distributed Cognition and Situated Learning in Children's Development

Learning does not occur in a social vacuum. Development happens through children's participation in activity settings. Socially distributed cognition appears in children's group activities; each child plays a part in furthering the goal of the activity, according to her developmental competence level and social status. According to Rogoff, research has told us little about the nature of socially distributed cognition in children's peer interactions. Notable examples of the study of children's coordinated action include Goodwin's (1990) ethnography of children's talk embedded in activities in a neighborhood in Philadelphia and Corsaro's (1985) study of preschool culture in Italy. In this volume, Helen Davis shows how preschool children in Costa Rica gain social knowledge about participation in peer activities directly through those interactions, and through the teacher's management of the classroom setting. She shows how the children's initiation into the culture of play is similar to adults' initiation into new communities of practice by situated learning.

Children learn in their daily activities how to negotiate their social worlds (Corsaro, 1985; Goodwin, 1990). Parents, teachers, peers, and child-caregivers shape this learning. One way they do this is by socializing their attention. Socializing attention is a process by which both adult- and child-caregivers, peers, and teachers point out culturally relevant topics for the child to focus on (Zukow, 1989; Zukow-Goldring & Ferko, 1994). Caregivers of young children do a lot of this by their speech and their nonverbal gestures such as orienting children to objects. The chapter by Kana`iaupuni and Else describes the way that attention to the child's Hawaiian name creates a learning situation for culture and for verbal interaction as well. The authors show how mundane events provide a "basic, recurrent grounding for the socialization of cultural meanings" (Schieffelin & Ochs, 1996, p. 256).

The Role of Language

Language is a powerful tool in the socialization of children. Through linguistic interactions in social contexts children acquire their culture's values, rules, and roles (Ochs, 1986; Schieffelin, 1990; Triandis, 1994). Parents, teachers, and other socializing agents express to children linguistic information (which is also cultural information) to indicate the appropriate behavior expected of the child (Ochs, 1982). In this volume, Laurie Schick describes the way that a teacher of adolescent dance classes uses that activity setting to socialize moral behavior.

As another example of the impact of language use in interaction, parents who use imperatives in communicating with their children socialize the development of comprehension and obedience (Greenfield, Brazelton, & Childs, 1989; LeVine, Dixon, LeVine, Richman, Leiderman, Keefer, & Brazelton, 1994). On the other hand, parents who use interrogatives in communicating with their children socialize the development of self-expression and inquisitiveness (LeVine et al, 1994; Greenfield & Suzuki, 1998). Maynard and Greenfield's chapter on the Zinacantec Maya cultural model of teaching and learning illustrates the emphasis placed on obedience in the everyday cultural contexts of learning to weave, making tortillas, and carrying firewood.

FAMILY LEARNING AND FAMILY LINKS TO SCHOOL LEARNING

The family context is taken to be the first learning context for children. Parents and siblings may provide examples and opportunities for the engagement in linguistic settings, cultural activities, and cultural models. At times, there may be implicit or explicit guidance in the performance of activities, and children may take initiatives themselves in participating in the family activities (Rogoff, 1990; Rogoff, Paradise, Mejía Arauz, Correa-Chavez, & Angelillo, 2003). The chapter by Weisner and colleagues makes the family the center of nested levels of contexts that impact child development, and they focus on family adaptation as a learning process itself. They use an ethnographic interview to uncover the variables involved in learning at the family level. Their approach fits squarely in the sociocultural paradigm in that it provides a way to think about child and family outcomes that are missed by the typical individualistic, non-contextualized assessments.

Likewise, the typical assessments used to gauge children's learning may not always be the most informative indicators, particularly across sociocultural contexts. Kana`iaupuni and Else show that, for Hawaiian children, the family context of interaction that results in the child's knowing his or her Hawaiian name is the best indicator of successful gains in knowledge in preschool. The importance of the link between home and school characterizes their sociocultural approach.

Home and school connections are the focus of much recent research on learning and development. In this volume, DeBaryshe and Gorecki report their method and findings in a preschool intervention aimed at creating and strengthening the partnership between parents and teachers. By engaging the parents in the intervention, they were able to produce significant gains in the children's performance and to increase consumer satisfaction among the parents.

INSTITUTIONAL CONTEXTS OF ADOLESCENT LEARNING: LEARNING ACROSS BOUNDARIES

One of the goals of the volume is to make the link from everyday contexts of learning to gain insights about what might improve school learning. Several chapters are focused on later learning, in adolescence. Links between everyday learning and improvements in the school context are the central focus of the chapter by Yamauchi, Wyatt-Beck, and Carroll and the chapter by Buchanan. Their research emphasizes the effective re-culturing of schools to enhance learning.

PLAN OF THE BOOK

The book begins with a focus on everyday contexts of learning and transitions to more institutional contexts in a developmental manner. Section I focuses on learning in informal, everyday contexts. Section II reports work on culturally-motivated approaches to supporting children's early learning. Section III reports research programs that center around learning in middle- and high-school contexts. Each section is preceded by a brief introduction to each of the chapters that comprise it.

REFERENCES

Butterworth, G. (1993). Models of cognitive growth. In: P. Light and G. Butterworth (eds.), *Context and cognition: Ways of learning and knowing*, Lawrence Erlbaum Associates, Hillsdale, NJ, pp. 1–13.

Cole, M., Gay, J., Glick, J. A., and Sharp, D. W. (1971). *The cultural context of learning and thinking*. Basic, New York.

Corsaro, W. A. (1985). *Friendship and peer culture in the early years*. Ablex Publishing Corporation, Norwood, NJ.

Goodwin, M. H. (1990). *He-Said-She-Said. Talk as social organization among black children*. Indiana University Press, Bloomington, IN.

Lave, J. (1991). Situating learning in communities of practice. In: Resnick, L. B., Levine, J. M., and Teasley, S. D. (eds.), *Perspectives on socially shared cognition*, American Psychological Association, Washington, DC, pp. 63–82.

Lave, J., and Wenger, E. (1991). *Situated Learning. Legitimate peripheral participation*. Cambridge University Press, Cambridge, England.

LeVine, R. A., Dixon, S., LeVine, S., Richman, A., Leiderman, P. H., Keefer, C. H., and Brazelton, T. B. (1994). *Child care and culture: Lessons from Africa*. Cambridge University Press, Cambridge, England.

Light, P., and Butterworth, G. (1993). *Context and cognition: Ways of learning and knowing*, Lawrence Erlbaum Associates, Hillsdale, NJ.

Maynard, A. E. (2002). Cultural teaching: The development of teaching skills in Maya sibling interactions. *Child Development* 73(3):969–82.

Ochs, E. (1982). Talking to children in Western Samoa. *Language in Society* 11:77–104.

Ochs, E. (1986). From feelings to grammar: A Samoan case study. In: Schieffelin, B. B., and Ochs, E. (eds.), *Language socialization across cultures*, Cambridge University Press, Cambridge, England, pp. 251–272.

Resnick, L. B., Levine, J. M. Levine, and Teasley, S. D. (1991). *Perspectives on socially shared cognition*. American Psychological Association, Washington, DC.

Rogoff, B. (1990). *Apprenticeship in thinking: Cognitive development in social context*. Oxford University Press, Oxford, England.

Rogoff, B. (2003). *The cultural nature of human development*. Oxford University Press, Oxford, England.

Rogoff, B., Paradise, R., Mejía Arauz, R., Correa-Chavez, M., and Angelillo, C. (2003). First-hand learning through intent participation. *Annual Review of Psychology* 54:175–203.

Schieffelin, B. B. (1990). The give and take of everyday life: Language socialization of Kaluli children. Cambridge: Cambridge University Press.

Schieffelin, B., & Ochs, E. (1996). The microgenesis of competence: Methodology in language socialization. In: Slobin, D. I., Gerhardt, J., Kyratzis, A., and Guo, J. (eds.), *Social interaction, social context, and language. Essays in honor of Susan Ervin-Tripp*. Lawrence Erlbaum Associates, Mahwah, NJ, pp. 251–263.

Tharp, R. G. (1994). Intergroup differences among Native Americans in socialization and child cognition: An ethnogenetic analysis. In: Greenfield, P. M., and Cocking, R. R. (eds.), *Cross-cultural roots of minority child development*, Lawrence Erlbaum Associates, Hillsdale, New Jersey, pp. 87–105.

Tomasello, M., Kruger, A. C., and Ratner, H. H. (1993). Cultural learning. *Behavioral and Brain Sciences* 16:495–552.

Triandis, H. C. (1994). Major cultural syndromes and emotion. In: S. Kitayama, S., and Markus, H. R. (eds.), *Emotion and culture: Empirical studies of mutual influence*. American Psychological Association, Washington, D.C., pp. 285–306.

Valsiner, J. (1989). Collective coordination of progressive empowerment. In: Winegar, L. T. (ed.), *Social interaction and the development of children's understanding*. Ablex, Norwood, NJ, pp. 7–20.

Vygotsky, L. S. (1978). *Mind in society*. Cambridge University Press, New York.

Zukow, P. G. (1989). Siblings as effective socializing agents: Evidence from Central Mexico. In: Zukow, P. G. (ed.), *Sibling interaction across cultures. Theoretical and methodological issues*, Springer-Verlag, New York, pp. 79–105.

Zukow-Goldring, P., and Ferko, K. R. (1994). An ecological approach to the emergence of the lexicon: Socializing attention. In: John-Steiner, V., Panofsky, C. P., and & Smith, L. W. (eds.), *Sociocultural approaches to language and literacy. An interactionist perspective*, Cambridge University Press, Cambridge, England, pp. 170–190.

AUTHOR NOTE

The NSF-funded workshops from which this volume emerged spanned the course of one academic year, and the conversations it inspired are ongoing. In the fall of 2001 and the spring of 2002, seven prominent researchers who conduct sociocultural investigations visited the University of Hawai`i. They gave colloquia, and they each spent a day with the local researchers discussing sociocultural theory and research, and the specific research interests of each member of the team. This book emerged from those colloquia and workshops. Several of the chapters were written by the visiting scholars, and others were prepared by the local investigators in Hawai`i. A few other chapters were invited from scholars whose work focuses on sociocultural methods and theory.

Thanks to Darnell Cole and Su Yeong Kim for their helpful comments on this chapter, and to Tasha Hicks for her assistance in formatting the references for the volume. Special thanks to Ned Davis for support and encouragement during the preparation of this book. We dedicate this book to the memory of Rod Cocking, who was committed to optimizing children's learning. He inspired and supported our efforts, for which we are very grateful.

Section I

Cultural Practices and Ways of Learning in Informal Settings

The three chapters in this section are focused on learning in everyday, informal settings. The first chapter is Mary Gauvain's comprehensive review of the literature on everyday contexts of learning. Gauvain traces the history of the sociocultural school, beginning with Vygotsky, who is seen by many as the father of this school of thought. She shows how social processes that occur in the seemingly mundane activities of everyday life provide opportunities for children to learn and to practice cognitive skills. Various kinds of everyday learning are considered, such as observational learning, the regulation of attention in infancy, learning from deliberate teaching, and cognitive socialization through narrative. Methods for the study of learning in context are discussed throughout the chapter, paying special attention to the adjustments that must be made in order to obtain ecologically valid results in cultural or cross-cultural research.

Tom Weisner, Cathy Matheson, Jennifer Coots, and Lucinda Bernheimer focus on learning at two levels in their chapter on sustainability of daily routines as a family outcome. As researchers engaged in the study of family adaptation to the needs of a child with a disability, their chapter emphasizes not only the learning of the families under study, but also the learning of the researchers as they engage in the research process. The researchers have developed an in-depth ethnographic interview, the Ecocultural Family Interview (EFI), that gets at the heart of the family as a context for development at the same time that the family is engaged in other contexts to which they must adapt, such as the children's schools, community organizations, and the like. They consider the extension of the use of the EFI to other contexts, such as mothers' control of infant pain during inoculation and emergent literacy in preschool children.

Using excerpts from ethnographic fieldnotes, Ashley Maynard and Patricia Greenfield present an indigenous cultural model of teaching and learning. Based on their work with the Zinacantec Maya of Chiapas, Mexico, they describe and analyze a model of informal education that epitomizes the apprenticeship of tasks that girls and women perform every day in Zinacantán: weaving, making tortillas, and chopping and carrying firewood. The analyses in the chapter add to the literature on cultural models by showing that the model of teaching and learning can be extended across domains of daily life and to a person from another culture as well.

Chapter 1

Sociocultural Contexts of Learning

Mary Gauvain

INTRODUCTION

A sociocultural approach to children's learning emphasizes the role that social and cultural experiences play in the acquisition, organization, and use of knowledge. In this approach, culture, described in general terms as a system of shared meaning and action transmitted across generations (Bruner, 1990), is considered a necessary and defining feature of human psychological development. Cole (1996) states this point clearly when he characterizes human biology and culture as the dual legacy or inheritance of our species. In other words, biology and culture co-evolved, with the connection between them mediated by social-cognitive processes (Donald, 1991). Cognitive capabilities critical to this developmental process, both in evolutionary and ontogenetic terms, include the ability to understand the self and others, to understand and use the accumulated knowledge of the group, to transmit this knowledge to subsequent generations, and to adapt historically formulated courses of intelligent action, the products of culture, to local and immediate needs (Tomasello, 1999). Critical social capabilities include the ability to engage in reciprocal exchanges, social behaviors that facilitate access to the thinking of other people, and the ability to participate in social arrangements in which the valued knowledge of the group is made available and supported in both rudimentary and advanced forms.

A sociocultural approach is consistent with the ecological perspective in that both concentrate on the reciprocal nature of maturation and experience in human psychological growth (Bronfenbrenner, 1979). However, a sociocultural approach advances understanding of the ecological niche of human development by attending to the contributions of social and cultural experiences to psychological growth. Some research based on this approach has concentrated on the socioemotional aspects of development in cultural context (Super & Harkness, 1986), other research has emphasized cognitive development in cultural context (Gauvain, 1995). This chapter discusses learning, a critical component of cognitive development that has important links to the sociocultural context in which growth occurs.

Like many other contemporary approaches to cognitive development, a sociocultural approach is constructivist in its theoretical orientation. That is, intellectual development is seen as the result of active efforts by the child to make sense of the world. Of particular interest to socioculturalists is how the child's own efforts to learn about the world are coordinated with the opportunities for learning that are provided by the social and cultural setting. This approach owes much of it theoretical formulation to the writings of the Russian psychologist L. S. Vygotsky. For Vygotsky (1978), the relation between learning and cognitive development is ongoing and bi-directional. As children learn, their level of development increases; changes in developmental level then affect the child's ability to learn new concepts and skills. Following up on this basic idea, one aim of a sociocultural approach to cognitive development is to describe in detail what it is that children and other people do that affects children's learning and, thereby, helps lead cognitive development.

From a sociocultural perspective, cognitive development is the process by which the child's emerging maturational capabilities interact with the cultural context of development as it is instantiated in social experience. The outcome of this dynamic process is a mature individual in whom the culturally specific nature of experience is an integral part of what and how the person thinks. The main assumptions of a sociocultural approach are that 1) learning and cognitive development rely in good measure on the child's participation in the activities and practices in the settings in which growth occurs, 2) these activities and practices are largely organized by culture, and 3) more experienced cultural members play vital roles in determining the nature and timing of children's participation in these activities and practices. In this approach, the child's participation in cultural activity is the primary unit of analysis (Rogoff, 1998).

This chapter discusses the social processes that occur in the course of everyday experiences that provide children with opportunities to learn about and practice cognitive skills, what Serpell and Hatano (1997) refer to as cultural arrangements for learning. Different social processes offer different opportunities for learning. Some social processes directly involve other people, such as social interaction and instruction. Other social processes are less interpersonally direct, yet they are also social in that they entail ways of thinking and carrying out intelligent action that have been devised by culture and are transmitted from more to less experienced members of the group (Cole, 1996; Gauvain, 1995). Children may use such tools of thinking even when they are working alone. For example, mathematical notations, products of culture, are transmitted socially to children when they learn mathematics. From this point forward, these tools are used by children when they solve mathematics problems, regardless of whether they solve these problems alone or with others. Many intelligent human actions bear the stamp of the social and cultural bases of learning in the content, form, and goals of the activities in which children engage.

Both direct and indirect social processes that provide children with the knowledge and skills that are useful in and valued by their culture are fertile sources for learning and cognitive development. This is because they are rich in culturally specific information and they are related to one another over time and across circumstances. That is, children not only have social experiences that guide them in the development and use of situationally specific cognitive skills; there is a commonality or redundancy across many of the social experiences that children have that involve these skills. This commonality, which is largely rooted in culture, increases the opportunities that children have to develop and practice valued cognitive skills. Although direct and indirect social processes play significant roles in learning and cognitive development, this chapter concentrates on direct social processes.

Researchers have studied several direct social processes that promote children's learning including observational learning, the social regulation of attention in infancy, deliberate efforts to transfer knowledge from more to less experienced partners, social coordination during joint cognitive activity, and cognitive socialization through conversation and shared narratives. Taken together, this research suggests that social opportunities for children's learning appear in many forms and that culture determines the frequency and manner with which these processes occur during childhood. Thus, better understanding of these social processes from a cultural perspective will advance knowledge of children's learning. It will also increase understanding of the social psychological mechanisms that lead to cognitive change (Gauvain, 2001). Cognitive development may result from social experience because children have opportunity to evaluate and refine their thinking as they are exposed to the ideas of other people (Rogoff, 1990), to participate in creating shared understanding (Rommetveit, 1985), and to learn how to use material and symbolic tools to support intelligent action (Goody, 1977). These types of experiences have all been linked to changes in cognitive functioning.

Although social experience is crucial for cognitive development, the universality of any particular social process as a mechanism of cognitive change is not known. More empirical evidence of children's learning and development in different cultural settings will help address this issue. Investigating the universality of social processes that contribute to cognitive development is important for understanding the range of species general cognitive capabilities as well as the role that cultural and social experiences play in the development and expression of these capabilities. Research that attends to the universality of a developmental process can also scrutinize existing developmental theories in ways that are not possible from the vantage point of a single culture (Rogoff, Gauvain, & Ellis, 1984). A lesson from cross-cultural research on language acquisition is instructive in this regard.

Child-directed speech, a type of simplified speech used in speaking to young children and sometimes referred to as motherese, was long considered critical to language learning. Its prevalence among middle-class parents in the U.S. helped reinforce this view. However, cross-cultural research demonstrated that child-directed speech is less common, and therefore less essential to language learning, than initially presumed (Ochs & Schieffelin, 1984). In cultures where child-directed speech was uncommon, other social processes that were important to language learning were documented, such as direct instruction and opportunities for children to overhear adults when they speak to each other. This research also demonstrated that the social processes that are used in cultural communities to support learning are not arbitrary; they fit with broader cultural practices and goals. In cultures in which interactions between adult caregivers and young children tend to be adjusted to fit with children's activities and needs, such as middle-class families in the U.S., child-directed speech is common. In cultures in which the interactions of caregivers and young children mainly occur when adults are carrying out their own routine activities, the communication that is directed toward children tends to be instructional and children are privy to many adult-adult conversations.

The lesson for present purposes is that although research both within and across cultures supports the general claim that the social context contributes to language development, i.e., that social experience functions as a universal process or mechanism of language acquisition, the exact social processes that contribute to this development and whether these processes are universal in form and consequence continue to be studied and debated. It is important to note that the term "universal" is used in this chapter to describe the presence or absence of a social-developmental practice and not the ability of individuals to engage in or benefit from this practice. The absence in one culture of a social practice that has been identified as important for learning in another culture does not indicate that individuals in the former culture are incapable of using or benefiting from this practice. It simply means that this practice is used in some cultures and not used in others. This meaning of universal is quite different from the concept of universal that appears in deficit models in which the absence of a behavior or practice is interpreted as lack of ability in a group.

In general, research indicates that the nature and timing of social processes that support children's learning reflect two forces, the child's maturational readiness and cultural values and practices (Bransford, Brown, & Cocking, 1999). Even changes that seem wholly maturational, such as the development of motor control over the first year of life, reveal the intricate links between maturation and the social and cultural context of development. As the baby's ability to control her neck improves, caregivers are able to hold the baby differently. Different patterns of infant holding lead to different experiences for the baby with objects and people in the world and, thereby, introduce different learning opportunities for the infant (Martini & Kirkpatrick, 1981). These experiences then facilitate further development, including changes in motor, cognitive, emotional, and social functioning (Super & Harkness, 1982). Research on language developmental also illustrates how sociocultural processes that support children's learning are coordinated with children's maturational capabilities. In some cultural communities, such as the Kaluli of New Guinea, there is the belief that children learn language through deliberate efforts or instruction by adults (Ochs & Schieffelin, 1994). However, among the Kaluli language instruction does not commence until children are deemed ready, which is when children speak their first words. Other maturational changes that research has shown influence the timing of the learning opportunities provided in the sociocultural context include motor strength and coordination (Hopkins & Westra, 1990), attentional control (Ruff & Rothbart, 1996), and memory (Mistry, 1997).

Cultural beliefs and practices that influence social processes that contribute to learning and cognitive development include patterns of group composition, such as whether children mostly interact with same-age peers or with children of different ages (Konner, 1975), whether social interaction tends to be dyadic or involve several partners or large groups (Martini, 1994), and the extent to which children are integrated into the everyday activities of the community (Rogoff, Paradise, Mejía Arauz, Correa-Chavez, & Angelillo, 2003). Social processes are also regulated by culturally preferred ways of interacting with children that are related to the long-term goals and values of the group. For example, there is a tendency in cultures in which formal schooling is important, such as middle-class families in the U.S., for parents to interact with children in ways that promote cognitive skills that are valued in school, such as asking questions of preschoolers for which the parents already know the answer or displaying mock excitement when toddlers manipulate objects offered by the parent (Rogoff, 2003). This type of social interaction reflects what LeVine and colleagues (1994) call the pedagogical model of child socialization, which emphasizes the development of individual skill and achievement and the rewards associated with such performances. It is quite different from socialization approaches in which social intelligence and responsibility toward the community are emphasized (Super, 1983).

In sum, human social organization in the form of culture provides the framework that unites children's social experiences across situations and helps structure the content and process of cognitive socialization (Goodnow, 1990). Analysis of children's learning in relation to the sociocultural context can provide insight into the role that social processes play in cognitive development. In addition, it can increase understanding of the flexibility and responsiveness of the developing human organism to social input as children learn about the world in which they live. Finally, this research can increase understanding of the intricate connection between culture and intellectual functioning.

SOCIAL PROCESSES THAT CONTRIBUTE TO CHILDREN'S LEARNING AND COGNITIVE DEVELOPMENT

In this section, several social processes that have been studied in relation to learning and cognitive development are discussed. These processes include observational learning, the social regulation of attention in infancy, deliberate efforts to transfer knowledge from more to less experienced partners, social coordination during joint cognitive activity, and cognitive socialization through conversation and shared narratives. As much research exists on each of these processes, this chapter is not intended to review them in detail. Rather, it focuses on the sociocultural contributions to children's learning that may emerge during these processes. The purpose for discussing these processes together is to highlight the large and pervasive impact that culture has on cognitive development. Although these processes are discussed individually for purposes of explanation, it is important to remember that they are related to each other and often occur side-by-side in a culture, sometimes even in the same learning situation. In addition, they sometimes build on one another, for example deliberate efforts to instruct children rely on earlier developments in the regulation of attention, which is a maturational and social process.

Observational Learning in Social and Cultural Context

Children learn much by watching others. Other people often model behavioral approaches or strategies for solving problems in front of children and these demonstrations may influence children's future behaviors. Observational learning has a long history of study in developmental psychology, most notably by Bandura (1962) who studied how children learn social behaviors. More recently, this approach has incorporated cognitive processes as a central feature of observational learning (Bandura, 1986). However, much of the research stemming from this tradition remains focused on the role of observational processes in children's learning of social behaviors (e.g., Crick & Dodge, 1994).

Although observational learning of cognitive skills has not been a central focus in developmental research in recent years (Siegler, 2000), some illustrations of this type of learning exist and underscore the importance of examining this process both within and across cultural contexts. For instance, infants as young as 6 months of age are able to imitate novel actions toward objects that they have seen adults do (Barr, Dowden, & Hayne, 1996) and by 14-month of age infants can remember such actions for as long as a week after they first saw them demonstrated (Meltzoff, 1988). Strategies for solving problems among children as young as 30-months of age can be learned by watching same-age peers solve a problem (Brownell & Carriger, 1991). Observing a partner can also lead to improvements in individual skill. Azmitia (1988) showed that five-year-old children who observed their peer partners as they worked on problem solving tasks gained more skill and showed more improvement in their later individual performance on similar tasks than children who worked with peers and did not observe their partners or children who worked alone. Findings such as these make it clear that the social world provides information about intelligent action, that even very young children take notice of this information, and, most importantly, that they can learn much from social observation including ways of carrying out their own goal-directed actions at a later point in time.

Opportunities for children to learn cognitive skills by observing others are also evident in many of the detailed descriptions provided in research on social interaction and cognitive development. The coding schemes that are used to describe behaviors that occur during these interactions often include information about instances when the learner watches the behavior of his or her partner. Sometimes the partner promotes these observations ("watch me do it") and sometimes they emerge spontaneously on the part of the learner. In several studies, these junctures have been related to children's learning in social context, especially when children work with peers who are less likely than adults to verbalize their strategies or thought processes (Gauvain, 2001).

Sociocultural research on children's learning has made unique contributions to the developmental literature on this topic by describing the role that observational learning plays in the acquisition of cultural values and practices (Rogoff, 2003) and by introducing a form of observational learning that had been previously overlooked. Lave and Wenger (1991) introduced the concept of legitimate peripheral participation to describe learning in cultural settings where observation is the primary means by which valued and complex skills are acquired. The term "legitimate" in this concept refers to the fact that the learner, who may be an adult or a child, is allowed or expected to have sustained but non-intrusive contact with a person who is engaged in and experienced with the activity that is the focus of the learning.

In many situations and domains of learning, cognitive skills are not conveyed via direct guidance or instruction and much learning occurs as children live alongside others who are participating in and therefore demonstrating specific skills (Rogoff, 2003). Legitimate peripheral participation is especially important in settings in which explicit adult-child instruction is less common that in Western communities. For example, in their research on weaving among the Zinacantecans, a Mayan community in Mexico, Greenfield and Childs (1991) found that much of this skill is transferred across generations as apprentice weavers, who are usually young girls, sit or stand quietly alongside and watch as their mothers, older sisters, and other women in the community weave. The learner's attention is focused on the behavioral components of the process that are important to learning the skill and this attention is permitted and sustained over time. Thus, both the learner and the teacher value this type of behavior in this circumstance, which in other situations might be considered intrusive or rude.

Culturally organized opportunities to learn by watching others not only occur in relation to the development of expertise in particular domains. They also occur in mundane, routine activities as adults make their actions available to children and children learn by attending carefully to what adults do. In many cultures, children are incorporated into the regular, daily activities in a way that affords them ample opportunity to observe the mature practices of their community. Even children as young as 2–3-years of age in some communities, such as the Efe foragers of the

Democratic Republic of Congo and Mayan children in rural Guatemala, have frequent experience with the work activities of adults in the community (Morelli, Rogoff, & Angelillo, 2003). Observations of adult activity also convey to children strategies for learning and instruction that are practiced by the group. For example, Rogoff, Mosier, Mistry, and Goncu (1993) observed middle-class mothers in the U. S. and Mayan mothers in rural Guatemala as they played with their toddlers with a set of nesting dolls. These investigators observed significantly more reliance on verbal communication among the U.S. mothers, whereas the Mayan mothers relied more on nonverbal communication such as eye gaze, facial expression, and postural changes in relation to the objects. By the same token, the children displayed behaviors that meshed with their mothers' behaviors and assisted the children in learning, with U. S. children more talkative and Mayan children relying more on nonverbal communication.

In sum, opportunities to learn by observing others abound in social and cultural contexts. Current thinking on this topic suggests that observational learning in humans is a cognitive process that entails understanding the intentions of other people, as well as the affordances of their actions and the objects that support their actions (Tomasello, Kruger, & Ratner, 1993). Moreover, imitation is often combined with innovation, which is the "nest egg" that enables the adaptation of observed actions to new circumstances (Tomasello, 1999). Research has made it clear that observational learning plays an important role throughout childhood, that children learn both social behaviors and cognitive skills from observing others, and that this process is not restricted to imitation in which the learner reproduces the behavior of another person in the hope of achieving the same goal as the model. In other words, observational learning is an active, constructive process that embodies information about culture in its content, form, and goals for action. Children's ability to learn from social observation changes with development, as their skills at encoding, retaining, retrieving, and reproducing information derived from these observations improve. Research from non-Western cultures has introduced new ways of thinking about when and how this type of learning occurs, such as the observation of routine cultural practices and the process of legitimate peripheral participation. Limitations to learning cognitive skills by observing others are also evident in research that examines cultural contributions to this type of learning. In particular, learning by observing others is not effective for transferring what has been learned to new tasks (Segall, Dasen, Berry, & Poortinga, 1999) or when innovation is important (Greenfield, 1999).

The Social Regulation of Attention in Infancy

Research on the development of the attention displayed by infants in social situations provides insight into a social process that relies on the early capabilities that infants have to attend to and follow the gaze of others as a means of learning about the world. In the latter part of the first year, infants display a set of social behaviors and interactional patterns referred to as joint attention. At this time infants begin to look reliably and flexibly toward the place where adults are looking and they begin to use active means to direct adult's attention to outside entities (Carpenter, Nagall, & Tomasello, 1998). Joint attention is the tendency of social partners to focus on a common reference, which may be an object, person, or event, and to monitor one another's attention to this outside entity. Interactions involving joint attention help children learn much about the world around them, including what objects and events are important to pay attention to and how these objects and events are valued by others in the community. Because these interactions are set in the context of interpersonal relationships, they are a rich source and motivating setting for learning.

Joint attention is an important process for children's learning and cognitive development for several reasons (Adamson & Bakeman, 1991). First, joint attention helps direct infant attention toward certain information in the environment. This guidance helps children learn about the world, especially what parts of the world are important for them to pay attention to, as well as how people around the infant feel about this information. Enthusiastic and positive attention affects the child differently than neutral or negative attention. A second function that joint attention plays in cognitive development is that it communicates to infants that other people play instrumental roles in identifying objects worthy of their attention. In other words, by attending to objects with another person, infants learn that other people can be helpful for learning about the world. This experience leads to the understanding of others as intentional agents, which is a chief component of social cognition (Tomasello, 1995). A third function of joint attention is its contribution to language development, in particular the development of referential communication skills as children learn how to label objects, events and people in ways that are conventional in their language (Bruner, 1975). And, finally, joint attention allows children and adults to share experiences with one another, which has profound social, emotional, and cognitive consequences and underlies many of the social interactional processes discussed in this chapter.

Joint attention has been studied primarily with infants and their caregivers because of its emergence between 9 and 15 months of age (Adamson & Bakeman, 1991; Tomasello & Farrar, 1986). Most of this research focuses on the infant's visual orientation toward and away from the caregiver, with this visual orientation used as evidence of the sharing and monitoring of attention between social partners. In order for an interaction to involve joint attention, attention monitoring by both partners is crucial. Thus, this shared experience does not involve the passive sharing of foci, but the active construction of attention by the participants in relation to the task and activity at hand (Bruner, 1995). Of course, the means by which adults and children contribute to these interactions differ. Adults monitor the infant's focus of attention and adjust their own gaze to support shared attention. Adults can elicit attention from the infant by either redirecting the child's attentional focus or by following the child's already established attentional focus. Research has shown that infants learn more when adults respond to cues of interest from infants rather than when they attempt to redirect an infant's attention (Tomasello & Farrar, 1986). Infants contribute to this process through the attentional, social and emotional skills they have available and their contribution changes as these skills develop. This process reaches a particularly interesting juncture late in the first year of life when infants begin to seek and use the emotional information conveyed by adults in joint attentional episodes to organize the infant's own emotional response to objects or events, especially ones that are unfamiliar or ambiguous, a process known as social referencing (Campos & Stenberg, 1981).

Cross-cultural research indicates that the development of joint attention is similar across very different communities (Adamson & Bakeman, 1991). However, cultural variation in the communicative styles and cultural practices with which caregivers establish joint attentional episodes are also evident. For example, among the !Kung San, a hunter-gatherer society that resides in Africa, adults neither encourage nor prohibit the infant's exploration of objects (Bakeman, Adamson, Konner, & Barr, 1990). However, if the infant initiates interactions by offering objects to caregivers, joint attention and object exploration follow the same course observed in other communities.

The focus of interest during joint attentional episodes may also differ across cultural contexts. Some variation exists across cultures in how infants learn to allocate their attentional resources. Chavajay and Rogoff (1999) observed the interactions of Guatemalan Mayans and U. S. middle-class mothers and their 12- to 24-month-old children. Mayan children and adults were more likely to attend to several events simultaneously, whereas U. S. children and mothers usually attended to one event or object at a time or alternated back and forth between two items in the environment. This study suggests that the distribution of attentional processes may be an aspect of socialization and thus reflect cultural values and practices. In addition, the researchers argued that attention to one or multiple objects or events in the environment at a time may reflect more of a cultural value than attentional capacity.

Other research has pointed to cultural variation in how mothers and infants direct their attention. Bornstein, Tal, and Tamis-LeMonda (1991) conducted home observations of mothers and their 5-month-old infants in the U.S., France, and Japan. This cross-cultural comparison is interesting in that all the participants were middle class and lived in large, modern, urban settings. Cultural similarities as well as differences emerged in mothers' engagement of the infants' attention toward objects in the environment and toward the mother herself. Mothers in all three cultures directed their infants' attention more towards objects than toward the mother. However, mothers in the U.S. were more likely than the other mothers to direct their infants' attention to objects, and American and Japanese mothers were similar and had higher rates of directing their infants' attention to the mothers themselves than French mothers did. Although mothers in these three cultures were similar in their nurturance and responsiveness toward their infants, suggesting commonality in socioemotional support and involvement, they differed in the rate with which they tried to engage their infants with information in the environment. These patterns suggest that culture influences both the content and rates of joint attentional episodes as early as 5-months of age.

These studies support the view that caregivers in different social and cultural circumstances are similar in many ways in their efforts to coordinate infants' attention between objects and people. However, this goal is accomplished in culturally appropriate and valued ways. Culture provides a framework that determines the initiation of joint attentional episodes, the communicative behaviors that occur during these exchanges, and the nature of the attentional focus.

Deliberate Efforts to Transfer Knowledge from More to Less Experienced Partners

According to Vygotsky (1978), higher mental functions, such as conceptualization, memory, problem solving, and other complex forms of knowledge acquisition and use, have their origin in human social life as children interact with more experienced members of their community. This process involves a child as an active participant working with a more competent partner to come to some shared understanding or solve a problem. To facilitate children's participation and learning, more experienced partners target their assistance to a child's zone of proximal or potential development, defined as "the distance between the actual developmental level as determined by independent problem solving and the level of potential development as determined through problem solving under adult guidance or in collaboration with more capable peers" (Vygotsky, 1978, p. 86). For Vygotsky, the child's prospective accomplishments, that is, what the child is capable of knowing, thinking, or doing with appropriate support is what cognitive development is all about. This view is quite different from approaches that emphasize what the child is already capable of doing on his or her own, which Vygotsky considered already developed and not particularly useful for describing the future course of development.

Interaction in the child's zone of proximal development involves exposing children to increasingly more complex understanding and activity than they are capable of doing on their own. The more experienced partner helps a child use his or her current capabilities to support higher levels of competence. New ways of thinking are first experienced collaboratively or intermentally. After some competence and understanding are achieved by the learner, these new ways of thinking are then experienced individually or intramentally. In other words, understanding is initially a social experience. For Vygotsky, the structure of social interaction reflects the larger sociocultural context in which the interaction is embedded. The sociocultural context shapes the communication that occurs between people and this communication serves as a support or scaffold for the learner by providing contact between old and new knowledge (Wood & Middleton, 1975). More experienced partners rely on a variety of communicative techniques to scaffold children's learning in the zone of proximal development including suggestions, prompts, hints, questions, praise, directives, and demonstration. Researchers have studied how these communicative devices influence children's emerging understanding, as well as how an adult's use of these techniques changes over the course of an interaction. By adjusting the support or scaffold provided for children's learning in social context, an adult can tailor the learning situation to the changing needs and skills of the learner as revealed over the course of the interaction.

The notion of the zone of proximal development has inspired research on the transmission of cognitive skill during adult-child and peer interactions (Rogoff, 1998). It has also been used to study the organization of instruction in relation to more formal learning situations (Palinscar & Brown, 1984). These findings support the general claim that cognitive development can result from solving problems with an experienced partner who targets her assistance to the learner's needs. To account for the child's active role in procuring or appropriating understanding through social interaction, Rogoff (1990) introduced the idea of guided participation. In this view, the child is not seen as merely a naive actor who follows the instructions or prompts of the more experienced partner. Rather, the child is a full participant, albeit a participant whose contribution at any point in time is defined by his or her current understanding, maturation, interests and so forth. An emphasis on the child's active contribution not only underscores the dynamic nature of children's learning in social context, it provides a way of conceptualizing cognitive development. According to Rogoff (1998), cognitive development is evident in changes in the child's roles and responsibilities during joint cognitive activity.

The types of deliberate instructional interactions described in relation to the zone of proximal development and the process of scaffolding may be more common in cultures in which formal schooling is highly valued. In cultures in which formal schooling is less common or nonexistent, mothers provide instructional support for their children's learning, however, their support differs from that which is often found among American mothers when they teach their children. LeVine and his colleagues (1994) videotaped mothers in the Gusii community of Kenya and in middle-class U.S. families as they taught their young children age-appropriate tasks that were based on tasks from the Bayley Scales of Infant Development. There were three age groups in this study, 6–8-month olds, 12–14-month olds, and 19–25-month olds and all the tasks involved the manipulation and arrangement of small objects, such as blocks and pegs. The Gusii mothers tended to instruct their children verbally and would often demonstrate the entire task in advance of asking their children to try to do it. The mothers' instructions were clear and unambiguous and the goal they communicated to their children was to complete the task exactly as demonstrated. If a child was inattentive, mothers would reinstruct them in the task. These mothers rarely demonstrated part of the task while their children were trying to do it and when their children completed the task successfully the mothers did not praise them. In contrast, American mothers relied heavily on verbal instruction throughout the task, they often demonstrated part of the task while their children worked on it, they encouraged exploration of the task, and when the children were finished their mothers praised the accomplishment. Gusii children were more cooperative with mothers overall than American children were, however Gusii children completed the task less often than the American children did. LeVine and colleagues explain these differences by pointing out that the Gusii mothers and children were in an unfamiliar situation. Normally, young children in this community learn skills in their interactions with older children and siblings, whom young children observe and imitate. Compliance is highly valued because it is considered critical for children as they become increasingly responsible for domestic activities around the household. In addition, praise is avoided at all ages in this community because adults think it leads to conceit, which then draws attention to the individual and may threaten individual belongingness and group solidarity.

What this research suggests is that some modes of mother-child instructional interactions are more common in some cultures than in others. It also indicates that the instructional encounters that do occur reflect cultural values and practices pertaining to the long-term goals for children's learning and social behavior in the community. In communities in which formal schooling is rare or does not occur, deliberate efforts to instruct children may not rely as heavily on verbal instruction as has been the case in research conducted in Western communities. For example, Kagitcibasi (1996) cites early anthropological research by Helling (1966) which describes parental teaching in a rural Turkish village. In this community, parental teaching that incorporated demonstration and imitation, mostly pertaining to household tasks, was common. This type of "teaching by doing" rarely included verbal instruction or positive reinforcement. Greater reliance on demonstration and imitation in deliberate teaching efforts has been observed in many communities throughout the world (Serpell & Hatano, 1997), as well as among Latino-American mothers in the U.S. who have had few years of formal schooling (Laosa, 1980). Finally, research also suggests that deliberate efforts to transfer skills to younger members of the community may not only involve adults and children. Older children, especially siblings, may be more involved in these instructional encounters worldwide than current research describes. Recent research by Maynard (2002) underscores the important role that siblings may play in children's learning in cultural communities and in specific domains of cognitive development.

In sum, deliberate efforts to make knowledge available to children, along with active efforts by children themselves to procure knowledge as they participate in social situations, affect children's learning and cognitive development in a number of ways. These efforts provide children with an introduction to and practice with activities that foster the development of particular cognitive skills. They also provide children with opportunities to learn how more experienced partners understand a problem and what knowledge and skills are useful for solving that problem. They also provide children with experience with cultural tools, both symbolic and material, that are useful for solving the types of problems regularly encountered and considered important to solve in a culture.

Social Coordination and Opportunities for Learning

The collaborative nature of cognition and cognitive development has been a central focus of psychological and educational research for well over a decade (Joiner, Littleton, Faulkner, & Miell, 2000; Rogoff, 1998). This research covers a broad spectrum of issues, such as the processes that are involved in collaborative learning, the contribution of social coordination to cognitive development, and the application of these ideas to classroom practice. This section examines one facet of this topic, specifically the types of social coordination that have been the primary focus of research in children's learning and how cultural values and practices relate to these processes. This discussion concentrates on social coordination during peer learning situations because this has been the main focus of research in this area. However, effective functioning in the child's zone of proximal development and during joint attention and guided participation is contingent on social coordination by the interactive partners.

When children work on a cognitive activity together, their interaction can proceed in any number of ways. Psychologists have been especially interested in the consequences for children's learning when an interaction is cooperative and when interactions are conflictual. Piaget (1932) argued that conflict between partners during joint cognitive activity could benefit cognitive development. For Piaget, the primary impetus behind cognitive development is disequilibrium, which is discordance between what the child knows and the information available in the environment. Although Piaget stressed that disequilibrium is largely an intrapsychological process, he did contend that certain social arrangements could thrust a child into disequalibrium and thereby instigate mental growth as the child strives to reestablish equilibrium. Thus, a social agent may mediate the equilibrium-disequilibrium process by making evident to a child the mismatch between what is known and some state of the world. For Piaget, this occurs when peers close to but not identical in their understanding engage in cognitive conflict. The process of cognitive conflict requires open communication in that one person needs to be free or confident enough in speaking to another person in a conflictual way, that is in a way that contradicts or criticizes the partner's current knowledge state.

Piaget's claim that cognitive conflict may promote cognitive development among peers has garnered much support from research (Doise, Mugny, & Perret-Clermont, 1975). However, variability on this count has been observed and this variability, in some cases, has been explained by consideration of the sociocultural context of the interaction. For example, Mackie (1983) found differences between European-New Zealand and Maori children when they worked with peers on a set of Piagetian tasks. The European-New Zealand participants did benefit from cognitive conflict, as Piaget proposed. However, the Maori children were less likely to benefit from conflict. This pattern of results reflects differences in the cultural communities in which these two groups of children lived. These cultural communities differ in the extent to which they value cooperation in social activity, with the Maori placing greater value on cooperation than children in New Zealand whose ancestry is European. Thus, this study suggests that Piaget's assertion regarding conflict is conditioned upon factors that exist outside the immediate task context. Without attention to cultural information, in this case information regarding a social value and how this value is related to the children's social and cognitive performance, it would be difficult to interpret these group differences without resorting to a deficit model.

Other than Piagetian-based research on cognitive conflict, most research on social coordination and children's learning has emphasized the more cooperative aspects of joint cognitive activity. Research has focused on a range of issues, including how shared understanding is created during peer interaction, how working with peers influences children's affective response and motivation for learning, how the skills and learning of individuals can be understood in the midst of peer activity, and how and when children develop the ability to participate in collaborative learning (Joiner et al., 2000). In terms of development, research has shown that children are able to cooperate with peers as early as 18-months of age and that by 24–30 months of age children can coordinate their actions with same age peers to reach a goal (Brownell & Carriger, 1991). Thus, by 2 years of age some of the skills required for social coordination, and therefore opportunities to learn from these types of social situations, are already in place. These rudimentary skills continue to develop in the third year of life. Ashley and Tomasello (1998) studied joint problem solving involving same-age dyads who were 24, 30, 36, and 42 months of age on a task that required them to manipulate objects to get a reward. The 24-month-olds were not very successful at working together even when they received assistance from an adult. The 30- and 36-month-olds were successful when they received adult assistance, with the 36-month-olds capable of adjusting their behaviors to accommodate the behavior of a partner. By 42-months of age, children were highly cooperative with one another and they could even demonstrate successful behaviors for their partners.

Knowing that children are capable of collaboration does not answer the question of whether collaboration benefits learning, however. Glachen and Light (1982) investigated this topic by comparing the performances of 8- to 9-year-old children who worked together on a puzzle task that required collaboration or they worked on the task alone. They also assessed children's individual skill level and their strategic approach to the problem at the beginning and end of the observational session. Results showed that collaboration benefited children's learning. However, regardless of initial ability level, only children who were systematic and strategic during the pretest, that is before they even worked with a partner, benefited from collaboration. This pattern suggests that opportunities to learn from collaborative interactions are not independent of learning-related behaviors that children bring with them to social problem solving situations.

In general, research supports the contention that social collaboration can enhance children's learning (Johnson & Johnson, 1987). However, just putting children together does not guarantee that learning will occur. Research has shown that when partners share responsibility for thinking about and carrying out a cognitive activity, children learn more than when responsibility is not shared (Gauvain & Rogoff, 1989). Sharing task responsibility aids learning in that it encourages joint understanding or intersubjectivity (Rommetveit, 1985) during the interaction, that is, it helps children understand the cognitive problem from the perspective of another. During interactions in which responsibility for the thinking or decision making about the task is shared, children are also more likely to have opportunity to practice cognitive skill. Communication skills are very helpful in establishing joint understanding and age-related changes in the ability to participate and benefit from cooperative activities parallel the development of communicative competence (Ding & Flynn, 2000).

Much of the research on the benefits of peer cooperation has been conducted with U.S. samples, with no differences found for children from different ethnic groups. There has been less research on cultural influences on children's social coordination during problem solving interactions. This is surprising in that in some cultures, peer assistance as children learn all types of skills is a common and critical component of the social fabric (Martini & Kirkpatrick, 1992; Rogoff, 2003). The research that exists suggests that cultural values and practices related to social coordination play an important role in children's learning in social context. For example, one study compared European-American and Navajo children on a task that involved pairs of 9-year-old children teaching a 7-year-old child how to play a game (described in Ellis & Gauvain, 1992). The European-American child teachers relied more on verbal instruction than the Navajo child teachers did. In addition, the contributions of the European-American teachers tended to provide two parallel and unrelated lines of instruction whereas the contributions of the Navajo teachers tended to build on each other. The Navajo children, both teachers and learners, remained engaged in the task even when they were not directly involved in a problem solving activity by observing the partners' actions. European-American children were often distracted, sometimes to the point of leaving the task, when not directly involved in the problem themselves. Finally, Navajo teachers did not rush the learner's activity and they offered little praise to the learners. European-American children tended to rush their partner's activity and provided the learner with much more praise than Navajo teachers did. These differences raise interesting questions about the contribution of culture to social coordination in peer learning situations.

In sum, social coordination that leads to learning can be conflictual or cooperative. It can involve dyads or groups of participants. Although there is substantial support for the view that social coordination among partners contributes to learning and cognitive development, descriptions of these processes in relation to cultural values and practices are limited. Research that includes information about cultural context goes beyond the question of whether and how social coordination benefits learning by investigating how cultural values and practices influence the process of social coordination and how these processes are related to children's learning. Social interaction among peers, the processes they entail, and the learning that ensues may vary substantially across cultures. More attention to the cultural values and practices that determine the nature and frequency of these interactions is needed.

Cognitive Socialization through Conversation and Shared Narratives

Adults and children talk to one another about many things. Over the preschool years, the rapid explosion of children's language along with their conversational abilities provides one of the main avenues for learning in social context. In their conversations with adults children learn many things about the world, including information about themselves and other people. The conversations that children have with adults can bolster conceptual development as well as inform children about the intentions behind people's actions (Siegel, 1996). These early conversations are also fruitful for the development of memory in early childhood, both in terms of the content of children's memories and the processes through which certain types of memories are organized and retrieved. Of particular interest in terms of memory is the role that early conversations play in the development of children's understanding and use of narratives.

A narrative is a structure for remembering and communicating memories. It contains a unique sequence of events that involve human beings as characters (Bruner, 1986). It can be about a real or an imaginary event and it includes information about the intentionality of the actors as well as information about the cause and evaluation of the event. Narratives appear to be developmentally significant; they appear early and occur frequently in children's conversations with their parents and other adults. The narrative form has both social and psychological functions. It is often used in everyday conversations about the past, as well as for storing and retrieving information. Researchers interested in the sociocultural context of children's learning have studied how early conversations in general, and the narrative structure in particular, may influence the way that children learn to organize, store, and retrieve certain memories about themselves and their social group, such as their family and their culture. In fact, much of what is conveyed to children about family and cultural values occurs in the context of narratives. Shared narratives or storytelling are common in sustained social groups and this activity may stimulate the development of social ties, individual and group identity, and other cognitive and linguistic skills (Ochs, Taylor, Rudolph, & Smith, 1992). Because narratives can take various forms, e.g. some are highly embellished and others attempt to stick close to the facts, conversations containing narratives also convey information to children about the content of stories and ways of remembering that are valued in their culture.

Conversations that entail narratives are effective for children's learning for several reasons. First, they are highly motivating because they are often about the children themselves or the world they inhabit. Second, they often involve other people who are familiar to the children and therefore occur in the context of social relationships that have much meaning and affection for the children. Third, they are frequent in that stories about events of the past are a regular part of human conversation. Finally, these conversations are socially dynamic, that is they change as the participants add information and challenge and rework each other's contributions (Ochs et al., 1992). As a consequence, these conversations involve children as authentic participants whose own contributions and memories help shape the focus and direction of the conversation. In short, conversations involving shared memories are socially constructed memories as interlocutors provide unique contributions that are then parlayed into some socially negotiated form. This process not only leads to an interesting way to conceptualize memory itself, i.e. as a social product, but also underscores the active role of the child in this process. The engaging and motivating aspects of these conversations, along with the fact that children provide authentic and meaningful contributions, are critical components of this process. These aspects, in turn, fit with the child's emerging sense of agency that is so crucial to the development of the self-system (Bruner, 1990).

When parents and children discuss the past, parents communicate to children what events are worth learning and remembering (Snow, 1990). Researchers estimate that social interactions involving young children and their parents include discussion of past events as often as five to seven times an hour (Fivush, Haden, & Reese, 1996). Event memory concerns things that happen in everyday life and emerges in childhood once children are capable of reflecting on their own ideas or representations, which occurs shortly after the second birthday. Early on in these interactions, parents provide substantial scaffolding for children's participation in memory talk. When children are very young, parents ask many questions, and in some instances parents provide the answers to their own questions that they ask their children to repeat. Early in the child's life shared memories are mostly one-sided, with the parent taking on much of the responsibility for reminiscing. With time, as their language and social skills develop, children participate more in these conversations (Nelson, 1996). By 3 years of age, children's contributions to shared remembering are quite evident and their memories begin to endure rather well. By this age children can remember specific event information for as long as 18 months after the event (Hamond & Fivush, 1991). The structure of memory interactions and the way in which adults draw children into conversations about the past are important features of this process. During memory talk, the adult, usually a parent, essentially co-opts the child into what Middleton (1997) calls conversational remembering. Such social remembering typically begins by the adult evoking the child's memory of an event and, once the child acknowledges remembering the event, the adult guides the child into a more elaborate, and often emotionally laden, recollection of the event. Conversations that involve shared narratives about the past are especially interesting in terms of memory development because they are clearly a cognitive act. Unlike recognition memory, which can happen without explicit awareness the something is being remembered, shared event memory involves explicit awareness that something is being remembered. When children engage in conversations about past events, there is understanding that the event being discussed is in the past and that what is being discussed are people's ideas about or memories of the event.

In addition to creating shared knowledge and developing skill with a technique for remembering, conversations between parents and children contribute in significant ways to the development of autobiographical memories which are important to the child's emerging sense of self. Hudson (1990) recorded the conversations of 10 mothers and children over a four-week period when the children were between 24 and 30 months of age. Many of these conversations pertained to shared personal events involving the mother and child. Hudson found that early in the observational period the children had limited ability to talk about past events and they depended on their mothers to remind them. However, as they got older and their experience with such conversations increased, the children became more active participants in these conversations. Moreover, during their participation the children did not simply repeat what their mothers had said, they included new information about the event. This research suggests that in the second year of life children begin to recollect past experiences, that this cognitive ability emerges in conversations that are heavily scaffolded by adults and organized around a narrative structure, and that children do not merely imitate the information in prior conversations that was provided by others but develop a unique memory of the event based on the social transaction. Children's participation in conversations is also related to better memory by the children for these events, suggesting that conversation serves as a form of rehearsal (Hamond & Fivush, 1991), and aids the development of children's memory more generally (Ratner (1980, 1984).

Research also demonstrates that the early conversations that parents and children have about past events reflect cultural values. Mullen and Yi (1995) recorded the home conversations of Korean and European American mothers and their children when the children were between 37 and 44 months of age. European American dyads talked more about the past than Korean dyads did. In addition to differences in the amount of conversation, the content of the conversation differed. European American mothers made more references to the thoughts and feelings of the children in their memory talk than Korean mothers did. In contrast, Korean mothers included more references to social norms in their memory talk with their young children. These patterns are consistent with socialization goals and values in these two communities and suggest that during mother-child conversations about the past, children not only learn how to organize memories for communication, they also learn what aspects of the past are important to talk about and remember.

Research also indicates that personal storytelling is a routine socializing activity that contains culturally specific expectations about child behavior by the time the child is 2-1/2-years of age. Miller, Wiley, Fung, and Liang (1997) studied naturally occurring stories about the past experiences of 2-1/2-year-old children in middle-class Taiwanese and European-American families. Although the frequency of these conversations did not differ in these two groups and the range of issues discussed in these two groups were similar in many regards; some differences in relation to cultural practices were evident. The Taiwanese stories were more likely to emphasize moral and social standards, especially when the story focused on the child's past transgressions. Values pertaining to proper conduct, respect for others in the group, and self-control were highlighted in these stories. In contrast, European-American stories were more likely to focus on entertainment and affirmation of the child as an individual. When the child's past transgressions were the object of the discussion, the child's misdeeds were understated and recast to emphasize the child's strengths. These parents were not indifferent to transgressions by their children, they just tended to handle them at the time of the transgression and not incorporate them into their later conversations. This research highlights both the commonalities as well as the cultural uniqueness of shared narratives and indicates that these types of transactions and the cultural values they contain are part of the child's socialization experiences from very early in life.

In sum, research suggests that adults, especially parents, provide guidance for young children during their conversations about the past that contributes to the development of event and autobiographical memory. Conversations about the past and the narrative structure they assume compose a substantial portion of young children's experience with adults, especially parents, during the early years of childhood. The narrative form is useful for organizing event knowledge in children's memory as well as for helping children communicate with others about the past. Shared remembering has many potential benefits for the development of children's memory. These benefits include learning how to remember, especially strategies for aiding memory; helping shape the child's self-concept; informing the child about his or her personal and social history; and communicating family values. Sociocultural research has contributed to this research by emphasizing the influence of culture in both the content and form of narratives. This research also demonstrates how this social process is used to convey information to children about cultural values, which in turn fosters individual identity in relation to the cultural group and promotes social solidarity.

CONCLUSIONS

Cognitive development is a process of socialization to the cultural context of development so that the knowledge base and cognitive skills that children learn make sense and are useful in that context. Although learning is an inseparable and critical component of cognitive development, it has received scant attention from researchers in recent years. However, as Siegler (2000) points out, a renaissance in the study of learning in cognitive development is in the offing. Research based on a sociocultural approach has and will continue to play a central role in this endeavor by concentrating on the links between cultural context and what and how children learn through their experiences with others in their cultural community. The discovery and documentation of both similarity and variation across cultures in the social processes that support children's learning will contribute to theoretical development and refinement of these processes and help clarify the role that they play in cognitive development. A question that researchers will need to keep in mind as they do this work is how much variation across cultures in a particular social process or its learning outcomes can exist before it no longer qualifies as the same psychological process.

Examination of research on the various social processes of learning discussed in this chapter suggests that these processes are often implicitly assumed to be similar in form or consequence across cultural groups (Ellis & Gauvain, 1992). However, as research has shown, this assumption is problematic in that cultural norms and practices of social interaction are likely to play an important role in any learning that occurs in social settings. Research has also made it clear that many of the questions themselves that guide the study of social processes of learning present difficulty when they are considered from a cultural vantage. For example, much of the research conducted to date on deliberate efforts to transfer knowledge to children is tied in with values and practices that are more common in cultures in which formal schooling is an important part of childhood (Rogoff, 2003).

Conventional methods of study may also obscure important information about children's learning in sociocultural context. LeVine and colleagues (1994) discussed this issue explicitly in their research that compared mothers in two cultural communities, U.S. middle class and the Gusii in Kenya, as they taught their children how to do several standard age-appropriate cognitive tasks. These researchers went to lengths to make their study as comparable across the groups as possible while still respecting cultural differences in the groups, e.g. by conducting the observations in surroundings and with experimenters that were familiar to the mothers. Their results revealed differences, discussed earlier in the chapter, in adult instruction and child learning in these two groups. However, as these investigators point out, their efforts did not result in a truly comparable situation. In everyday life, Gusii mothers are less involved than U. S. mothers in deliberate efforts to instruct their young children. Among the Gusii, many community members, particularly older siblings, are involved in teaching young children. Thus, the Gusii and U.S. mothers were quite different in their familiarity and practice with the social situation. Moreover, these two groups of mothers also differed in their own educational experiences, a factor which has been shown in U.S. samples to be related to maternal instruction (e.g., Laosa, 1980).

Given these differences, several questions emerge. What do the observed patterns of maternal instruction in these two groups tell us about children's learning in these two cultural settings? More generally, what can these differences tell us that will improve our understanding of the role of this social process of learning? And, along empirical lines, what would have been the more appropriate comparison groups in these two cultures for studying this particular social process? Would it have been better to compare the instruction provided by mothers in the U.S. and older siblings in the Gusii community? Perhaps, but this type of comparison would raise other questions, such as how the different developmental status of these two types of teachers contribute to the learning process and outcomes. Research on the zone of proximal development suggests that the adult instructors would provide more help and, therefore, more opportunities for learning, than the child instructors would. However, because one of the chief differences in adult versus peer instruction is verbal exchange, adult instruction may only surpass that provided by siblings if verbal information is critical to learning the particular skill. In addition, the smaller status differential between children in peer interaction relative to adult-child instruction may help learners in peer situations steer the instruction to better meet their needs (Duran & Gauvain, 1993). In brief, our ability to answer questions such as these or to draw more general conclusions about the contribution of social processes to children's learning requires further study both within and across cultures.

Several other issues are important to emphasize in relation to social processes of learning. For all the processes discussed in this chapter, it is clear that learning from others entails more than imitation. Sustaining a culture requires imitation and innovation, and research on the social processes of learning discussed here indicates that both imitation and innovation are emergent properties of these experiences. Children actively construct what they learn during social learning experiences and they actively reconstruct this information later on for their own needs. The situations in which children use what they have learned previously invariably differ in some way, small or large, from the original learning context. Therefore, what children learn socially would not be expected to be reproduced in the exact form as when this information was initially learned. Investigating social processes of learning by focusing only on imitation is insufficient for capturing all that children can and must learn from these experiences. To date, research on the innovative consequences of children's learning in social and cultural contexts is limited.

Maturational processes are a nontrivial component of children's learning in social situations. A sociocultural approach may make a unique contribution to understanding the role that maturation plays in cognitive development by providing naturally occurring evidence of the range of maturational responsiveness produced by the human organism to social input that supports learning. Research conducted both within and across cultures has identified how social support is calibrated to the maturational capabilities of the child. An intriguing question is how information about maturation gets built into social processes of learning. Sociocultural research suggests that the beliefs or expectations that parents have about the nature and timing of development, which reflect cultural values, help regulate the opportunities that parents provide for children to develop cognitive skills (Sigel, McGillicuddy-DeLisi, & Goodnow, 1992). Thus, by considering cultural beliefs, along with cultural values and practices, as critical components of cognitive development, a sociocultural approach to children's learning also offers unique information about how the long-term historical contributions that make up a culture are coordinated with processes of maturation and, over time, become instantiated in cognitive functioning.

Finally, it is important to emphasize that understanding cultural contributions to children's learning is not equivalent to, and therefore cannot be reduced to, the analysis of social contributions. Even though cultural contributions are often introduced to and made available to new cultural members via social processes, the cultural aspects of cognitive development in social context are important to delineate. Better understanding of the cultural framing of social processes of children's learning will not only broaden the scope of research on cognitive development, it will also be helpful for understanding why certain social processes that support learning take on the form or significance they do in particular cultural contexts. A sociocultural approach to cognitive development tries to wed children's present cognitive capabilities, opportunities for further learning and development of these capabilities that are provided by social experiences, and the relation of social experiences to the values and practices of the culture in which development occurs. This effort coincides with calls for an integrated systems analysis of psychological development (Horowitz, 2000). Understanding when and how culture contributes to children's learning is part of this overall effort and such information can have far reaching implications for both the theory and practice of research in cognitive development.

REFERENCES

Adamson, L. B., and Bakeman, R. (1991). The development of shared attention during infancy. In: Vasta, R. (ed.), *Annals of child development*, Volume 8. Kingsley, London, pp. 1–41.

Ashley, J., and Tomasello, M. (1998). Cooperative problem solving and teaching in preschoolers. *Social Development* 17:143–163.

Azmitia, M. (1988). Peer interaction and problem solving, When are two heads better than one? *Child Development* 59:87–96.

Bakeman, R., Adamson, L. B., Konner, M., and Barr, R. G. (1990). !Kung infancy, The social context of object exploration. *Child Development* 61:794–809.

Bandura, A. (1962). Social learning through imitation. In: Jones, M. R. (ed.), *Nebraska symposium on motivation*, Volume 10. University of Nebraska Press, Lincoln, NE, pp. 211–271.

Bandura, A. (1986). *Social foundations of thought and action, A social cognitive theory*. Prentice-Hall, Englewood Cliffs, NJ.

Barr, R., Dowden, A., and Hayne, H. (1996). Developmental changes in deferred imitation by 6- to 24-month –old infants. *Infant Behavior and Development* 19:159–170.

Bornstein, M. H., Tal, J., and Tamis-LeMonda, C. (1991). Parenting in cross-cultural perspective. In: Bornstein, M. H. (ed.), *Cultural approaches to parenting*. Erlbaum, Hillsdale, NJ, pp. 69–90.

Bransford, J., Brown, A. L., and Cocking, R. R. (1999). *How people learn, Brain, mind, experience, and school*. National Academy Press, Washington, DC.

Bronfenbrenner, U. (1979). *The ecology of human development*. Harvard University Press, Cambridge, MA.

Brownell, C. A., and Carriger, M. S. (1991). Collaborations among toddler peers, Individual contributions to social contexts. In: Resnick, L. B., Levine, J. M., and Teasley, S. D. (eds.), *Perspectives on socially shared cognition*. American Psychological Association, Washington, DC, pp. 365–383.

Bruner, J. (1975). The ontogenesis of speech acts. *Journal of Child Language*. 1:1–19.

Bruner, J. (1986). *Actual minds, possible worlds*. Cambridge, MA, Harvard University Press.

Bruner, J. (1990). *Acts of meaning*. Cambridge, MA, Harvard University Press.

Bruner, J. (1995). From joint attention to the meeting of minds, An introduction. In: Moore, C., and Dunham, P. J. (eds.), *Joint attention, Its origins and role in development*, Erlbaum, Hillsdale, NJ, pp. 1–14.

Campos, J. J., and Stenberg, C. R. (1981). Perception, appraisal, and emotion: The onset of social referencing. In: Lamb, M. E., and Sherrod, L. R. (eds.), *Infant social cognition, Empirical and theoretical considerations*, Erlbaum, Hillsdale, NJ, pp. 273–314.

Carpenter, M., Nagall, K., and Tomasello, M. (1998). Social cognition, joint attention, and communicative competence from 9 to 15 months of age. *Monographs of the Society for Research in Child Development*, 63(Serial No. 255). University of Chicago Press, Chicago.

Chavajay, P., and Rogoff, B. (1999). Cultural variation in the management of attention by children and their caregivers. *Child Development* 35:1079–1090.

Cole, M. (1996). *Cultural psychology, A once and future discipline*. Harvard University Press Cambridge, MA.

Crick, N. R., and Dodge, K. A. (1994). A review and reformulation of social-information processing mechanisms in children's social adjustment. *Psychological Bulletin* 115:74–101.

Ding, S., and Flynn, E. (2000). Collaborative learning, An underlying skills approach. In: Joiner, R., Littleton, K., Faulkner, D., and Miell, D. (eds.), *Rethinking collaborative learning*, Free Association Books, London, pp. 3–18.

Doise, W., Mugny, G., and Perret-Clermont, A. (1975). Social interaction and the development of cognitive operations. *European Journal of Social Psychology* 5:367–383.

Donald, M. (1991). *Origins of the modern mind: Three stages in the evolution of culture and cognition*. Harvard University Press, Cambridge, MA.

Duran, R. T., and Gauvain, M. (1993). The role of age versus expertise in peer collaboration during joint planning. *Journal of Experimental Child Psychology* 55:227–242.

Ellis, S., and Gauvain, M. (1992). Social and cultural influences on children's collaborative interactions. In: Winegar, L. T., and J. Valsiner, J. (eds.), *Children's development within social context*, Volume 2, *Research and methodology*, Hillsdale, NJ, Erlbaum, pp. 155–180.

Fivush, R., Haden, C., and Reese, E. (1996). Remembering, recounting, and reminiscing, The development of autobiographical memory in social context. In: Rubin, D. C. (ed.), *Remembering our past, Studies in autobiographical memory*, Cambridge University Press, Cambridge, pp. 341–359.

Gauvain, M. (1995). Thinking in niches, Sociocultural influences on cognitive development. *Human Development* 38:25–45.

Gauvain, M. (2001). *The social context of cognitive development*. Guilford, New York.

Gauvain, M., and Rogoff, B. (1989). Collaborative problem solving and children's planning skills. *Developmental Psychology* 25:139–151.

Glachen, M., and Light, P. (1982). Peer interaction and learning, Can two wrongs make a right? In: Butterworth, G., and Light, P. (eds.), *Social cognition, Studies of the development of understanding,* University of Chicago Press, Chicago, pp. 238–262.

Goodnow, J. J. (1990). The socialization of cognition, What's involved? In, Stigler, J. W., Shweder, R. A., and G. Herdt, G. (eds.), *Cultural psychology,* Cambridge University Press, Cambridge, pp. 259–286.

Goody, J. (1977). *The domestication of the savage mind.* Cambridge University Press, Cambridge.

Greenfield, P. M. (1999). Cultural change and human development. In: Turiel, E. (ed.), *New directions in child development.* Jossey-Bass, San Francisco, CA, pp. 37–60.

Greenfield, P. M., and Childs, C. P. (1991). Developmental continuity in biocultural context. Cohen, R., and Sigel, A. W. (eds.), *Context and development,* Erlbaum, Hillsdale, NJ, pp. 135–159.

Hamond, N. R., and Fivush, R. (1991). Memories of Mickey Mouse, Young children recount their trip to Disneyworld. *Cognitive Development* 6:433–448.

Helling, G. A. (1966). *The Turkish village as a social system.* Occidental College, Los Angeles, CA.

Hopkins, B., and Westra, T. (1990). Motor development, maternal expectations, and the role of handling. *Infant Behavior and Development* 13:117–122.

Horowitz, F. D. (2000). Child development and the PITS, Simple questions, complex answers, and developmental theory. *Child Development* 71:1–10.

Hudson, J. A. (1990). The emergence of autobiographical memory in mother-child conversation. In Fivush, R., and Hudson, J. A. (eds.), *Knowing and remembering in young children,* Cambridge University Press, Cambridge, pp. 166–196.

Kagitcibasi, C. (1996). *Family and human development across cultures.* Erlbaum, Mahwah, NJ.

Konner, M. (1975). Relations among infants and toddlers in comparative perspective. In Lewis, M., and Rosenblum, L. A. (eds.), *Friendship and peer relations.* Wiley, New York.

Johnson, D. W., and Johnson, R. T. (1987). *Learning together and alone: Cooperative, competitive, and individualistic learning,* 2nd. ed. Prentice-Hall, Englewood Cliffs, NJ.

Joiner, R., Littleton, K., Faulkner, D., and Miell, D. (2000). *Rethinking collaborative learning.* Free Association Books, London.

Laosa, L. (1980). Maternal teaching strategies in Chicano and Anglo-American families: The influence of culture and education on maternal behavior. *Child Development* 51:759–765.

Lave, J., and Wenger, E. (1991). *Situated learning, Legitimate peripheral participation.* Cambridge University Press, Cambridge.

LeVine, R., Dixon, S., LeVine, S., Richman, A., Leiderman, P. H., Keefer, C. H., and Brazelton, T. B. (1994). *Child care and culture, Lessons from Africa.* Cambridge University Press, Cambridge.

Mackie, D. (1983). The effect of social interaction on conservation of spatial relations. *Journal of Cross-Cultural Psychology* 14:131–151.

Martini, M. (1994). Balancing work and family in Hawai`i, Strategies of parents in two cultural groups. *Family Perspective* 28:103–127.

Martini, M., and Kirkpatrick, J. (1992). Parenting in Polynesia: A view from the Marquesas. In: Roopnarine, J. L., and Carter, D. B. (eds.), *Parent-child socialization in diverse cultures,* Volume 5, *Annual advances in applied developmental psychology,* Ablex, Norwood, NJ, pp. 199–222.

Maynard, A. E. (2002). Cultural teaching: The development of teaching skills in Maya sibling interactions. *Child Development* 73:969–982.

Meltzoff, A. N. (1988). Infant imitation and memory, nine-month-olds in immediate and deferred tests. *Child Development* 59:217–225.

Middleton, D. (1997). The social organization of conversational remembering: Experience as individual and collective concerns. *Mind, Culture, and Activity* 4:71–85.

Miller, P. J., Wiley, A. R., Fung, H., and Liang, C. (1997). Personal storytelling as a medium of socialization in Chinese and American families. *Child Development* 68:557–568.

Mistry, J. (1997). The development of remembering in cultural context. In: Cowan, N. (ed.), *The development of memory in childhood*, Psychology Press, Hove, East Sussex, UK, pp. 343–368.

Morelli, G. A., Rogoff, B., and Angellilo, C. (2003). Cultural variation in young children's access to work or involvement in specialised child-focused activities. *International Journal of Behavioral Development* 27:264–274.

Mullen, M. K., and Yi, S. (1995). The cultural context of talk about the past: Implications for the development of autobiographical memory. *Cognitive Development* 10:407–419.

Nelson, K. (1996). *Language in cognitive development*. Cambridge University Press, Cambridge, UK.

Ochs, E., and Schieffelin, B. (1984). Language acquisition and socialization: Three developmental stories. In Shweder, R., and LeVine, R. (eds.), *Culture theory, Essays on mind, self and emotion*, Cambridge University Press, Cambridge, UK, pp. 276–320.

Ochs, E., and Schieffelin, B. (1994). The impact of language socialization on grammatical development. In Fletcher, P., and MacWhinney, B. (eds.), *Handbook of child language*. Oxford, UK, Blackwell.

Ochs, E., Taylor, C., Rudolph, D., and Smith, R. (1992). Storytelling as a theory-building activity. *Discourse Processes* 15:37–72.

Palinscar, A. S., and Brown, A. L. (1984). Reciprocal teaching of comprehension monitoring activities. *Cognition and Instruction* 1:117–175.

Piaget, J. (1932). *The moral judgment of the child*. Free Press, New York.

Ratner, H. H. (1980). The role of social context in memory development. In: Perlmutter, M. (ed.), *Children's memory*, Jossey-Bass, San Francisco, pp. 49–67.

Ratner, H. H. (1984). Memory demands and the development of young children's memory. *Child Development* 55:2173–2191.

Rogoff, B. (1990). *Apprenticeship in thinking: Cognitive development in social context*. Oxford University Press, New York.

Rogoff, B. (1998). Cognition as a collaborative process. In Damon, W. (Series ed.) and Kuhn, D., and Siegler, R. S. (Vol. eds.), *Cognition, perception and language*, Volume 2, *Handbook of child psychology*, 5th ed. Wiley, New York, pp. 679–744.

Rogoff, B. (2003). *The cultural nature of human development*. Oxford University Press, Oxford, UK.

Rogoff, B., Gauvain, M., and Ellis, S. (1984). Development viewed in its cultural context. In Bornstein, M. H., and Lamb, M. E., (eds.), *Developmental psychology*, Plenum Press, New York, pp. 261–290.

Rogoff, B., Mosier, C., Mistry, J., and Goncu, A. (1993). Guided participation in cultural activity by toddlers and caregivers. *Monographs of the Society for Research in Child Development, 58* (7, Serial No. 236). University of Chicago Press, Chicago.

Rogoff, B., Paradise, R., Mejía Arauz, R., Correa-Chavez, M., and Angelillo, C. (2003). First-hand learning through intent participation. *Annual Review of Psychology* 54:175–203.

Rommetveit, R. (1985). Language acquisition as increasing linguistic structuring of experience and symbolic behavior control. In J. V. Wertsch (ed.), *Culture, communication, and cognition, Vygotskian perspectives*, Cambridge University Press, Cambridge, UK, pp. 183–204.

Ruff, H. A., and Rothbart, M. K. (1996). *Attention in early development, Themes and variations*. Oxford University Press, Oxford, UK.

Segall, M. H., Dasen, P. R., Berry, J. W., and Poortinga, Y. H. (1999). *Human behavior in global perspective: An introduction to cross-cultural psychology*, 2nd ed. Allyn and Bacon, Boston.

Serpell, R., and Hatano, G. (1997). Education, schooling, and literacy. In: Berry, J. W., Dasen, P. R., and Saraswathi, T. S. (eds.), *Handbook of cross-cultural psychology*, Volume 2. *Basic processes and human development*, Allyn and Bacon, Boston, pp. 339–376.

Siegel, M. (1996). Conversation and cognition. In Gelman, R., and Au, T. (eds.), Carterette, E. C., and Friedman, P. (Gen. eds.), *Handbook of perception and cognition*, 2nd ed., *Perceptual and cognitive development*, Academic Press, San Diego, CA, pp. 243–282.

Sigel, I. E., McGillicuddy-DeLisi, A. V., and Goodnow, J. J. (1992). *Parental belief systems: The psychological consequences for children*, 2nd ed. Erlbaum, Hillsdale, NJ.

Siegler, R. S. (2000). The rebirth of children's learning. *Child Development* 71:26–35.

Snow, C. E. (1990). Building memories: The ontogeny of autobiography. In Cicchetti, D., and Beeghly, M. (eds.), *The self in transition, Infancy to childhood*, University of Chicago Press, Chicago, pp. 213–242.

Super, C. M. (1983). Cultural variation in the meaning and uses of children's intelligence. In Deregowski, J. G., Dziurawiec, S., and Annis, R. C. (eds.), *Explorations in cross-cultural psychology*, pp. 199–212. Lisse, Swets and Zeitlinger.

Super, C. M., and Harkness, S. (1982). The infant's niche in rural Kenya and metropolitan America. In Adler, L. L. (ed.), *Cross-cultural research at issue*, Academic Press, San Diego, CA, pp. 47–55.

Super, C. M., and Harkness, S. (1986). The developmental niche: A conceptualization at the interface of child and culture. *International Journal of Behavioral Development* 9:545–569.

Tomasello, M. (1995). Joint attention as social cognition. In Moore, C., and Dunham, P. H., (eds.), *Joint attention, Its origins and role in development*, Hillsdale, NJ, Erlbaum, pp. 103–130.

Tomasello, M. (1999). *The cultural origins of human cognition*. Harvard University Press, Cambridge, MA.

Tomasello, M., and Farrar, M. J. (1986). Joint attention and early language. *Child Development* 57:1454–1463.

Tomasello, M., Kruger, A. C., and Ratner, H. H. (1993). Cultural learning. *Behavioral and Brain Sciences* 16:495–552.

Vygotksy, L. S. (1978). *Mind in society*. Harvard University Press, Cambridge, MA.

Wood, D. J., and Middleton, D. (1975). A study of assisted problem solving. *British Journal of Psychology* 66:181–191.

Chapter 2

Sustainability of Daily Routines as a Family Outcome

Thomas S. Weisner, Catherine Matheson,
Jennifer Coots, and Lucinda P. Bernheimer

A mother of a nine-year-old boy says....

"Monday, I do carpool duty and so I have to drive into Burbank. I pick up my [age 11] son at 1:00, then we dash over to Burbank and pick up 6 kids and they all get off at different times. Even on days that it's not my carpool day, I still have an hour and fifteen minutes drive to pick up my son. Some days it's really hectic. There are days when I have a night class, so we stop and get dinner on the way home, but that's only one day a week. Then, we do homework, I get the kids bathed and in bed. And we found a new, more appropriate school for [my daughter]. We have an impossible schedule. We had to reshuffle our whole lives. We had to give up a lot to have her go to this school, but I felt like for years we'd given up so much to take care of my son's therapy and she [the older sister] was miserable. I thought we've got to try something else. Every once in a while, I get really tired of the 2 hour drive, and then my daughter will say 'Please, I'll do anything, don't pull me from the school. I've never been happier in my life.' Well, as a result, I get up at 4:30 in the morning, and then I don't get to bed until after midnight. We probably have the worst life of all the parents in your study. We are going to die young. As far as sleep, we don't sleep. We exist. I'm lucky, because I'm kind of a night person, but we tend to get sick easily."

INTRODUCTION

The time when parents recognize their child has a developmental delay is one they never forget. In addition to dealing with the emotional consequences, parents begin to reorganize their resources, their family activities, and their goals and priorities. Parents begin to reshape their daily family routine to accommodate to their child with delays, using what resources they have, responding to the nature of their child's conditions. This is an achievement worthy of our respect and worthy of scientific inquiry.

The mother whose voice we hear in the opening quote has a 9-year-old son with ADD and pervasive developmental disorder. She does not work outside the home, due to the fact that, in addition to her son, she has 2 daughters (ages 11 and 7) with hearing impairments and mild learning disabilities. However, she recently started back to school to earn her bachelor's degree. She volunteers in her son's class as much as she can, and actively monitors all 3 children's school placements. Her desire to find the best programs for her children led to both her daughters being placed in a school district over 50 miles away from the family home. Her husband just accepted a new full-time job with a very long commute, so while he is supportive, he will be less available than before. The family is high moderate in SES, and the father's new job provides insurance coverage that they didn't have previously. Mother is always upbeat and has seemingly endless energy. However, with all that this family tries to do, their daily routine shows obvious strains, conflicts, and struggles.

We call this ongoing project of reshaping the family daily routine, sustaining a family social ecology. Our qualitative and quantitative measures of sustainability, and their associations with other measures of family ecology and environment, are the subject of this chapter. The comparative advantage of understanding and assessing sustainability is that a family's own cultural goals are central to the construct and its measurement, and that it is a holistic and contextualized assessment of family strengths. Barring substantial pathology of some kind in individuals or in family life, all families manage to sustain a routine of life of some sort. At the same time, daily routines depend on several dimensions of coherence and integration—that is, sustainability varies across families in a community, and across communities around the world. A family that has a more sustainable daily routine has a family ecology that 1) fits with available resources; 2) has meaning with respect to goals and values; 3) balances inevitable family conflicts; and 4) provides some stability and predictability for family members.

Development Along Pathways

Sustainability of family life puts developmental research and the study of learning squarely in the context of children and families engaged in activities within a cultural community. Development occurs along pathways given to us by culture and society, and actively chosen and engaged in by parents and children within some particular cultural ecology. Imagine these pathways as consisting of everyday activities (getting ready for bed, sleeping, having breakfast; going to church; sitting in classrooms; visiting relatives; playing video games; doing homework; hanging with your friends; going to the mall; dating; "partying", watching TV). Those activities and their cultural and ecological contexts are the "stepping stones" we traverse as we move along a pathway through the day and the day's routine. These activities make up our life pathways, which we engage in each day. This activities-on-a-pathway conceptual framework is not only useful for thinking about human development; it encourages and expects the use of multiple methods. How can one conceptualize development as such a journey on a pathway consisting of activities in some specific cultural-ecological context, and imagine that we could use only one method to find out about it (Weisner, 2002; also drawn from Weisner, in press)?

A pathways framework encourages understanding what children do in their everyday activities, grasping the personal experiences of parents and children in those contexts, and knowing the cultural psychology—the shared beliefs, motives, and scripts organizing behavior and thought—of the communities the parents and children are in. Children not only actively and joyously engage in those activities, they also resist and transform them as active agents.

Children's daily engagement in these routines is an important part of child development. Communities share patterned features of daily routines and a cultural psychology, though of course there are local, familial, and individual variations of them. These are the "population-specific" patterns that shape the local pathways of life children engage:

> No account of ontogeny in human adaptation could be adequate without the inclusion of the population specific patterns that establish pathways for the behavioral development of children. (LeVine et al., 1994, p. 12)

LeVine describes the socialization of children as "... the intentional design of psychologically salient environments for children's development." (LeVine, 2003, p. 1). Population-specific, shared patterns are a powerful way in which environments are designed. The sociocultural perspective situates human development in the population-specific, intentionally-designed everyday worlds and paths through life. These provide the cultural careers (Goldschmidt, 1992) that families and societies afford us.

The developmental pathway approach to human development comes at an important time. New conceptions of development and new methods are being called for in many fields, but there are as yet few examples of findings based on those concepts and methods. Journals and research funders are looking for better ways to include mixed methods as the standard for research, rather than an occasional add-on—but are unsure how to evaluate such work if made standard. Diversity in the United States and elsewhere is increasing, demographic "majority minorities" are emerging in states throughout the country, yet ways to understand these communities are lagging behind. Schools and other institutions that support families are looking for better ways to train and assist children and their families, but are struggling to find policies that work. How can we enhance the chances for success in youth development—that is, the provision of supports and opportunities that can guide children onto successful pathways and help keep them there—unless we fully and holistically study those pathways in the first place?

A sociocultural perspective on development also offers ways to conceptualize and assess child and family outcomes missed by individualistic, non-contextual perspectives. Well-being for children, for example, can be viewed as the engagement by children and parents in everyday routines and activities, part of a life pathway of such activities, that are deemed desirable by them and their community. These kinds of engagement produce the positive psychological experiences (effectance, pleasure, attachments, flow, competence) that go along with sociocultural well-being. Empirical study of how to promote the supports and opportunities for children that contribute to successful pathways and promote more engagement in them, requires integration across the methods in the social sciences. In this chapter, for example, we use a fieldwork and interview procedure, the Ecocultural Family Interview, that taps the family daily routine of activities. The interview ensures that content specific to the community being studied is incorporated into the data (Lieber, Weisner, & Pressley, 2003; Weisner, 2002).

Sustainable Family Routines and Families with Children with Developmental Disabilities

Focusing on the family routine as a way into understanding family social ecology is not a new idea in the field of developmental delays, but it is of relatively recent vintage. Historically, research on outcomes for families adapting to children with developmental delays featured mental health outcomes, usually of parents, or focused on stress and coping. While mental health is an important and significant outcome, too exclusive focus on mental health can lead to the notion "that a family with a child who has a disability is a family with a disability" (Glidden, 1993). A growing body of work questions this model of "expected impairment" (Boyce & Barnett, 1993), as well as the association between adapting to childhood disability and increased family maladjustment or dysfunction (Dyson, 1991; Hanson & Hanline, 1990; Keogh, Bernheimer, Gallimore, & Weisner, 1998; Sloper, Knussen, Turner, & Cunningham, 1991). Keogh, et al. (1998), among others, have pressed for consideration of other, more positive family outcomes. Response to stress and major perturbations of life through effective coping no doubt is an important family capacity, but the family ability to sustain a daily routine of life that is viable the rest of the time, surely deserves serious study and increased recognition as a complementary family strength.

Of course, effective coping as a response to various forms of stress certainly can be a way for parents to construct a supportive, protective social ecology (Baldwin, Baldwin, & Cole, 1990; Bristol, 1984; Caldwell & Bradley, 1994). Many approaches to family ecology begin with the classical model of response to crisis, and examine family ecology in terms of coping and stress (Hill, 1949; McCubbin & Patterson, 1983; Patterson 1988). Another way to measure supportive family circumstances is to index them by family income, social class, or social support scales (Cohen & Syme, 1985; Crnic, Dunst, Trivette, & Deal, 1988; Dunst & Trivette, 1990; Friedrich, & Greenberg, 1983). Family environment scales focus on interactional quality and literacy-related stimulation such as the FES (Moos & Moos, 1986), and HOME (Caldwell & Bradley, 1984). These measures index aspects of family status related to interactional quality among family members and child stimulation.

As useful and productive as these approaches have been, they have limitations. First, the structural/categorical variables, such as SES or income or ethnicity, are only proxies for the processes and activities of the family social ecology. Income level may correlate with better child outcomes, but why, and at what cost for other family members, or at what opportunity cost for pursuing other activities? Second, most of these proxies tap material aspects of life, as opposed to cultural and family values, beliefs, or other "family capacity" variables which can be powerful mediators of child outcomes (Gallagher, 1989). Third, some measures of family environment define the "goodness" of the social ecology for only one individual, e.g. the child with delays, thereby confounding a potential family outcome with one focused on a single member. Since a family outcome is always concerned with outcomes for all members, and since family members are to some extent in competition and conflict as well as cooperation, it is dubious to use as a family outcome a measure that taps how "good" the social ecology is only for a single individual. Family adaptations have a collective outcome benefiting or harming each member somewhat differently. Excessive focus on cognitive or socioemotional stimulation benefiting primarily one particular child ignores the collective goals of family adaptation.

And finally, the relevance for policy and intervention of these other approaches is limited. Distal structural features (income, employment prospects, community supports, service availability, insurance policies) indeed are important and may require systematic change, yet not be within our or the family's power to change very easily, except through longer term political and community involvement. Similarly, interactional characteristics of families and overall family climate are consequential, but, taken out of the context of the daily routine, they may be hard to change or even identify. Focusing on everyday family routines and activities meaningful to parents and children can be a useful level of analysis for intervention (Moes & Frea, 2000). A sociocultural theory of family learning based on child and parental engagement in developmental pathways in cultural context can have policy relevance.

Sustaining a Meaningful Family Routine: Definition and Examples from Families with Children with Disabilities

Sustaining a daily routine is a universal adaptive problem for all families, and emerges out of ecological-cultural (hereafter ecocultural) theory (LeVine, 1977; Munroe, Munroe, & Whiting, 1981; Weisner, 1984; 1993; Whiting, 1976; 1980; Whiting & Edwards, 1988). Ecocultural family theory applies Super and Harkness' notion of a developmental niche for the child (Super & Harkness, 1980; 1986), to the study of the family. A culture is conceptualized as practices and activities embedded in everyday routines, and the shared cultural models and interpretative meanings those activities have in a community (Weisner, 1997). Ecocultural theory combines social ecology indicators known to influence development (such as basic health and mortality threats, material and social resources, social support for mothers, peer networks, and so forth) with measures of activities and shared cultural meanings. Parents' goals for family life, parenting and development drawn from their cultural niche, are important to understanding family ecology. Family daily routines represent the operationalization or instantiation of what cultures and parents jointly have constructed to achieve these personal and cultural goals. The Ecocultural Family Interview taps this dimension of family life.

Sustainable Daily Routines: A Definition

The unit of analysis in assessing sustainability is neither individual behavior, nor the family social address (e.g., SES level, single mother, Euro-American). Instead, it is the daily routine of activities and events. Sustainability of family routines differs from the stress and reactions attending the crisis of the discovery of delay and the psychology of coping with these stressors. Sustainability captures another, more enduring project: juggling ongoing demands and meeting long term goals, rather than coping with crisis and stress (Gallimore, Bernheimer, & Weisner, 1999; Glidden, 1993). This project is of course common to all families everywhere, not uniquely different for families with children with delays (although demands and stress are clearly often high in these families), and so families with children with delays should respond in similar, more than in unique, ways to the challenge.

Sustainable routines of daily activities share at least these four features, which affect the well being of family members.

Social Ecological Fit. Parents have to balance their family ecology with available resources and limitations. For instance, how should parents allocate scarce time and money and attention to their child with delays and other family members? Should they focus on their work, on health insurance, on stimulation for the child with delays, on siblings, on the spouse, on seeking services and information, on friends, on church or other areas? Ecological fit means to find stability given family resources, competing interests, and goals, to be able to juggle and balance these resources in a functional adaptation.

Ecological fit does not just mean more resources; it means that the resources available roughly match and support the activities that the family weaves into a daily routine. Although more income and wealth and greater education and job status certainly matter for sustainability, our theory specifically differs from those in which more is better—where merely having more income, for instance, would be the central feature associated with a more sustainable routine, or better developmental outcomes. Our theory suggests that even families with limited income can organize a sustainable routine.

Congruence and Balance. Parents have to assess the inevitably competing interests of family members. Which family members' concerns should take precedence, when there are always inconsistent, conflicting concerns among family members? Some parents strive for a cultural ideal of "equal" treatment of siblings for example, or spend nearly all their time with the child with disabilities because the child needs so much more attention. Neither of these ways to balance conflicting needs are easy to sustain. Sustainable routines show the results of parental efforts to fit their routines to individual needs and competencies of different family members.

Meaning.   Parents try to organize their routine in a personally, culturally, and morally right way. After all, there are many possible ways to respond to their child and organize their family life, but only a small set of ways would be acceptable to any particular family—that would meet the criterion of being meaningful or appropriate for that family and its cultural community. In whatever ways families respond to their concerns about their child—will they feel that they have made the <u>right</u> choices? The right choices are those that will be more meaningful, choices, which fit with morally and culturally significant values and goals. These are experienced as meaningful in part because they are concordant with implicit and explicit cultural models of parenting and development shared by parents in a community. Meaningfulness involves asking parents about the interpretive meaning them of their routine. Does the routine meet the goals of and for development and family life from the points of view of family members, rather than from the points of view of service providers, researchers, or others. Sustainability is greater if family ecology has meaning with respect to personal goals.

Stability/predictability.   Change is required for sustainability of daily routines, and is often a positive sign. Sustainability requires adaptation and is a dynamic process. However, constant change without meaning or fit or balance is not a sign of sustainability, and is not good for children or parents. Frequent change in a chaotic, unpredictable daily routine is not a sign of sustainability.

RESEARCH QUESTIONS

Five research questions regarding sustainability are considered in this chapter. Each of these questions offers a sociocultural perspective on family life and child development:

- Is sustainability of family routine a goal families talk about, is it understandable to them, and can it be reliably rated? If not, then use for research and practice will be restricted and it is largely perhaps of conceptual but not substantive interest. Is it meaningful to parents' concerns? If so, it should be given serious attention, but if it is confusing and distant from what matters to parents and families, it might not be worth the effort to assess.
- What are the descriptive, qualitative characteristics of families with different patterns of sustainability?

- How is sustainability related to parental education, SES and other variables? Is it merely a proxy for family SES and resources? If so, then the notion of sustainability might still be useful to discern the mechanisms through which resources matter in families and development, but its status as an additional, complementary family assessment weakens. Our expectation is that higher SES, and more years of formal education are not going to be strongly associated with sustainability, except when resources are very few and formal education precludes sustainability due to associated poverty. Workload and social network connectedness, however, are more likely to show associations, because they are more proximal measures that directly impact the daily routine and its activities.

- How is sustainability related to conventional measures of family functioning and home environment (e.g. the HOME, FES, FACES)? If it is highly correlated with existing questionnaire measures of family functioning across child ages, this is of interest for validity reasons, but for ease of measurement, we might as well use existing family measures.

- How does sustainability change or remain stable in families over a 10 year period? Sustainability does not mean life is unchanging, but rather dynamic adaptation and balance, and it may well change as children get older or other family circumstances change. Are families with resource fit, balance, meaningfulness with respect to goals, and relative predictability when children are age 3, still like that when their child is 13?

We show that sustainability can be assessed, is meaningful to parents and reflects their concerns, is not strongly related to existing family measures, and is not simply a proxy for SES, and is fairly stable for 75% of families. Hence we argue that on conceptual and empirical grounds, a holistic, sociocultural assessment of the family project of sustaining a meaningful routine of life deserves consideration.

SAMPLE AND MEASURES

Sample

We used data from Project CHILD, a 10 year study of families of children with delays living in Southern California (Gallimore, Coots, Weisner, Garnier, & Guthrie, 1996; Gallimore, Weisner, Kaufman & Bernheimer, 1989; Gallimore, Weisner, et al, 1989; Nihira, Weisner, and

Bernheimer, 1994; Weisner, 1993; Weisner, Beizer, & Stolze, 1991; Weisner, Matheson, & Bernheimer, 1996). A cohort of 102 Euro-American families with delayed children aged three to four years old were recruited into a longitudinal study in 1985-86 (there were 103 children—one family had twins, both delayed). The children and their families were recruited through Regional Centers, early intervention programs, community preschools, and pediatricians.

Parents were primarily in their early to mid-30's when we first contacted them, with 12% single mothers. If there was a divorce or separation during the course of the study, we stayed with the child and his/her main caregiver(s). Altogether, 19.4% of the children were in a single parent household (mother, father, grandmother, or other relative). About 25% of the mothers were employed full-time initially, and about 50% by age 13. The mean family socioeconomic level, assessed with the four-way Hollingshead (a standard scale combining education and employment status), was 44.7 ("middle-middle-class"), with a range from below poverty level in a number of families, to a family with income over $150,000 a year.

Each family in our sample has a child who had been judged to be "developmentally delayed" by a professional or an agency. Developmental delay is a term of relatively recent vintage and lacks definitional specificity (Bernheimer & Keogh, 1986). It is essentially a nonspecific "clinical" term with less ominous overtones for the future than "retarded" (Bernheimer & Keogh, 1988; Bernheimer, Keogh, & Coots, 1993). Children with known genetic abnormalities were excluded from the sample, as were children whose delays were associated with either known prenatal alcohol or drug usage, or with postnatal neglect or abuse (Bernheimer and Keogh 1986, 1982).

At entry the mean child chronological age (CA) was 41.8 months (SD = 6.2; range = 32 to 55). The mean Gesell developmental quotient (DQ) was 72.32 (SD = 15.97; range = 38 to 117). At entry, all but 18 of the children had DQs below 90, and all 103 had significant delays in one or more areas (motor, speech, behavior, or cognition) in spite of some relatively high DQs. When the children were between 67 and 99 months old (mean = 84; SD = 6), another round of testing was conducted in a manner that replicated the original procedures. The mean Binet IQ was 71.40 (SD = 18.26, range = 24 to 114). At age 11, the children were tested again with a mean Binet IQ of 66.68 (SD = 20.29, [range 27 to 122]). The cognitive/developmental scores were quite stable with a correlation from age 3 to 7 of .69 (Bernheimer, Keogh, and Coots, 1993) and from age 7 to 11 of .83 (Gallimore, et al, 1996).

Attrition has been remarkably low. Out of 102 initial families, 6 were lost or declined contact by age 13, and 3 children are deceased. We have maintained contact with 91% of the sample. At age seven N = 97 and at age

11 N = 95. At age 13, a 50% sample (45 families) was randomly selected for interviews. (Age 13 data are representative of our total sample, but should be viewed as tentative due to reduced sample size.)

Measures

We developed qualitative and quantitative assessments of family sustainability, and have independent measures of family ecology, accommodations, environment, demographics, and child characteristics, which we then related to family sustainability.

Assessment of Family Sustainability

Sample families were visited by a trained interviewer at child ages 3, 7, 11, and 13. These interviewers conducted semi-structured interviews with the parents, the Ecocultural Family Interview (EFI); each interview lasted from one to three hours. Parents were encouraged to "tell their story" about their child and about how they were or were not adapting their family routine, and in response to what or whom. There were no false negatives; if parents did not bring up topics, we used probes that carefully covered standard ecocultural domains (resources, supports, child services, siblings, work schedules, goals, etc.). Each family also completed a questionnaire covering standard demographic information and socioeconomic status characteristics of the family. Field notes were also compiled for each family. For additional information on the various methods used in the study, see Gallimore, et al, 1993; 1996: Nihira, Weisner, & Bernheimer, 1994; Weisner, 1984; Weisner et al, 1996.

Our fieldwork staff held a series of meetings to discuss, case by case, the nature of sustainability and well being across the families. We attempted to develop specific indicators that would differentiate what we knew of family strengths and weaknesses, within the overall framework of ecocultural theory. The typology we eventually developed emerged from these dynamic discussions, closely related to our comprehensive knowledge of the families and children. Fieldworkers and interviewers carefully reviewed each family, using the four criteria for assessing a daily routine (ecological and resource fit, balanced interests, meaningfulness, and stability/predictability). Assessments were made at child ages 3, 7, 11, and 13. Fieldworkers doing assessments had no knowledge of test scores, scores on other family assessment measures, or any of the quantitative measures of family or child status subsequently related to our sustainability judgments. (Additional details regarding coding and reliability are available from the authors.)

Qualitative assessment of each family required <u>contextual</u> knowledge about each family as well as across families; <u>depth</u> of understanding; <u>breadth</u> of knowledge about the family; and <u>accuracy</u> and <u>precision</u> about what such features as material and social resources, or family goals, or the child's behavioral problems actually look and feel like in the context of everyday family life (Becker, 1996; Weisner, 1996).

Ecocultural Features

SES, workload, social supports, and other indicators were scored using interviews and questionnaires (Gallimore, et al, 1989; Weisner, 1993). Twelve ecocultural domains were assessed: socioeconomic status; career work orientation; efforts to structure the home environment; help for family; help available within the family; workload related to the child; connectedness of the family; formal/support assistance; integration of child into nondisabled networks; integration of child into disabled networks; and use of information from professionals. Internal-consistency reliability was established for the EFI domain scores and is reported in Nihira, Weisner, & Bernheimer, 1994. Three summary ecocultural factors (SES/Resources, Family Workload, and Connectedness/Family Help) were derived at each time period from the ecocultural domains.

Assessment of Family Accommodation

Accommodation is defined as a family's functional responses or adjustments to the demands of daily life with a child with delays (Gallimore, et al., 1989; 1993; 1996). Accommodations include actions taken, avoided, or delayed in order to create and sustain a daily family routine. Accommodations that were wholly or mainly made to other family members, such as siblings, were excluded. Reliabilities of these ratings were: age 3–78%; age 7–70%, and age 11–82% (Gallimore, et al., 1993, p. 192; Gallimore, et al., 1996, p. 222; Weisner, et al., 1991, p. 654):

Four measures of accommodation were used: Internal Accommodation, External Accommodation, Accommodation Intensity, and Accommodation Frequency (Gallimore et al, 1996; Keogh, Bernheimer, & Guthrie, 1997). These measures are available at ages 3, 7, and 11 only. Internal and External factors reflect accommodations directed within the family and those directed outside the family respectively. Accommodation Intensity was rated on a 9-point scale from low to high. Accommodation Intensity measures the extent to which accommodations across all the accommodation domains was a theme or dominant *focus* of family adaptation to childhood disability. Accommodation Frequency reflected the total number of family accommodation activities that fit within 82 categories of family accommodation scored for all families.

Family Environment Scales

Measures of family and home environment included the Home Observation for the Measurement of Environment (HOME) (Caldwell & Bradley, 1984), the Family Adaptability and Cohesion Evaluation Scale (FACES) (Olsen, Partner, & Lavee, 1985), and the Family Environment Scale (FES) (Moos & Moos, 1986). The HOME was rated by fieldworkers following family visits. The FACES and FES were administered to parents in a mail-out questionnaire when children were age three and seven only.

Child hassle

"Hassle" is an ethnobehavioral term often used by parents to describe child problems that have an impact on the daily routine of family life. We rated each child on a 9-point scale from low to high across six areas: medical, behavioral, communication, interaction rate, responsiveness, and behavioral appropriateness. Reliabilities are: age 3 (88%), age 7 (77%) and age 11 (93%) (Gallimore, et al., 1996).

RESULTS

Sustainability of Family Routines: Meaning to Parents; Reliability

Parents' narrative accounts of family adaptation confirmed at least one theoretical assumption—a sustainable daily routine of family life is a readily articulated parental goal. Parents understood the task of sustaining a routine, and spontaneously would talk about it. Asking parents to "walk me through your day", or "tell me how things have been going", or "what has been working for you and what hasn't" will lead to a rich, often emotional account. We identified five overall patterns of family sustainability, which were comprehensively described and reliably rated using qualitative case and pattern analyses. Raters were able to assess the components of sustainability as well as ecocultural features influencing sustainability, such as loss of jobs or child services, or changes in supports. The final criteria we used for placing a family in one of five overall sustainability groups is presented in Appendix A, for children at age 11 (fieldworkers took into account variations in families and children reflecting differences in developmental concerns at each age). Appendix A also summarizes the family constellation among resources, conflict, meaning, and stability characteristic of thatsustainability group Disagreements regarding sustainability processes and overall criteria for sustainability were initially discussed in fieldworker meetings and resolved by one of the authors (CM). We were successful in achieving interrater agreement in judging these five groups.

An independent blind rater reviewed a randomly selected set of 10% of the interviews and fieldnotes with 74% agreement at age 3, 67% at age 7, 74% at age 11, and 100% at age 13.

Sustainability: Five Qualitative Patterns

The four holistic family adaptive patterns that make up sustainability for each family varied within and across the families. Some families struggled with resources yet had quite high meaningfulness and stability, but considerable conflict, for instance. Others had seemingly very adequate resources but the couple argued over what to do about their child, changed their routines a lot, and did not report that they had much "peace of mind" with regard to their family routine.

Although there was a fair amount of independence across the holistic patterns, these were patterns. Families with less conflict did tend to have more meaningfulness, somewhat more resources, and somewhat more stability, for instance. Hence, differences in overall sustainability could be discerned looking across each adaptive concern. The processes that lead to differences in sustainability were clustered together to some extent.

Multiply Troubled—Low Sustainability Families (Age 3–1%; Age 7–8%; Age 11–8%; Age 13–2%)

The families with the lowest levels of sustainability of a routine would be recognizable even without extensive qualitative or quantitative assessments. We described their family routines as multiply troubled. They had problematic fit with their ecology and resources, little balance or stability, and the lowest sense that their routine fit their goals and was meaningful for them. Stability was an ongoing concern of parents.

A few of these parents had serious personal problems, such as alcoholism, or experiences of spousal abuse, or had disabilities themselves. In addition, parents had few religious contacts or other forms of social support. Parents often seemed overwhelmed, responding reactively rather than proactively. As would be expected, the daily routines of these families were unstable, unpredictable, sometimes chaotic; some fieldworkers called these families' circumstances "precarious". There was little balance across different family members' interests.

These parents and their children had multiple, severe problems in at least three and often more, of the following areas: resources (jobs, income, financial and health insurance), child hassle, marital relationships, the extent of the family workload, social and familial support, and the health problems of the parent him or her self, or the sibs. For example one family was living on $12K–$15K a year, with the father's business failing, few supports, parents angry and upset, siblings rebellious (one with developmental delays of his own), with their child diagnosed with "autistic-like" behaviors, needing constant supervision. Over ten years, these troubles never really improved; family routine could not fit with their resources, their family could not develop a balance and coherence, and their expressed goals and values were unrealized in their routine of life.

Vulnerable but Struggling—Low-Moderate Sustainability (Age 3–16%; Age 7–16%; Age 11–17%; Age 13–9%)

These families were sometimes described as "hanging on". They usually missed the Multiply Troubled classification because of a focus on goals and meaning-related strengths. These parents were more likely to be actively religious, for instance. They sometimes talked about just "taking things as they come", or being "slow and steady", to endure or accept what their problems are. These families, unlike Low sustainability family situations, had at least one domain of life in which they seemed to be doing fairly well. As one mother said to us about her struggles, "This is all the reasons why I need God. . . . you either go crazy or you question why and you find out why and you find the peace and the help that is out there just sitting there waiting for you and so that's how I came to have God mean so much to me." Their resources and resource fit are still quite precarious, and they have significant difficulties in sustaining their routines in 3 or even more of the domains indicated in Appendix A—financial resources, jobs, connectedness in the family, connections outside the family, services, marital or couple relationships, and others. Balance and stability are difficult to sustain at times, but show intermittent improvement.

One family struggled with a child with significant behavioral problems, committing to a time and effort-consuming series of interventions over many years, which caused family discord and low balance amongst family members. Ecological and resource fit was adequate but the family had to move closer to father's work, which was disruptive.

Improving/Resilient—Moderate Levels of Sustainability (Age 3–32%; Age 7–25%; Age 11–29%; Age 13–32%)

These parents had resource fit problems, but in fewer domains than the Troubled or Struggling groups. They also reported that things were improving over time. Their balance and stability was higher, and they reported feeling less overwhelmed, although they reported being busy and active. It took effort and "grit", proactivity and some good fortune at times to sustain their routine. The sense of meaning and fit with goals was not very high however—few of these families had real peace of mind with respect to their goals. Families in this group showed effective adaptive responses in the face of threat—that is, they had some resilience, but not an easily sustainable routine. In some other cases these parents thought that their child was making good enough progress, or thought their child was nearly normal in development, so that active accommodation and concern was not particularly important in parents' opinions (although not always according to others' opinions, such as teachers, professionals, other family members, or fieldworkers). These parents may not have as many resources, and may have more conflicts and difficulties in their families, and less balance, than parents in our higher sustainability groups. On the other hand, they do not report high levels of dissatisfaction with their lives, nor with special services they have obtained. A fairly common reason for this is that some do not believe their child is on a particularly delayed developmental path.

One family had financial struggles and uncertain income from the entertainment industry, yet managed to make ends meet, and received help from relatives. These parents have a child that is average in terms of behavioral hassle but with serious speech and communication problems. The child was able to benefit from special services from the school in their local area. Parents agreed generally on what to do, and the two children from the mother's first marriage help out some in caring for the child with disabilities. The parents compare their situation favorably with that of other families: "... even though we have a problem, it's lighter than anyone else's.... he's a handful, but I can imagine what it is for some of the others."

Active—Moderately High Sustainability (Age 3–18%; Age 7–18%; Age 11–17%; Age 13–18%)

These families are dissatisfied with the balance amongst differing family members' goals (reported conflicts and disagreements are relatively high), and in the meaningfulness of their routines. At the same time, their resource fit is the highest of any of our sustainability groups. Some of these parents do not have a sense of peace of mind regarding their family routine. Some continue to be concerned over schools, placements, services, or what it has taken for them to monitor the sometimes, difficult behavior of their children. A number of parents in this group have struggled to balance career and work with their child. Compared to the first three groups, these parents are likely to have a higher functioning, lower hassle child, few or no job, income or work-related problems, fewer marital problems, better personal health, and on average, more of a support network consisting of at least one of the following: spouse, live-in help or roommate, extended family, church, or professionals.

One family has quite high income, and the mother spends full time as a homemaker and advocate for her son, who has developmental delays and communication problems. But she doesn't feel that the services she has found are meeting her child's needs: "...even though [these service providers] are special educators and psychologists," they "...continually try and tell us what is best for [our son]." She has spent considerable time in his classroom "training" teachers, as well as her relatives and friends, in how best to work with her son. The family has met some goals and values in their everyday lives, but not others, and there is an imbalance in how they have distributed their time and energy, and a continuing dissatisfaction with their routine.

Stable/Sustainable—Highest Sustainability (Age 3–34%; Age 7–32%; Age 11–28%; Age 13–49%)

This group shares many features of the Moderately High group, but this group has an underlying attitude of satisfaction or contentment regarding their child's situation, their ongoing family adaptation, and the way the child's needs are fit into the daily routine of the entire family. Most of the families in this group have reduced needs for services, better assistance with care, less need for career changes and acceptance of the choices made in the past. These families are similar to the Moderate group with quite similar levels of family adaptive challenges. But they differ in the meanings and goals they have. They frame their challenges as opportunities, as being "acceptable", with the result generally meeting their own sense of balance and meaningfulness. These families are not spending much time getting involved with the child's schooling nor with most other services. There is also little sense of tension and conflict regarding finances, marital adjustment, or siblings. Balance among competing family interests exists but at low to modest levels. In general, these families could be described as having high "peace of mind" regarding their family accommodation and the meaningfulness of what they have done to alter their daily family routines. These families have adapted most clearly in a sustainable, meaningful, and congruent way, although by no means easily or without proactive efforts. Their routines are relatively stable, and they show resilience when changes come.

One family combined active church membership, a successful business, and declining involvement in direct care or teaching for their child, who has significant speech and language difficulties. The daily routine is described as relaxed, quiet, and busy. "Either I'm just getting used to it [her child's delays and their routine], or it's not as bad, I don't know which," the mother remarked. The younger brother spends time with the child with delays and with parents. Their social network outside of church is not strong, nor is family support, but they say that will come eventually.

How is Sustainability Related to Parental Education, SES, Workload, and Social Network Connections?

We next turned to the associations of family sustainability with other common indicators of social ecology and family circumstances. Mothers with high school or less education were more often in the Low and Low Moderate sustainability groups, and fewer were in the Moderately High group then expected by chance at ages 3 and 7. College-educated fathers were more likely to be in the Moderately High group and less likely to be in the Moderate group. Overall, mothers' levels of education were significantly related to our five sustainability groups when children were 3 ($X^2 = 31.99, n = 98$) and 7 ($X^2 = 26.22, n = 98$), but not at age 11. Fathers' education showed a significant difference only at 11 ($X^2 = 31.54, n = 84$). Sustainability shows some associations with parents' formal education, but at the same time, sustainability is not the purview only of more educated families.

Single parents had more difficulties sustaining a daily routine however. There were more single parents ($X^2 = 17.80, n = 100$) in the Low Moderate and Moderate groups when children were 3 and 11. Expanded families (usually single parents living with their own parents or other kin) were also more likely to have more difficulties in family sustainability at age three, but not later ages ($X^2 = 15.39, n = 100$). Conjugal/married families show no significant differences in their levels of sustainability—for instance, there were proportionately as many couples in the Vulnerable/Struggling and Improving/Resilient groups as in the Stable/Sustainable group.

Family SES and Resources

Sustainability is certainly related to family resources. More resources translate into better resource fit, but only to a limited extent does this relationship extend into other sustainability patterns. The first rows of Table 1 for ages 3, 7 and 11 shows significant mean differences in socioeconomic status. (Too few families were in the lowest group to include them in the analysis at age 3.) However, note that the Moderate, Low Moderate and Low groups are not significantly different from each other on SES. The High and Moderately High families differ on SES only at child age 7. The High groups are actually <u>lower</u> in SES than the Moderately High. Overall, SES distinguishes the two highest groups from the three lower sustainability groups, but otherwise characteristics of families other than SES come in to play in shaping family sustainability.

There are a number of families with relatively low income, who nonetheless appear to have constructed a reasonably sustainable daily routine even while struggling with fitting together scarce resources.

Table 1. ANOVAs Comparing Sustainability Ratings and Ecocultural Ratings at Ages 3, 7, and 11

Ecocultural Ratings	Sustainability Ratings					
	Low	Low Moderate	Moderate	High Moderate	High	F
Age 3						
Socioeconomic Status	NA	44.15^{ab}	46.53^{cd}	53.30^{ac}	53.20^{bd}	7.28***
Family Workload	NA	48.58	49.60	54.29	48.57	
Connectedness	NA	45.00^{ab}	45.53^{cd}	54.59^{ac}	53.76^{bd}	7.73***
Age 7						
Socioeconomic Status	42.82^{ab}	49.02^{c}	47.71^{d}	56.77^{acde}	51.12^{be}	4.14**
Family Workload	46.69	55.11^{ab}	48.06^{ac}	54.49^{cd}	46.57^{bd}	3.10*
Connectedness	46.11	49.32	48.40	51.02	51.38	
Age 11						
Socioeconomic Status	40.91^{ab}	48.74^{cd}	45.73^{ef}	57.03^{ace}	55.40^{bdf}	8.51***
Family Workload	51.10	53.86^{a}	48.02^{b}	55.29^{bcc}	46.04^{ac}	3.14*
Connectedness	41.83^{ab}	48.86	46.88^{c}	52.28^{a}	54.91^{bc}	3.98**

Note. Means followed by the same superscript differ significantly in pairwise posthoc tests.
*** $p < .001$, ** $p < .01$, * $p < .05$.

Religion provides meaning in some families, and leads to a belief that they have an opportunity, not a burden, to care for their child. Many of these lower income/higher sustainability families are typically troubled by only one additional issue, for example a child that is high in behavioral or medical problems, or marital discord, but no other issues. These families seemed able to concentrate their accommodation efforts and limited resources on this one central problem. Further characteristic of these families, one parent (usually the mother) is either unusually proactive and dynamic, *or* slow and steady, just taking things one day at a time. In relatively lower SES families, parental goals and temperaments often allow for a relatively sustainable routine.

Family Workload and Connectedness

When family workloads are very high or unpredictable, family routines are more difficult to sustain. However, the absolute amount of workload, (except at <u>very</u> high or very low levels), is not the key for sustainability. Rather, workload influences family sustainability through the way the workload is integrated, balanced, shared, and its meaning constructed by parents. The High sustainability group is different from the Moderately High in having a relatively low workload, but this group also has the highest average Connectedness score of the five groups at all three child ages. The level of Family Workload involving the child with delays discriminates sustainability groups at ages 7 and 11, and Connectedness does so at ages 3 and 11 (the second and third rows under each age in Table 1).

How is Sustainability Related to Conventional Measures of Family Functioning?

Traditional Family Measures

We expected that there would be relatively few and scattered relationships between these standard family measures and sustainability, and that is generally what we find when we compared a wide range of subscales of traditional family assessment scales to overall sustainability. Table 2 shows mean scores for FES, HOME, and FACES on each subscale for ages three and seven (data were not collected at age 11). Three FES scales, eight HOME scales, and two summary FACES scores were compared to sustainability. None of the FES scales are related to sustainability at age three, and the Expression scale is the only one significant at age seven (i.e., only one of six Anovas is significant). Three of eight HOME subscales are significant at child age three, and four at age seven (i.e., seven of a possible sixteen). Only the FACES Cohesion scale is significant at age three and no FACES scale is significant at age seven (i.e., only one of four FACES scales was significant). At age seven, the Lowest sustainability families score significantly lower than the other four groups on the FES or HOME subscales five of 13 times. The other four groups of families, however, are either indistinguishable or only weakly differentiated by the traditional measures, even though, in fact, daily life is very different across these four groups according to our sustainability assessments.

The Lowest sustainability group accounts for nearly all of the statistically significant group differences. The Low sustainability families at age seven have somewhat lower scores on HOME subscales. This is consistent with our fieldwork reports: it is not difficult to spot concerns in the Lowest sustainability group. But to discern the strengths and concerns of families in the other four groups, conventional family assessment questionnaires seemed insufficient. Understanding meaning/goals, balance, and stability was required. In addition, it is striking that no one sustainability group contributes disproportionately to the Anova differences for FES, HOME, OR FACES measures. Active Stable families for example, are not uniformly high across the various scales in traditional family measures.

Sustainability is certainly not a proxy for traditional family measures. Families relatively low in sustainability can and do offer their children

Table 2. ANOVAs Comparing Sustainability Ratings and FES, HOME, & FACES Ratings at Ages 3 and 7

FES, HOME, & FACES	Sustainability Ratings					
	Low	Low Moderate	Moderate	High Moderate	High	F
Age 3						
FES Achievement	NA	4.59	5.39	5.33	5.58	
FES Expression	NA	4.91	5.67	6.04	6.48	
FES Religion/Morality	NA	1.69	1.52	1.83	1.78	
HOME Learning Stimulation	NA	7.82	8.26	9.61	9.18	
HOME Language Stimulation	NA	5.59[a]	5.68[b]	6.50[ab]	6.12	3.13*
HOME Physical Environment	NA	6.12	5.97[ab]	6.94[a]	6.72[b]	3.94**
HOME Warmth & Affection	NA	6.47	6.32	6.67	6.54	
HOME Academic Stimulation	NA	2.65	2.94	3.50	3.24	
HOME Modeling	NA	3.35	3.77	4.17	4.03	
HOME Variety in Experience	NA	4.71[abc]	6.00[a]	6.89[b]	6.24[c]	5.37***
HOME Acceptance*	NA	5.50	5.33	7.20	6.17	
FACES Cohesion	NA	36.19[ab]	38.25[cd]	44.11[ac]	42.39[bd]	6.56***
FACES Adaptation	NA	22.69	23.07	22.50	22.45	
Subsample n		n = 17	n = 31	n = 18	n = 33	
Age 7						
FES Achievement	5.04	5.12	5.07	5.38	4.79	
FES Expression	3.33[a]	6.23	6.63[a]	6.30	6.21	2.66*
FES Religion/Morality	6.75	6.58	6.20	6.42	6.93	
HOME Learning Stimulation	6.75[abcd]	9.07[a]	9.28[b]	9.75[c]	9.52[d]	4.00**
HOME Language Stimulation	6.25	6.53	6.67	6.94	6.72	
HOME Physical Environment	4.50[ab]	6.27	6.17	6.75[a]	6.52[b]	2.79*
HOME Warmth & Affection	4.50[ab]	5.87	6.39[a]	6.25[b]	6.08	3.01*
HOME Academic Stimulation	4.00	4.07	4.72	4.69	4.52	
HOME Modeling	3.25[a]	4.47	4.11	4.88[a]	4.28	3.28*
HOME Variety in Experience	6.25	6.47	7.17	7.44	7.44	
HOME Acceptance	3.50	3.87	3.89	3.94	3.80	
FACES Cohesion	37.20	40.15	41.63	41.94	41.40	
FACES Adaptation	24.20	25.32	24.01	22.19	24.82	
Subsample n	n = 5	n = 15	n = 19	n = 18	n = 25	

Note. Means followed by the same superscript differ significantly in pairwise posthoc tests.
Results for Age 3 HOME Acceptance represent reduced samples: Low Moderate-$n = 4$, Moderate-$n = 12$, High Moderate-$n = 5$, adn High-$n = 12$.
*** $p < .001$, ** $p < .01$, * $p < .05$.

similar levels of stimulation and warmth in the home compared to families with higher sustainability. Families with varied levels of sustainability of family activities and routines, can nonetheless show similar levels of cohesion and adaptation. This is an important result: quality of interaction, or home environment characteristics, are not the same as sustainability of a daily routine (except perhaps among Multiply Troubled families), and sustainability should not generally be confused with these kinds of assessments of family environments.

Stability of Sustainability Over 10 Years

Are families relatively stable in their patterns of family sustainability over time? We are able to compare sustainability at four points in time, from age three to 13. Our central finding is that families remain fairly stable over this 10-year period in sustainability, although there is a significant increase in families with High sustainable routines from age 11 to 13. Basically about 75% of the families have a quite similar pattern over time.

But there are shifts. Gina and her family exemplify a situation in which sustainability went up and down over the years. When Gina (pseudonym) was 3, her family was well established in an area they liked, with a good deal of social support. Father had a good job with benefits, Gina's seizures were under control, she was making good progress in her early intervention program, and her older brother was quite helpful with her. The family was excited about their impending purchase of a new, larger home nearby. Their sustainability rating: Stable/High.

By age 7, Father's job situation had become unpredictable, and Mother had to return to work to help with mortgage payments and insurance benefits. Gina's seizures had increased, she was diagnosed with CP, and she was having serious difficulties with self-esteem. Mother found she had to push hard to get the right school placement and equipment for Gina. In general, the family's situation was much less stable, their routine had become much more demanding, less congruent with parental goals, less fitted to their configuration of resources. Their sustainability overall went to Vulnerable but Struggling, and Low-Moderate Sustainability.

When Gina was 11, both parents had jobs with good benefits, but Father was becoming increasingly dissatisfied with his career. Gina's self-esteem had been built back up through intense intervention. Mother continued to do battle with the school system to obtain appropriate services, and searched out the best therapies, even if it meant long drives. The older brother continued to be of great help with Gina, and was doing well in school. Sustainability moved again to Active—Moderately High Sustainability.

At age 13, Mother was quite satisfied with Gina's school, and her full-time income was supporting the family while Father went back to school for a career change, which both Mother and Father had agreed on. Mother had established an excellent network of support and information for herself and Gina through her work. As Gina embarked on her adolescent years, her daily routine was back to being Stable/High.

Families of course did shift from one sustainability group to another over time, like Gina's family, but about 75% remained fairly stable until early adolescence. Families starting out with relatively sustainable routines are likely to continue on that path. Families with lower levels of sustainability are more likely to vary, struggle in the middle childhood years, but in some cases, show moderately higher sustainability at child age 13. The highest correlations between age periods are between ages 3 and 7 (.57) and ages 11 and 13 (.61). The seven to 11 period shows somewhat lower correlation (.41) suggesting greater change in patterns of family sustainability during the early grade school years. Parents described several reasons that might account for changes in family sustainability during this period, including the adjustment to school, which frequently included decisions about special education and programs, and the increasing recognition that their child was not delayed but disabled and unlikely to catch up.

To better understand change over time, we categorized the families for whom we had complete data into four groups based on their pattern of change from age 3 to 15: Stable Low Sustainability; Unstable Moderate to Lower; Improving Over Time; and Stable High. Stable Low families (n = 30, 32%) had low or low/moderate sustainability ratings at all time periods. Unstable Moderate/Low families (n = 15, 16%) typically improved from low to moderate between 3 and 11, but by age 11 and 13 dropped lower again. Improving Over Time families (n = 22, 23%) started out with lower levels of sustainability, but ended up moderately high or high by 11 and 13. Stable High families (n = 28, 29%) remained moderately high or high at all age periods.

We then ran a series of Anova analyses using the same set of measures (demographic, ecocultural, and family measures) used to compare the original five sustainability groups. (We present only the measures with significant differences in Table 3.) The major finding is that the Stable Low (n = 30) families appear to have significantly fewer resources than other families, engage in less accommodation and child stimulation activity, and have children rated as more disruptive of their daily routine. Beyond this pattern, however, few of our measures distinguished the other change patterns from each other.

More families have achieved Highly sustainable routines at age 13 than at earlier ages: from 28% at age 11 to 49% at age 13. We reviewed each of these cases, using data from interviews and field notes, and examined the pathways they followed. Why the increase in sustainability, when adolescence is often seen as a time of increased concern? One reason actually is that early adolescence for most of these children, is not yet that time of increased concern for parents of children with disabilities as it might be for typically developing children. However, early adolescence is a time when many of these parents seemed to have completed changes in their daily routines. Some families finally felt their child had a confirmed diagnosis and this brought a sense of closure, leading them to make clearer

Table 3. Significant ANOVAs Comparing Sustainability Change Groups by Ages 3, 7, and 11

	Sustainability Change Groups				
	Stable Low	Unstable Moderate to Lower	Improved	Stable High	F
Age 3					
Ecocultural Ratings					
Socioeconomic Status	43.37[abc]	50.12[ad]	49.75[be]	56.51[cde]	11.60***
Connectedness	44.17[abc]	51.28[a]	51.40[b]	54.41[c]	6.49***
HOME & FACES					
HOME Learning Stimulation	7.87[a]	9.07	8.68	9.36[a]	3.64*
HOME Language Stimulation	5.40[a]	6.00	6.05	6.29[a]	4.91**
HOME Physical Environment	5.80[abc]	6.67[a]	6.64[b]	6.79[c]	5.56**
HOME Variety in Experience	5.07[abc]	6.47[a]	6.50[b]	6.32[c]	5.70**
FACES Cohesion	37.00[a]	40.07	41.40	43.04[a]	4.06**
Subsample n	n = 30	n = 15	n = 22	n = 28	
Age 7					
Ecocultural Ratings					
Socioeconomic Status	43.56[ab]	48.89[c]	51.65[a]	54.55[bc]	7.95***
Accommodation Ratings					
External Accommodation	−.51[ab]	.49[ac]	−.30[cd]	.36[bd]	4.92**
HOME & FACES					
HOME Learning Stimulation	8.46[a]	9.29	9.33	9.92[a]	4.40**
HOME Language Stimulation	5.46[ab]	6.50	6.61[a]	6.75[b]	4.77**
HOME Physical Environment	3.83[a]	4.50	4.33	4.63[a]	3.28*
HOME Variety in Experience	6.58[a]	7.36	7.67[a]	7.13	3.26*
FACES Cohesion	38.94[a]	40.36	43.81[a]	41.76	3.47*
Subsample n	n = 24	n = 14	n = 19	n = 25	
Age 11					
Ecocultural Ratings					
Socioeconomic Status	43.04[abc]	50.71[ad]	52.40[b]	56.39[cd]	10.96***
Connectedness	42.85[abc]	52.77[a]	52.40[b]	53.67[c]	7.92***
Child Status					
Behavior Hassle	5.77[ab]	5.00	3.82[a]	3.64[b]	5.12**
Subsample n					

Note. Means followed by the same superscript differ significantly in pairwise posthoc tests.
*** $p < .001$, ** $p < .01$, * $p < .05$.

decisions. Some mothers at this point in their child's life moved back into careers, or their jobs improved and/or additional caretakers (kin, or hired help) were available to help out. Some parents divorced or remarried, after staying together in a difficult relationship when the child was younger. Such changes often led to a subsequent increase in satisfaction, stability, and sustainability of their routines after an initial rocky transition between ages 7 and 11. In several cases, child placement outside the home for all or part of the week, dramatically improved sustainability of family routines. One child, for example, moved from living with a full time working mother, to living with her father and homemaker stepmother. Another family moved out of a large urban area to a rural community with strong kin and community help and support from their church.

DISCUSSION

Family achievement of a sustainable routine is a useful family outcome, complementary to the use of other measures, and is meaningful to parents. It can be reliably rated and provides a holistic assessment of how parents weave together the routines and activities of daily life. We found a range of patterns, ranging from quite troubled and struggling, to coherent, balanced and meaningful. Sustainability scores are related to family composition (it is lower for single parents), SES and family income (higher for higher SES and income). Resources are not a proxy for achieving a sustainable daily routine, however, since there is considerable variation in income and SES within sustainability groups. Higher levels of family sustainability are associated with high social and interpersonal Connectedness and lower Family Workloads, but the relationships are not linear; how families integrate and <u>balance</u> work and use connections, is important for sustainability, not simply the amount of either. The FES, HOME, and FACES showed quite low to moderate associations. Sustainability is fairly stable for most families, dips around age 7, but shows a surprising increase when children are 13. Increases in sustainability as children get older, are associated with higher SES, more family connectedness, and less child hassle. These are the same features, which distinguished family sustainability within age periods.

The traditional measures of family adjustment include useful items, but the valence of each item is predetermined and not considered in relationship to the whole family system. What might be a "good" score for one family on an item may not be relevant, or in fact may be negative for another, depending on the holistic appraisal that is part of understanding and assessing sustainability. Sustainability starts not with items that have predetermined valence, but with a holistic appraisal of the family's goals, the context of their daily routine, and the varied features that seem to sustain a routine (resource fit, balancing conflicts, meaning with respect to goals, and stability/predictability).

We do not have a comparison sample of families who do not have children with disabilities, and so are not able to differentiate qualities of sustainability unique to families with children with disabilities. However, the EFI and questionnaire has been used in a number of other populations. These include South Asian immigrant, Navajo, and Japanese families with children with disabilities (Begay, Roberts, Weisner, & Matheson, 1999; Raghavan, Weisner, & Patel, 1999; Sakagami, Kanenaga, Nihira, Sakurai, & Suzuki, 1996) and families with typically developing but at-risk children (Reese, Goldenberg, & Loucky, 1995; Weisner, et. al., 1999). A recent study linked home cultural ecology to infant reactivity to pain responses among North Italian families (Axia & Weisner, 2002). In each case, both common and unique features of family goals and daily routines were found. This is what our theory and methods would expect: a common set of universal family adaptive concerns, with significant variations due to culture and (in the case of families with children with disabilities) child developmental variations. Thus ecocultural theory and sustainability of family routines opens the topic of ethnic and cultural variations in family life, to empirical study with or without a child with disabilities. Ethnic groups are not well served by homogeneous group trait or social address labels. Our approach provides a way to assess which practices and meanings do or do not vary across cultural groups at the family level.

The EFI model of understanding family activities and routines can also be used in experimental research for topics with applied and policy implications. For example, a version of the EFI for working poor families and children has been developed as part of a prospective, longitudinal experimental intervention, New Hope (Weisner, Gibson, Lowe, & Romich, 2002). Over 1300 adults in two zip codes in Milwaukee, Wisconsin were recruited for a study of the impact of supports for working poor families. Half were randomly selected for eligibility for supports. The supports included wage supplements, child care vouchers, health care subsidies, and a community service job if needed. The other half were in the control group. A survey, child assessments, teacher reports, and administrative records were also used in the mixed method design (Bos, Huston, Granger, Duncan, Brock, & McLoyd, 1999; Huston, Duncan, Granger, Bos, McLoyd, 2001; Huston, Miller, Richburg-Hayes, Duncan, et al, 2003). The EFI focused on how families organized their daily routine in the face of low incomes, jobs which often were episodic and poorly paid with few or no benefits, and other stresses in their lives. The EFI also focused on parenting and children's lives, since a central focus of the overall study was on the impacts of the intervention and of concurrent welfare reforms on children's development. How parents learned about and used the New Hope program depended in part on their family sustainability and their prior beliefs and expectations regarding support programs (Gibson & Weisner, 1992); similarly, how parents used the child care vouchers also depended on their beliefs and values about appropriate care, and how such formal care fit into their daily routines (Lowe & Weisner, 1993).

An interview version of the EFI, focused on pre-literacy skills of parents and children, has been developed for parents of preschool children in Head Start (in collaboration with JoAnn Farver, (PI), USC, and Chris Lonigan, Florida State). The study is also an experiment, and assesses an intervention in Head Start and in homes, designed to increase children's pre-literacy skills. There are three arms of the intervention: some families are in a control group where they receive typical Head Start programs; some families are in Head Start centers receiving the intervention, and in which the families also receive an additional in-home intervention with parents; a third group of families are in the Head Start centers receiving the intervention but do not in addition receive the home intervention. The pre-literacy EFI interviews with parents focus on parent and child experiences with pre-literacy activities, beliefs about learning and preschool, and home learning contexts of families in all three arms of the intervention. The EFI taps the beliefs, values, goals, and practices found in family activities that might show how the intervention had its impacts, if indeed there are impacts (the study is still underway in 2004). A focus on sustainability of the family daily routine is relevant, then, not only to families with children with MR/DD, but to a variety of populations and policy concerns.

Sustainability is certainly illuminating with respect to current policies in place for children with disabilities and their families. With the reauthorization of the Individuals with Disabilities Education Act (IDEA) (PL 105-17). Congress has maintained its commitment to considering families, as well as children, as beneficiaries of early intervention services. The IFSP, or Individualized Family Service Plan, may include family, as well as child, outcomes. The question has been, what are appropriate family outcomes that are within the purview of early interventionists, and that are congruent with family goals and values? Bailey and colleagues (1998) have suggested that a reasonable family outcome of early intervention is an enhanced quality of life. A sustainable daily routine is likely to be associated with quality of life. An intervention intended to assist families and children should lead to increased sustainability. At the very least, it should not lead to a decrease in sustainability.

The reauthorization of IDEA also includes a mandate, beginning at age 14, for planning the transition between secondary school and adult life for youth with disabilities. "Adult life" is defined as broader than vocational outcomes; it encompasses living arrangements and social relationships. This transition is a significant one for families as well, requiring a renegotiation of parental roles and adjustments to the daily routine. One way to understand the impact of this transition on families is to examine sustainability of the family's routine before, during, and after the transition.

The sustainability of the youth's daily routine after the transition also can be used to indicate the success of the transition planning.

Talking with families about sustaining a routine opens up the subject of family activities and what makes them happen—what it takes to keep the desired ones going and what it would take to change the troubling ones. Such conversations foreground how interdependent daily routines and activities are: pull on one to demand more time for something else— and unanticipated changes happen elsewhere. Such conversations help us as researchers to "get inside" the family routine of life. Many desirable interventions founder on just this point: the interventions can't easily get inside the daily routine and become an accommodated part of everyday practices; they don't fit the cultural models and concerns of parents; they unexpectedly disrupt the fit with resources, the balance among conflicting demands, the goals of the family, or the predictability of life (Bernheimer & Keogh, 1995; Coots, 1998; Gallimore, et al., 1999). Effective ways to assess sustainability of routines help open this difficult area to practitioner understanding and shared discussion with parents.

Family sustainability also opens a window onto this important, powerful sociocultural context shaping learning and development in children. After all, sustainability is the crystallized outcome of previous and concurrent accommodations, which are, in turn, evidence of family social-ecological learning in context. All changes are not adaptations, since not all changes are the result of learning in response to the environment. But accommodations are a form of learning in response to others and the local ecology. Ethnographic research, including research using the EFI, is essential to reveal how families learn to accommodate in order to sustain their routine.

REFERENCES

Axia, V., and Weisner, T. S. (2002). Infant stress reactivity and home cultural ecology. *Infant Behavior & Development* 140:1–14.

Bailey, D. D., McWilliam, R. A., Darkes, L. A., Hebbeler, K., Simeonsson, R. J., Spiker, D., and Wagner, M. (1998). Family outcomes in early intervention: A framework for program evaluation and efficacy research. *Exceptional Children* 64:313–328.

Baldwin, A. L., Baldwin, C., and Cole, R. E. (1990). Stress-resistant families and stress-resistant children. In: Rolf, J., Masten, A. S., Cicchetti, D., Nuechterlein, K. H., and Weintraub, S. (eds.), *Risk and protective factors in the development of psychopathology.* Cambridge University Press, Cambridge, pp. 257–281.

Becker, H. S. (1996). The epistemology of qualitative research. In: Jessor, R., Colby, A., and Shweder, R. (eds.), *Ethnography and human development. Context and meaning in social inquiry.* University of Chicago Press, Chicago, pp. 53–71.

Begay, C., Roberts, R. N., Weisner, T. S., and Matheson, C. (1999). Indigenous and informal systems of support. Navajo families who have children with disabilities. In: Fletcher,

T. V., and Bos, S. (eds.), *Helping individuals with disabilities and their families Mexican and U.S. perspectives. The Bilingual Review XXIV (1 & 2).* Bilingual Review/Press, Tempe, AZ, pp. 79–94.

Bernheimer, L. P., and Keogh, B. K. (1982). Research on early abilities of children with handicaps. (Final report, longitudinal sample). University of California, Los Angeles. (Unpublished Manuscript).

Bernheimer, L. P., and Keogh, B. K. (1986). Developmental disabilities in preschool children. In: Keogh, B. K. (ed.), *Advances in Special Education,* Volume 5. JAI Press, Greenwich, CT, pp. 61–94.

Bernheimer, L. P., and Keogh, B. K. (1988). The stability of cognitive performance of developmentally delayed children. *American Journal of Mental Retardation* 92:539–542.

Bernheimer, L. P., and Keogh, B. K. (1995). Weaving interventions into the fabric of everyday life: An approach to family assessment. *Topics in early childhood special education* 15(4):415–433.

Bernheimer, L. P., Keogh, B. K., and Coots, J. J. (1993). From research to practice: Support for developmental delay as a preschool category of exceptionality. *Journal of Early Intervention* 17:97–106.

Bos, H., Huston, A., Granger, R., Duncan, G., Brock, T., McLoyd, V. et al. (1999). *New Hope for people with low incomes: Two-year results of a program to reduce poverty and welfare reform.* Manpower Demonstration Research Corporation Press, New York.

Boyce, G. C., and Barnett, W. S. (1993). Siblings of persons with mental retardation: A historical perspective and recent findings. In: Z. Stoneman and P. Berman (eds.), *Siblings of individuals with mental retardation, physical disabilities, and chronic illness.* Brookes, Baltimore, pp. 145–184.

Boyce, W. T., and Jemerin, J. M. (1990). Psychobiological differences in childhood stress response: I. Patterns of illness and susceptibility. *Journal of Developmental and Behavioral Pediatrics* 11(2):86–94.

Bristol, M. (1984). Family resources and successful adaptation to autistic children. In: Schopler, E., and Mesibov, G. (eds.), *The effects of autism on the family.* Plenum Publishing Corp, New York, pp.

Caldwell, B. M., and Bradley, R. H. (1984). *Home observation for measurement of the environment (revised edition).* University of Arkansas, Little Rock, AR.

Cohen, S., and Syme, S. L. (1985). *Social support and health.* Academic Press, Orlando.

Coots, J. J. (1998). Family resources and parent participation in schooling activities for their children with developmental delays. *Journal of Special Education* 31(4):498–520.

Crnic, K. A., Friedrich, W. N., and Greenberg, M. T. (1983). Adaptation of families with mentally retarded children: A model of stress, coping and family ecology. *American Journal of Mental Deficiency* 88:125–138.

Dunst, C. J. and Trivette, C. M. (1990). Assessment of social support in early intervention programs. In: Meisels, S. J., and Shonkoff, J. P. (eds.), *Handbook of early childhood intervention.* Cambridge University Press, Cambridge, pp. 326–349.

Dunst, C. J., Trivette, C. M., and Deal, A. G. (1988). *Enabling and empowering families: Principles and guidance for practice.* Brookline Books, Cambridge, MA.

Dyson, L. (1991). Families of young children with handicaps: Parental stress and family functioning. *American Journal on Mental Retardation* 95:623–629.

Gallagher, J. J. (1989). A new policy initiative: Infants and toddlers with handicapping conditions. *American Psychologist* 44:387–391.

Gallimore, R., Bernheimer, L. P., and Weisner, T. S. (1999). Family life is more than managing crisis: Broadening the agenda of research on families adapting to childhood disability. In:

Gallimore, R., Bernheimer, L. P., MacMillan, D. L., Speece, D. L., and Vaughn, S., (eds.), *Developmental Perspectives on children with high-incidence disabilities.* LEA Press, Mahwah, N.J., pp. 55–80.

Gallimore, R., Goldenberg, C., and Weisner, T. (1993). "The social construction and subjective reality of activity settings: Implications for community psychology." *American Journal of Community Psychology* 21(4):537–559.

Gallimore, R., Weisner, T. S., Kaufman, S. Z., and Bernheimer, L. P. (1989). The social construction of ecocultural niches: Family accommodation of developmentally delayed children. *American Journal of Mental Retardation* 94(3):216–230.

Gallimore, R., Weisner, T. S., Guthrie, D., Bernheimer, L., and Nihira, K. (1993). "Family response to young children with developmental delays: accommodation activity in ecological and cultural context." *American Journal of Mental Retardation* 98(2):185–206.

Gallimore, R., Coots, J. J., Weisner, T. S., Garnier, H. and Guthrie, G. (1996). Family responses to children with early developmental delays II: Accommodation intensity and activity in early and middle childhood. *American Journal of Mental Retardation* 101(3):215–232.

Gibson, C., and Weisner, T. S. (2002). "Rational" and ecocultural circumstances of program take-up among low-income working parents. *Human Organization. Journal of the Society for Applied Anthropology* 61(2):154–166.

Glidden, L. M. (1993). What we do not know about families with children who have developmental disabilities: Questionnaire on resources and stress as a case study. *American Journal on Mental Retardation* 97:481–495.

Goldschmidt, W. (1992). *The Human Career. The Self in the Symbolic World.* Blackwells, Cambridge, MA.

Hanson, M. J., and Hanline, M. F. (1990). Parenting a child with a disability: A longitudinal study of parental stress and adaptation. *Journal of Early Intervention* 14:234–248.

Harkness, S. and Charles M. S. (eds.). (1996). *Parents cultural belief systems.* Guilford Press, New York.

Hill, R. (1949). *Families under stress.* Harper and Row, New York.

Huston, A. C., Duncan, G. J., Granger R., Bos, J., McLoyd V., Mistry, R., Crosby, D., Gibson, C., Magnuson, K., Romich, J., Ventura, A. Work-based anti-poverty programs for parents can enhance school performance and social behavior for children. *Child Development* 72:318–336.

Huston, A. C., Miller, C., Richburg-Hayes, L., Duncan, G. J., *et. al.* (2003). *New Hope for families and children: Five-year results of a program to reduce poverty and welfare.* MCRC, New York.

Keogh, B. K., and Bernheimer, L. P. (1995). Etiologic conditions as predictors of children's problems and competencies in elementary school. *Journal of Child Neurology* 10(Suppl 1):S100–S105.

Keogh, B. K, Bernheimer, L. P., and Guthrie, D. (1997). Stability and change over time in cognitive level of children with delays. *American Journal of Mental Retardation* 4:365–373.

Keogh, B. K., Bernheimer, L. P., Gallimore, R. G., and Weisner T. S. (1998). Child and family outcomes over time: A longitudinal perspective on developmental delays. In: Lewis, M. and Feiring, C. (eds.), *Families, risks, and competence.* Lawrence Erlbaum and Associates, Mahwah, NJ, pp. 269–287.

Lazarus, R. (1984). Puzzles in the study of daily hassles. *Journal of Behavioral Medicine* 7:375–389.

Lieber, E., Weisner, T. S., and Presley, M. (2003). EthnoNotes: An internet-based fieldnote management tool. *Field Methods* 15(4):405–425.

LeVine, R. (1977). Child rearing as cultural adaptation. In: Leiderman, P., Tulkin, S., and Rosenfeld, A. (eds.), *Culture and infancy.* Academic Press, New York, pp. 15–27.

LeVine, R. (1988). Human parental care: universal goals, cultural strategies, individual behavior. In: LeVine, R. A., Miller, P. M., and West, M. M. (eds.), *Parental behavior in diverse societies.* Jossey-Bass, San Francisco, pp. 3–12.

LeVine, R. A., Dixon, S., LeVine, S., Richman, A., Leiderman, P. H., Keefer, C. H., and Brazelton, T. B. (1994). *Child Care and Culture. Lessons from Africa.* Cambridge University Press, Cambridge, UK.

LeVine, R. A. (2003). Childhood socialization: comparative studies of parenting, learning and educational change. *CERC Studies in Comparative Education* 12, University of Hong Kong Press.

Lowe, E., and Weisner, T. S. (2003). "You have to push it—who's gonna raise your kids?": Situating child care in the daily routines of low-income families. *Children and Youth Services Review* 25(3):225–261.

McCubbin, H. L., and Patterson, J. M. (1983). The family stress process: The double ABCX model of family adjustment and adaptation. In: McCubbin, H., Sussman, M., and Patterson, J. (eds.), *Social stress and the family: Advances and developments in family stress theory and research.* Haworth, New York, pp. 7–37.

Moos, B. S., and Moos, R. H. (1986). *Family environment scale manual*, 2nd ed. Consulting Psychologist Press, Inc., Palo Alto, CA.

Munroe, R., Munroe, R., and Whiting, B. (1981). *Handbook of cross cultural human development.* Garland STPM Press, New York.

Nihira, K., Weisner, T., and Bernheimer, L. (1994). Ecocultural assessment in families of children with developmentally delays: Construct and concurrent validities. *American Journal of Mental Retardation* 98(5):551–566.

Olson, D. H., Partner, J., and Labee, Y. (1985). *Family adaptability and cohesion evaluation scales.* University of Minnesota, Family Social Science, St. Paul.

Patterson, J. M. (1988). Families experiencing stress. I. The Family Adjustment and Adaptation Response Model. II. Applying the FAAR Model to health-related issues for intervention and research. *Family Systems Medicine* 6(2):202–237.

Raghavan, C., Weisner, T. S., and Patel, D. (1999). The adaptive project of parenting: South Asian families with children with developmental delays. *Education and Training in Mental Retardation and Developmental Disabilities* 34(3):281–292.

Reese, L., Goldenberg, C., and Loucky, J. (1995). Ecocultural context, cultural activity, and emergent literacy of Spanish-speaking children. In: Rothstine, S. W. (ed.), *Class, culture, and race in American schools: A handbook*, Greenwood Press, Westport, CT, pp. 199–224.

Sakagami, H., Kanenaga, H., Nihira, K., Sakurai, Y., Koga, H., and Suzuki, T. (1996). Family environment and accommodation for children with developmental disabilities: Ecocultural assessment method. *Japanese Journal of Family Research and Therapy* 13(3):41–52.

Sen, A. (1985). *Commodities and capabilities.* North-Holland Press, Amsterdam.

Sloper, P., Knussen, C., Turner, S., and Cunningham, C. (1991). Factors related to stress and satisfaction with life in families of children with Down Syndrome. *Journal of Child Psychiatry and Psychology* 32:655–676.

Super, C. and Harkness, S. (1986). The developmental niche: A conceptualization at the interface of child and culture. *International Journal of Behavior Development* 9:1–25.

Super, C., and Harkness, S. (eds.). (1980). *Anthropological perspectives on child development: New directions for child development*, No. 8. Jossey-Bass, San Francisco.

Weisner, T. S. (1984). Ecocultural niches of middle childhood: A cross-cultural perspective. In: Collins, W. A. (ed.), *Development during middle childhood: The years from six to twelve*, National Academy of Sciences Press, Washington, D.C., pp. 335–369.

Weisner, T. S., Beizer, L. and Stolze, L. (1991). Religion and the families of developmentally delayed children. *American Journal of Mental Retardation* 95(6):647–662.

Weisner, T. S. (1993). Siblings in cultural place: Ethnographic and ecocultural perspectives on siblings of developmentally delayed children. In: Stoneman, Z., and Berman, P. (eds.), *Siblings of individuals with mental retardation, physical disabilities, and chronic illness*. Brooks, Baltimore, pp. 51–83.

Weisner, T. S. (1996). Why ethnography should be the most important method in the study of human development. In: Jessor, R., Colby, A., and Shweder, R. (eds.), *Ethnography and human development. Context and meaning in social inquiry*. University of Chicago Press, Chicago, pp. 305–324.

Weisner, T. S. (1997). The ecocultural project of human development: Why ethnography and its findings matter. *Ethos* 25(2):177–190.

Weisner, T. S. (2002). Ecocultural understanding of children's developmental pathways. *Human Development* 45(4):275–281.

Weisner, T. S. (2002). Making a good thing better: Ways to strengthen sociocultural research in human development. *Human Development* 45(5):372–380.

Weisner, T. S. (in press). Introduction. In: Weisner, T. S. (ed.), *Discovering successful pathways in children's development: Mixed methods in the study of childhood*. University of Chicago Press, Chicago.

Weisner, T. S. et al. (1999). Understanding better the lives of poor families: Ethnographic and survey studies of the New Hope experiment. *Poverty Newsletter* Vol. 1, No. 3, pp.

Weisner, T. S., Matheson, C., and Bernheimer, L. (1996). American cultural models of early influence and parent recognition of developmental delays: Is earlier always better than later? In: Harkness, S., Super, C. M., and New, R. (eds.), *Parents' cultural belief systems*. Guilford Press, New York. pp. 496–531.

Weisner, T. S., Coots, J., and Bernheimer, L. (1996). *Ecocultural family interview field manual*. Ms, UCLA Center for Culture and Health.

Weisner, T. S., Gibson, C., Edward D., Lowe, and Romich, J. (2002). Understanding working poor families in the New Hope program. *Poverty Research Newsletter* 6(4): 3–5.

Willoughby, J. C., and Glidden, L. M. (1995). Fathers helping out: Shared child care and marital satisfaction of parents of children with disabilities. *American Journal on Mental Retardation* 99(4):399–406.

Whiting, B. (1976). The problem of the packaged variable. In: Riegel, K., and Meacham, S. (eds.), *The developing individual in a changing world: Historical and cultural issues*, Volume 1. Mouton, Netherlands. pp.

Whiting, B. (1980). Culture and social behavior: A model for the development of social behavior. *Ethos* 8:95–116.

Whiting, B., and Edwards, C. (1988). *Children of different worlds: The formation of social behavior*. Harvard University Press, Cambridge, MA.

Whiting, J., and Whiting, B. (1975). *Children of six cultures: A psychocultural analysis*. Harvard University Press, Cambridge, MA.

AUTHOR NOTE

This work is supported by Grants # HD19124 and HD11944 from the National Institute of Child Health and Human Development. The authors gratefully acknowledge the support of Robert B. Edgerton, Ronald Gallimore, Barbara Keogh and other colleagues in UCLA's

Neuropsychiatric Institute Center for Culture and Health. Weisner worked on this study while at the Center for Advanced Study in the Behavioral Sciences, with support while at the Center provided by National Science Foundation Grant #SBR-9022192 and the William T. Grant Foundation Grant #95167795. Address correspondence to: Thomas S. Weisner, University of California, Los Angeles, Box 62, Los Angeles, CA 90024-1759.

Chapter 3

An Ethnomodel of Teaching and Learning
Apprenticeship of Zinacantec Maya Women's Tasks

Ashley E. Maynard and Patricia M. Greenfield

INTRODUCTION: HUMAN CULTURAL MODELS

Human cultures have embedded, often taken-for-granted models for behavior, based on features of the ecocultural place which they inhabit (D'Andrade, 1992; Holland & Quinn, 1987; Weisner, 1984). Culture, as a system that informs its members of behaviors required for survival and correct performance, is unique to an ecocultural setting in the world. Several definitions of cultural models are found in the literature. A cultural model can be defined as a "shared, recognized, and transmitted internal representation" (D'Andrade, 1991, p. 230). Cultural models have also been defined as "presupposed, taken-for-granted models of the world that are widely shared by the members of the society and that play an enormous role in their understanding of that world and their behavior in it" (Holland & Quinn, 1987, p. 4). These cultural models are translated into scripts for socializing children along a particular pathway of development (Greenfield, 1994; Greenfield, Keller, Fuligni, & Maynard, 2000).

A cultural model can be likened to a grammar of a language. People know about and use grammar to speak and understand each other, but they do not state explicitly the grammar of their language without some linguistic training or some other influence that makes their grammar obvious to them. Similarly, people know about and use cultural models to participate in their social environments, but they do not talk about or state explicitly these embedded rules for behavior.

The Acquisition of Human Cultural Models

In the last two decades, a number of researchers have considered human cultural models (e.g., D'Andrade & Strauss, 1992; Holland & Quinn, 1987; Shweder & LeVine, 1984; Stigler, Shweder, & Herdt, 1990) and the acquisition of these models through apprenticeship (Greenfield, 1999; Greenfield, Maynard, & Childs, 2003; Lave & Wenger, 1991; Lave, 1988; Rogoff, 1990). Cultural knowledge, knowledge embedded in language, cultural myths, and cultural tools and artifacts, is learned from and shared with other humans (D'Andrade, 1995). Indeed, acquiring *cultural* competence seems to be one of the most important things for the social survival of an individual (Weisner, 1996).

The acquisition of human cultural models is a large part of this struggle for cultural competence. The understanding of cultural models can give researchers insight into what is important in a culture, what people need to do in order to succeed socially, and perhaps physically, in that culture. Ethnography, which typically includes longitudinal observation and interviewing of people in their own environment, is one method of research useful for the understanding of cultural models (Weisner, 1996; D'Andrade, 1995).

In this chapter, we apply the notion of cultural models to an understanding of cultural apprenticeship, which also lends itself to ethnographic study. Culturally important tasks are often taught in an apprenticeship between a learner and a master. In anthropology, an ethnographic tradition going back to Meyer Fortes (1937) has detailed the acquisition and practice of skills in everyday life (Carothers, 1953; Knapen, 1962). Later on, this tradition was extended by researchers working at the junction of psychology and anthropology (Childs & Greenfield, 1980; Greenfield & Lave, 1979/1982; Lave, 1988b; Guberman, 1996; Modiano, 1973; Rogoff 1990; Scribner & Cole, 1981). These researchers shifted the emphasis in the study of learning from learning by an individual in a classroom to learning by individuals or groups within their everyday cultural settings. Quite significantly, the initial research was done in cultures in which schooling was not indigenous, and out-of-school learning had pride of place. Nonetheless, this work has led to a general rethinking of what it means to learn and to know.

Ultimately, this evidence and line of thinking led researchers to investigate out-of-school learning in the United States (Guberman, 1992; Lave, 1988a; Lave & Wenger, 1991) including the learning and practice of manufacturing, service, and technological skills (Beach, 1992: Goodwin, 1994; Greenfield & Cocking, 1994; Hutchins, 1996; Scribner, 1984). The research reached full circle when scientific and technical learning in academic institutions was treated as an apprenticeship process (Ochs & Jacoby, 1997; Suchman & Trigg, 1996).

Investigators now conduct research with an assumption that people learn and demonstrate understanding within their natural, everyday settings (Chaiklin & Lave, 1996; Guberman & Greenfield, 1991; Rogoff & Lave, 1984). Under this paradigm, definitions of learning and intelligence encompass more environments and more ways of demonstrating knowledge (Greenfield, 1998; Sternberg & Grigorenko, 2004; Zambrano & Greenfield, 2004). Intelligence is thought of as the demonstration by the organism of succeeding in and adapting to its environment, whatever that environment may be (Scheibel, personal communication, March 15, 1996). With this definition in mind, apprenticeship has become a fruitful area of study, increasing our overall knowledge of human cognitive processes.

This chapter focuses on a particular cultural apprenticeship model, the Zinacantec model of teaching and learning, and the methods used to derive it. Our questions are two-fold: To what extent is there a single cultural model of apprenticeship that is applied to the learning of various everyday tasks and to various kinds of learners? What is the longitudinal nature of the apprenticeship model? That is, how does the model adapt to different stages of skill across time in a given learner?

The Study of the Acquisition of Zinacantec Cultural Models

The Zinacantec Maya have been the subjects of ongoing ethnographic and experimental inquiry for over 40 years (e.g., Cancian, 1992; Childs & Greenfield, 1980; Greenfield, 1973; Greenfield, Brazelton, & Childs, 1989; Greenfield & Childs, 1977; Greenfield, Maynard, & Childs, 2003; Maynard & Greenfield, 2003; Haviland, 1978; Laughlin, 1975; Vogt, 1970). It has been observed in prior ethnographic research that weaving, making tortillas, and chopping and carrying firewood are three tasks important to Maya womanhood in Highland Chiapas (Haviland, 1978; Modiano, 1973).

The transmission of weaving skill specifically has been the focus of over twenty years of empirical study (Childs & Greenfield, 1980; Greenfield, 1984; Greenfield & Childs, 1991; Greenfield, Maynard, & Childs, 2003). Girls are taught to weave by their mothers or other female relatives, or neighbors, in an informal apprenticeship. Childs and Greenfield (1980) videotaped 14 girls at different stages of learning to weave in 1970.

They analyzed the lessons, both verbal and nonverbal aspects, for the role of the learner and teacher in different parts of the weaving process. They found that the transmission of weaving skill was highly scaffolded through nonverbal communication and assistance, coordinated with verbal speech acts (Childs & Greenfield, 1980). However, there was no positive verbal reinforcement.

Findings from empirical study of the next generation of weavers in 1991 and 1993 indicate continued scaffolding and absence of positive verbal reinforcers as characteristic of the teaching and learning of weaving in Zinacantán, although there was a decline of scaffolding among families engaged in weaving commerce (Greenfield, Maynard, & Childs, 2000, 2003; Greenfield, 2004).

In terms of the Zinacantecs' procedural model of weaving apprenticeship, there has been no longitudinal inquiry into the entire process of teaching a girl to weave, from novice to independent weaving. Secondly, there has been no test of the within-culture generality of the procedural model of weaving apprenticeship to other domains of activity. In terms of the Zinacantecs' conceptual model of weaving apprenticeship, it proved impossible to elicit information concerning the Zinacantec concept of learning to weave by interviewing; the Zinacantecs would not or could not answer the questions (Greenfield, 1997b). Greenfield also tried to elicit comments about a learner's videotaped weaving session in 1970, as Tobin, Wu, and Davidson (1989) did in their study of preschools in Japan, China, and the United States. This approach also failed to elicit the Zinacantec concept, or model, of teaching and learning weaving skill; the Zinacantecs did not respond spontaneously as Tobin et al.'s (1990) subjects did. Most likely, it made no sense to them to be asked questions out of the context of actual activity and conversation (Devereaux, personal communication).

The present study of a single-subject teaching the entire weaving process to someone can tell us more about the Zinacantecs' procedural model of teaching and learning by elucidating more of this process from start to finish. Because the primary researcher was also the learner, her questions relevant to a conceptual model of weaving apprenticeship were "in context" and therefore answerable by her Zinacantec teacher. Finally, the ethnographic method of participant observation also lent itself to exploring the generality of apprenticeship procedures in two other important domains, making tortillas and carrying firewood.

The goal of the present chapter is to present a procedural and conceptual model of apprenticeship of the Zinacantec Maya of Southern Mexico. Deriving a model of teaching and learning in Zinacantán serves three purposes. One purpose is to have the model available as a cultural-historical account of apprenticeship of the Zinacantec Maya; it answers the question: What is teaching and learning like in Zinacantán?

The model can also be used to better answer the questions: How it is that people teach what they know? and How do people learn what they know? The exploration of teaching and learning in Zinacantán can inform research about human teaching and learning activities and processes generally.

Another purpose of formulating this model is to use the teaching-and-learning model to study cultural learning processes in Nabenchauk in further empirical studies. While several cultural psychologists have engaged in ethnographic inquiry before conducting experiments in a place, their ethnographic findings have not been published. Yet ethnography reveals a richness of findings—what Geertz (1973) calls "thick description"—that are generally lost in more controlled and structured studies.

It is important to know about Zinacantec teaching and learning styles before designing any empirical study involving learning, teaching, or even cognitive development to be conducted in this community. Ideas about the cultural place do not always fit the experimental design or the expectations of the researcher. Often a researcher will come to a new place with notions of behavior resembling and influenced by those of his or her home culture. It is crucial to the research process to do ethnographic inquiry about the models of a place before embarking on experimental work (Weisner, 1996).

This idea is further supported by Greenfield (1997a) who highlights the distinction between cross-cultural and cultural psychology. Where cross-cultural psychology makes assumptions about the features and the social world of a place, often borrowing tools from the home culture to test individuals in the study culture, cultural psychology makes no such assumptions. Cultural psychology takes the approach of inquiry, asking what is there to be studied. What is important to the people of the culture? And further, why is it important?

The present study further develops cultural psychology's methodological synthesis with anthropology. While drawing upon the anthropological method of ethnography, the present study adds from psychology a procedural awareness and explicitness about *how* the data were collected: hence, the innovation of a methods section in an ethnographic study.

ETHNOGRAPHIC METHODS IN THE STUDY OF THE ZINACANTEC MODEL OF TEACHING AND LEARNING

The current research explores the teaching and learning of three skills which virtually all Zinacantec Maya women: weaving, making tortillas, and chopping and carrying firewood. Maynard was taught to perform these tasks over a two month period in 1995 by a Zinacantec girl, Paxku'

Pavlu, who was about 13 years old at the time of the study. Paxku', a *muk'tah zeb* (big girl) and not yet considered a woman, had the skill of an adult woman in the three tasks considered for this study. All data were collected by Maynard, and the first-person-singular voice, used for clarity in the methods and results sections, represents her.

Before traveling to Mexico, I did an intensive study of the Tzotzil language in order to prepare for fieldwork. Using tapes and notebooks compiled by linguists who had done previous work in Zinacantán, I was able to learn the grammar of the language and many vocabulary words before I arrived. Immersion in the Tzotzil language made it easier to communicate, and I learned more of the language with ease in an immersion situation.

In 1995, Greenfield escorted me to the field site and introduced me to Paxku', her family, and her community. This is an important methodological point: How a researcher gets into a place influences how people respond to her. Greenfield gave me a personal introduction to many people in the community. Greenfield told them that I was interested in learning their language, learning to weave, and to learn what people do there. Because our research was in a female domain, Greenfield introduced me to other women and children in the village who seemed pleased that I wanted to learn their language and to learn to weave. A key aspect of the success of the introductions was the fact that Greenfield had begun work with Paxku's grandfather as her assistant in 1969; she had known Paxku's father and most of her uncles and aunts as children. She had met Paxku' in 1991, when she was nine years old. Even then, Paxku' had helped with the research (Greenfield, 2004). The Pavlu family also knew Greenfield's entire nuclear family and had worked with her daughter. In essence, I was accepted almost as another member of Greenfield's family. I also followed the research tradition of wearing Zinacantec clothes whenever I was in Nabenchauk.

Several times when I was introduced to someone new in the village, I was told a story of a man who was visiting years before who cried all the time because no one would talk to him and he would not eat their food. This man was not introduced by someone already accepted by the Zinacantecs and subsequently had a very difficult time working there. Thus, my personal introduction was crucial to my research experience in Zinacantán; without acceptance by members of the community, it would have been very difficult to learn about the cultural models of the Zinacantec Maya. Another aid was that the Tzotzil learning materials, developed by the Harvard Chiapas Project in the 1960s and updated by Carla Childs in 1991, included multiparty conversations that provided information about cultural routines.

Greenfield also provided other key instructions for how to be as "normal" a Zinacantec woman as a young, single, *gringa* (North American) woman could be. For example, she advised me never to go anywhere in the village unaccompanied. She told the story of a U.S. student working at the local clinic who was accused of being a witch. The evidence was that he walked around all alone, especially at night. The importance of the advice was not only for my research; it was also for Greenfield's future relationship with the community, for anything I did would reflect on Greenfield, then my academic advisor.

During two months of fieldwork in Mexico, I became a full participant-observer in the Zinacantec Maya daily routines and activities. Participant-observation is the method *par excellence* of ethnography. In this method, the researcher gets into the culture enough to learn what people do there and then actually learns the culturally important skills and, often, what people think about the skills and life in that culture, in an extended time period of becoming a participant in the culture. At the same time the researcher makes observations about what is going on and what she is doing in the activities. In order to use this method effectively, it is important to develop a clear participant role. I had one: Like Leslie Haviland (1978) before me, I was there to learn how to be a Zinacantec woman. More specifically, I wanted to learn how to pat tortillas, carry firewood, and weave, as I sharpened my Tzotzil abilities.

I used this ethnographic method of inquiry by becoming a participant-observer in the daily routines of the Zinacantec community. I lived in Southern Mexico for two months in the summer of 1995, spending part of the time in a Mexican city, San Cristóbal de las Casas, and the majority of the time in Nabenchauk, a Zinacantec Maya village. I traveled to the village for three or four days at a time, spending the days and nights with a family there. The family of eight lived in a one-room house with no sanitary plumbing. I paid the family a nominal amount for letting me stay in their home and for food each day. They were very generous in their hospitality.

On a typical day, I arose with the family or shortly after and began the day by talking with them. A few days into my stay, Paxku' asked if I wanted to learn to make tortillas and I said that I did. From then on, part of their daily routine was rising with the chickens around 6 in the morning and making tortillas for the family together, as Paxku' taught me how to do it. Paxku' also taught me to weave and to chop and carry firewood. She taught me to weave in eight sessions ranging from 2–5 hours each. I paid her a small amount for teaching me to weave. Paxku' invited me to come along on three trips to gather firewood and showed me how to chop and carry the wood home in a tumpline. I was accepted by the family as a participating member, learning how to do things around the house.

At the same time that I was learning how to carry out Zinacantec daily activities, I almost always had a notebook with me and wrote down everything I possibly could about what people said and did. While people noticed that I was writing things down and often joked about me and my *vun* (paper), the notebooks did not seem to interfere with participation in the daily routines. The Zinacantecs are accustomed to researchers coming to visit and carrying paper around with them and writing things down. The adults did not seem to mind the notebooks. Children were very interested in what I wrote down and often asked me to read it aloud to them. I spent many afternoons reading English, Spanish, and Tzotzil field notes to children who loved hearing aloud observations, conversations, and songs I had recorded.

It was very important that I used a notebook to record my observations, as opposed to a video camera or a tape recorder. Having a video camera would likely have caused Paxku' to set up the teaching space wherever the camera was. With the notebooks, I could go wherever Paxku' told me to go: inside the house, the front porch or courtyard, or the backyard. I could not have taken a video camera to gather firewood. A video camera would have severely interfered with the natural process of teaching and learning I was attempting to capture. An audio recorder would not have been of much use because there was not a lot of verbalization in the teaching and learning processes to record, as will be discussed in analyzing and presenting the model.

The Use of Questions in Ethnographic Research

One issue that arose in the collection of the data is the use of questions to gain information in Zinacantán. I went to Nabenchauk full of questions to ask about life there. I soon found, however, that inquisitiveness was not welcome socially, and that providing too much information about myself was also a bad idea. I was often frustrated when Paxku' did not answer my questions. I thought perhaps I was not asking the right question, or that I was asking the questions in the wrong way. An observation of cultural activity helps to explain this quandary: Zinacantec children are often observers of the conversations of the adults around them. Paxku' was probably not accustomed to having someone's undivided attention, and especially being asked questions by that person.

Paxku' was apparently unaccustomed to being asked "How?" and "Why?" questions. She often did not answer when I asked her such questions. I could not get at conceptual knowledge in an interview that was out of the context of weaving. Providing or using a concrete context for the "Why?" questions resulted in more answers from Paxku'. When I asked Paxku' "Why?" questions while we were weaving, which provided a concrete context, Paxku' could provide an explanation. The following excerpt from my field data illustrates this point.

I said, "Why is it difficult?" She said because it is so wide and pointed to how wide the piece of cloth is. After she had finished making the heddle she then started to make a few lines. She told me to watch her. I asked her why she was weaving it and not me and she said because it was difficult." (September 12, 1995)

Organizing the Fieldnotes

The data from which the model is derived are taken from my extensive fieldnotes. The fieldnotes include data of two types: direct quotes from Paxku' and her mother about the activities we were doing, either while we were doing the activity or after, and my thoughts about and observations of what we were doing. For the present analyses, we took the subset of the total collection that was about weaving, making tortillas, and carrying firewood.

These data fit into a framework of procedural and conceptual knowledge (Hatano & Inagaki, 1986), where procedural knowledge is characterized by "knowing how" and conceptual knowledge is characterized by "knowing that." Procedural knowledge is knowledge of *how to do* a task, the different actions required to do components of the task and ultimately the entire task. Conceptual knowledge is knowledge *about* the task, what one thinks about the task or knowledge overall of the task. Paxku' demonstrated her procedural knowledge with the actions she used when she taught me to do the various things. My field notes reflect Paxku's procedural knowledge as recordings of how she taught me. Paxku' demonstrated her conceptual knowledge when she spoke about weaving, making tortillas, and carrying firewood, or about teaching and learning generally. Paxku' also demonstrated conceptual knowledge of teaching and learning in what she said about the teaching and learning of weaving or the other tasks. This conceptual knowledge was communicated by specific verbalized examples of a concept, not by a generalization itself, as Paxku' did not make generalizations of the teaching-learning process. The fieldnotes also included my conceptual analyses of the teaching-learning process.

There were data that were about actual lessons I had in the three tasks in question: 8 weaving sessions, 10 tortilla sessions, 3 firewood sessions. There were also notes from conversations that occurred outside the context of the teaching-learning sessions. The subset of the fieldnotes regarding teaching and learning were entered verbatim into a word processing program and then qualitatively analyzed with computer software macros written for this purpose. With the help of an expert in qualitative data analysis, Gery Ryan, I created macros in Microsoft Word that I used in coding the data. Coding proceeded as I read through the fieldnotes and inserted codes that represented the levels and themes of interest in the study. For example, at one level there was the issue of the activity we were doing, such as "chopping wood, day 1." Another level had to do with the kinds of materials used, such as "yarn," and yet another level had to do with the discourse used in the instruction, such as "imperatives."

In this chapter we intend to model Zinacantec Maya teaching and learning, not the tasks from which the model is derived. The model of teaching and learning derived here is presumed to be a "shared, recognized, and transmitted internal representation" (D'Andrade, 1992, p. 230). Indeed, it is because this model is not explicitly represented in the culture that this research is undertaken. Further, it is important to do ethnographic research to find out what is important to the members in order to better understand their cultural models. Underlying features of the cultural model generate specific manifestations in practice. These specific manifestations form a pattern in the ethnographic observations.

We had initially intended to use only the weaving sessions to derive a model of teaching and learning of weaving. However, in reviewing the fieldnotes, there was an obvious general pattern in the way Paxku' taught the three activities: instruction was always scaffolded and learning always occurred through guided participation (Rogoff, 1990). In presenting the model we will focus on the training of weaving skill and discuss the training of making tortillas and gathering firewood as support for the teaching-learning model, drawing on the general pattern in the teaching behaviors across the three tasks.

Features important to the psychology of the model, in italics, are organized around the procedural-conceptual distinction.

THE ZINACANTEC MODEL OF TEACHING AND LEARNING: PROCEDURAL FEATURES

The procedural features are divided into two categories: those that involve scaffolding and those that do not. There are five sub-features related to scaffolding in the model.

Scaffolding in the Transmission of Cultural Skills

Scaffolding is a term used to describe the help provided to learners such that they will be able to perform a task, because of the help, that they cannot yet perform on their own. Scaffolding in all areas of highland Maya education has been highlighted in past research (Childs & Greenfield, 1980;

Greenfield, 1984; Modiano, 1973). Another important feature of the scaffold is that it should be developmentally sensitive: help can be gradually withdrawn as it is no longer needed. A second feature of the scaffold is that it can be sensitive to task difficulty: more help can be given on harder parts of the process (Childs & Greenfield, 1980; Greenfield, 1984).

Prior Work on Weaving Apprenticeship in Nabenchauk

Prior work on the teaching of weaving skill by Greenfield and Childs (1991; Childs & Greenfield, 1980; Greenfield, 1984) has indicated that the teaching of weaving skill is highly scaffolded, involving close contact between teacher and learner. One aspect of the scaffolding process was that the teacher would show the learner how to do various parts of the weaving process before letting her do them alone; almost invariably, the learner watched attentively (Childs & Greenfield, 1980). The importance of observational learning has been noted also by Jean Lave, who studied Vai and Gola tailors as their apprentices learned the trade in Africa (Lave & Wenger, 1991).

A second component of scaffolding occurred when the teacher worked cooperatively with the learner to help her with parts of the process that the learner could not do alone. Less help was provided for the more experienced learners and none at all was provided for the expert teenage weavers. The teachers also provided learners with more help on harder parts of the weaving process (e.g., getting started with weaving the first weft thread) and less help on the easier parts (e.g., weaving a later weft thread).

There was also more verbal guidance—in the form of imperatives—for the less experienced weavers and the harder parts of the process, less verbal guidance—in the form of statements—for the more experienced weavers and the easier part of the process. The predominance of imperatives early in the process signified a teacher-directed process and respect for the teacher's authority (Greenfield, 2004).

Multimodal interactions (speech plus action or gesture) predominated in teacher-initiated interactions for girls who had never woven before (68% of all teacher-initiated interactions were multimodal). Multimodal interactions declined with more experienced learners, for example, constituting only 33.6% of interactions for girls who had previously woven between two and four items. Help in the form of a single modality (action, gesture, or speech) is less redundant; redundancy is useful at the beginning of a learning process. In all of these ways, the scaffold was adjusted to the skill level of the learner and the difficulty of a particular task component (Childs & Greenfield, 1980).

Apprenticeship models of cognition have chronicled the ways in which people, especially children, learn to do things by participating in the activities themselves (Lave, 1988; Lave & Wenger, 1991; Rogoff, 1990; Rogoff & Lave, 1984). Based on our systematic video study of Zinacantec girls learning to weave in Nabenchauk, as well as these studies in other communities, we hypothesized that the instruction of all three tasks, weaving, making tortillas, and carrying firewood, would be scaffolded and acquired through practice. There are two features of the model that comprised the ethnographic findings about scaffolding in teaching and learning in Zinacantán. Both are consistent with the findings of Greenfield of Childs on Zinacantec girls learning to weave in 1970: 1) that the teacher pays attention to the learner and provide decreasing assistance as the learner improves, adjusting to the learner's ability; and 2) that the teacher will make choices for the learner about which parts to do on a certain day, rather than the learner choosing what to do. These, as well as the other findings, were generated inductively, out of the data themselves.

Scaffolding Features in the Zinacantec Model

Feature 1: The Teacher Pays Attention to What the Learner is Doing, More When She Doesn't Know and Less When She Knows More, Providing Less and Less Help As the Learner's Skill Improves

Paxku' gave me less and less help as the lessons progressed. Paxku' always provided the environment and the setup for weaving (the loom, the thread, etc.). She decreased the amount of help as I became more skilled. In the first lesson, Paxku' did almost all of the work. I was able to do only what a three- to five-year-old girl could do, as evidenced in the study of weaving apprenticeship by Maynard and colleagues (Maynard, Greenfield, & Childs, 1999). I mostly watched what Paxku' was doing and tried to learn. In the second lesson, I watched less, and Paxku' had to help with the most difficult parts and with keeping the weaving going. In the third lesson, Paxku' left me for several short periods, and I was able to keep the weaving going on my own. Paxku' came to check and knew when to intervene. This pattern was in line with the decline in observing the teacher as learner skill increases found for Zinacantec weaving learners (Childs & Greenfield, 1980).

By the end of the fourth lesson, I was weaving well on my own, needing only occasional help from Paxku' once the weaving process had started. I could pass the bobbin through on my own, but still needed Paxku' to help set up the loom, assist in the most difficult part of the weaving: finishing a piece once the threads were very tight in the warp and tying the piece off and take it off the loom. This trend toward more independent weaving ended when I attempted weaving a very large, more difficult piece for my skill level, as evidenced in the following passage:

"I sat down and tried to make a few lines. I had to ask Paxku' to come over and help me lift the heddle... I was unable to weave more than a few lines and asked Paxku' to finish the piece for me."

In the course of two months, I went from novice to independent weaving, though I still needed more practice to become an expert. The scaffolding Paxku' employed in teaching me to weave is a longitudinal demonstration of what Childs and Greenfield (1980) demonstrated cross-sectionally.

Another aspect of scaffolding observed with Zinacantec weaving learners was that the teachers adjusted the quantity and nature of the instruction to task difficulty: teachers intervened more on the harder parts and less on the easier parts (Childs & Greenfield, 1980). Paxku' coordinated this feature of scaffolding with my developmental progression of weaving skill. Thus, Paxku' provided me with easier parts of each process to do first, eventually giving more difficult parts for me to do on my own.

At the beginning of the third weaving lesson, Paxku' wanted to know whether I wanted to learn the most difficult part of weaving, tapestry brocade. I asked if it was possible to learn and Paxku' thought that it was. I indicated interest and Paxku' said, "Not yet." I never progressed to that expert level of weaving. Paxku' never mentioned the possibility again, after seeing what I could do in the lessons. Paxku' provided only what she thought I needed to know, giving more and more information as I improved in subsequent lessons.

Feature 2: The Teacher Makes Choices for the Learner About Which Parts to Teach First, Which Parts of the Process to Include in Succeeding Lessons, and in the Case of Weaving, Which Colors to Use

In all three tasks, Paxku' made all the decisions about what parts to give or to teach me on a given day. She did not ask me what I wanted to do, nor did she ask when I was ready to try something new. This reflects a collectivist value of respect for superior knowledge versus the individualist value of personal choice (Markus & Kitayama, 1991). This value had been manifest in the high rate of imperatives used by teachers to guide beginning Zinacantec weaving learners (Childs & Greenfield, 1980).

Paxku' made all the decisions about what she and I would weave, the colors to use, and how the winding would be set up. We had several conflicts about these issues. For instance, I would want to wind the thread one way and Paxku' would insist on a simpler way, more appropriate for my overall skill level in weaving.

I was often frustrated that Paxku' decided herself on what we were going to do during a lesson before I could even say what I wanted to do. These conflicts illustrate a cultural difference between me and Paxku':

Paxku' believed that she as the teacher could choose for me, and I wanted to choose for myself. One area in which we had our biggest conflicts was in choosing and assigning colors for a piece.

> "I was so excited about going back to the store to pick out colors... Paxku' was picking out colors for me. I started to pick out colors the way Paxku' groups them together. She was hanging near me to check what I was doing. She had the colors she thought were right... She did not like my colors. She took some of them away and put them back and showed me what colors were right and good ... This was a major conflict for us. I wanted to pick out colors that I liked and she had this other idea about it. She told me that it needs to be dark and light, dark and light... "

Paxku' structured all the lessons by setting up the activity and guiding me through it, eventually leaving me to do things on my own. This was clearly a cross-cultural value conflict between my more individualistic mode, valuing choice, and Paxku's more collectivistic mode, valuing the master's authority, based on a superior level of skill.

Another example of scaffolding is breaking down a complex task into simpler parts. I asked Paxku' one day, "Why are we winding on the *komen* today when before we were doing it on the loom?" She said, "You learn this way." This implies the idea that there are prerequisites in the stages of weaving. In another conversation about winding Paxku' said that winding on the loom was easier. Actually, winding on the loom is cognitively simpler, though it is manually more complex. Paxku' seemed to have some implicit knowledge that something that is cognitively easier should be learned first. She wanted me to learn how to wind on the loom, which is how the Zinacantecs start to weave.

Feature 3: Talk during the Lessons that Involve the Tasks should Accompany a Demonstration of the Action being Explained

Paxku' never taught me to weave in a solely verbal way. She did not speak much during the lessons, but when she did speak, it was in concert with the action she was describing. One possible explanation is that Paxku' did not verbally delineate the steps of the weaving process because I was not yet fluent in Tzotzil at that time. If it were true that Paxku' was aware of my developing language skills, then we would expect her to give more nonverbal instruction when I was first learning the language and weaving, and more verbal instruction as my facility with the language increased. It was interesting that Paxku' did not, however, increase the use of language in her teaching as the sessions progressed, even though my Tzotzil improved significantly. The more likely explanation is that the Zinacantecs use language to illustrate a process of weaving only when they are doing the task, and that linguistic instruction is not inherent in their culture. The study of Zinacantec weaving learners found that language is generally used deictically in conjunction with gestures or the action it is describing, particularly at the early stages of learning (Childs & Greenfield, 1980).

Feature 4: Observation is the First Step in Learning

Paxku' asked me to observe each step of the weaving process before she taught me how to do it. She told me to sit and watch her, later giving me the opportunity to do it myself. Observation could be considered the first step in the scaffolding of learning.

Feature 5: If the Learner Needs Guidance in How to Use Her Body in Weaving, it is Necessary to Touch the Learner to Direct Her Body in the Proper Movements

The model of teaching and learning was flexible to accommodate me as a non-native learner. Paxku' helped by directing my body during the weaving process, something she would not have had to do with a more mature Zinacantec learner (Maynard, et al., 1999). This is implicit in my weaving sessions. Paxku' touched me whenever I did not lean back far enough, or forward enough, or when I needed to kneel instead of sitting more cross-legged. Paxku' tried to direct my body so that I could weave in the proper Zinacantec way and "make the weaving easier" (Paxku', September 12, 1996). I was not, however, skilled in the bodily processes necessary for weaving (Maynard, et al., 1999), and I needed much guidance in this area.

This is one area where I differed from the native learners, most of whom did not need instruction in what to do with their bodies. A screening of a videotape of the oldest novice weaving-learner (15 years old) among the subjects studied by Greenfield and Childs (1991) showed no instruction in bodily technique. Although the learner is not as elegant as the younger weavers in the study, no one tells her what to do with her body. However, note that, although the actions differ, the principle is the same: scaffold the learner in whatever way is needed.

Other Procedural Aspects of the Model: Generality of the Model across Task Domains

Feature 6: Girls Begin to Learn the Three Tasks When They Are about Age Five, Though the Tasks Differ in the Age at which a Girl is Expected to Perform Them on Her Own

It is known from other research that Maya girls in Highland Chiapas typically begin to do some part of weaving, making tortillas, and carrying firewood at age four or five (Modiano, 1973). For instance, at age five a girl might begin to weave a very small piece of cloth on a play loom or she might learn to spindle wool yarn. A girl might be expected to make tortillas as early as age five, though she will not turn them over on the *cemete* (griddle) until about age nine or ten. Small children are expected to carry one piece of firewood beginning at about age five.

The age at which a girl is expected to perform by herself the tasks of weaving, making tortillas, and carrying firewood varies by the task. Paxku' said that girls learned to weave at age seven, that they learn to make tortillas by themselves at about age nine, and that they begin to carry a little bit of firewood when they are about five years old, carrying more firewood when they are bigger, about age nine. She also told me that these are the ages at which she was doing these things on her own, and she may have generalized from herself to other girls in Nabenchauk.

Feature 7: Continuity Across Tasks: Procedural Knowledge of Instruction in Making Tortillas and Gathering Firewood

The procedural features of the model for weaving instruction are continuous across the tasks of learning to make tortillas and learning to chop and carry firewood. Observation is important in all three tasks. Paxku' told me to watch her in the earliest lessons for each of the tasks. I would sit with Paxku' and watch while Paxku' did the activities. This was how Paxku' expected me to learn. This emphasis on observational learning is best exemplified by a quote from Marta Turok, a U.S. college student learning to weave from a Maya teacher in Chiapas. She says:

> Many times she [the teacher] would verbally call my attention to an obscure technical pint, or when she would finish a certain step she would say, "You have seen me do it. Now you have learned." I wanted to shout back, "No, I haven't! Because I have not tried it myself." However, it was she who decided when I was ready to touch the loom, and my initial clumsiness brought about comments such as *"Cabeza de pollo!* (chicken head) You have not watched me! You have not learned!" (Turok, 1972, pp. 1–2).

Like Marta Turok, I was expected to observe first, and to do so in all three of the tasks before doing them myself. For example, when we went to gather firewood the first time, Paxku' taught me to sit down and watch her and another girl chop the wood. Observation was stressed in making tortillas, also, when Paxku' told me to watch her do something and then later allowed me to try it.

Paxku' paid very close attention to what I did in each task as she taught me. Even when I performed the tasks more independently, Paxku' was quick to tell me when I did not press a tortilla correctly or how I could chop the wood better. Interestingly, applied research in Los Angeles showed that, in a manner similar to Paxku's, Latino immigrants come to the United States with an orientation toward a teaching style that points out errors to be corrected, rather than with a teaching style that tries above all to preserve self-esteem (Greenfield, Quiroz, & Raeff, 2000).

Paxku' always adjusted the instruction to my level of learning in each of the three domains. The lessons in weaving progressed the most slowly, followed by making tortillas, and, lastly, chopping wood. I had never woven nor made tortillas before, though I had chopped wood, but never directly from trees. Paxku' taught me to do each of these tasks in her way and she adjusted the lessons according to my performance. It took me much less time to chop wood independently to Paxku's satisfaction than it did to make tortillas or weave independently. This could be related to my prior experience with chopping wood, or to the lack of precision required by that task compared with making tortillas and weaving.

Paxku' also made choices for me on what I would learn first and what I was allowed to do in making tortillas and carrying firewood. She would direct me and decide what I was ready to do next. When I was learning to make tortillas, Paxku' decided that I would first learn to press a tortilla, and she put it on the fire for me. Later Paxku' allowed me to press the tortilla dough and then put it on the fire myself. Next, Paxku' gave me bowls of tortilla dough which I pressed and placed on the fire. Still later, Paxku' gave me a bowl of dough for me to shape into dough balls, followed by the sequence of cooking them on the griddle. Finally, Paxku' instructed me in how to prepare the ground corn meal from dried corn to be used for cooking.

Paxku' also made all the decisions about what I would do when we were gathering wood. On our first gathering excursion, Paxku' told me to watch, and allowed me to carry wood home. On the second occasion, she allowed me to chop wood from a small tree that she had already chopped down. That day, I was allowed to carry the wood home. During the third lesson, Paxku' again showed me how to cut down a small tree, to chop it into smaller pieces, and to carry it home.

There was relatively little talk in each of the tasks. When Paxku' did speak she always accompanied her words with the action she was describing. For example, she would place a ball of tortilla dough on the press, close the press, press down and say, "Like this." In chopping wood, she would chop and say, "Like this." There was no decontextualized language about making tortillas or carrying firewood, with the exception of occasions when Paxku' told her grandfather or other visitors that she was teaching me to do those things.

CONCEPTUAL FEATURES OF THE ZINACANTEC
MODEL OF TEACHING AND LEARNING

The conceptual features are divided into two categories: beliefs about teachers and beliefs about learners.

Beliefs about Teachers

Feature 8: The Teacher must Know How to Do the Complete Task Herself

This was made explicit with regard to weaving in a conversation with Paxku's mother, Maruch. "Paxku' told me that she can teach me to weave. I asked Maruch if Paxku' could help me learn to weave. She said, "Yes, she knows well already." (August 16, 1995).

This fact is also implicit in the data. Paxku' never asked her mother for assistance in teaching me to do any of the tasks. Paxku' knew how to do the task, could do the task alone, and was always my only teacher in the three tasks. Although her mother or other people were often nearby when we were doing an activity, they did not give Paxku' instruction in how to instruct me, nor did they tell Paxku' how to do the task differently.

Feature 9: Teaching Style is not Based on the Learner's Age but on Her Experience with a Task

There are normal or expected ages at which a Zinacantec girl will be expected to begin to weave and to be able to weave on her own. Weaving instruction usually begins with a pre-weaving stage, play weaving, at age four or five (Greenfield, 1995), and can include weaving on a toy loom, or performing a small part of the entire process, such as spinning wool thread on a spindle (Modiano, 1973). By age seven, many girls are able to weave a large piece of cloth on their own, with little assistance from teachers (Greenfield & Childs, 1991).

Paxku' knew that I was already an adult at the time of the study. In Zinacantec culture, almost all adult women would be expert weavers. Exceptions would be a few girls and women who had to work for wages and therefore did not weave clothing for the family as their work.

Paxku' taught me to weave according to my experience and actual ability, not according to my age. As a non-native learner, I was given much more instruction in weaving skill than the oldest first-time weaver, another girl named Paxku', a 15-year-old studied by Greenfield and Childs (Maynard, Greenfield, & Childs, 1999). This teenage Paxku', although she had never woven, was quite skilled in the process having seen it performed her entire life. She also reported doing play weaving when she was a little girl, an important source of learning (Greenfield, 2000, 2004). She did not require much assistance to keep the process going, once the loom had been set up. In contrast, my teacher, Paxku', was sensitive to my ability level and she stayed close to me to help when needed, leaving me to work more independently as my skill improved. She did not have an expectation that I should be able to weave as an adult, but tailored her instruction to my experience.

Beliefs about Learners

This part of the model of teaching and learning focuses on the implicit, and sometimes explicit, beliefs of the teacher about the learner. This is also part of the scaffolding in the model; the teacher gives the learner opportunities to perform tasks at her ability level. What the teacher knows about the learner affects how the teacher will construct the lessons. There are other features of the learner that affect the teaching; these are also part of the model.

Feature 10: The Learner will be Able to Progress Form Novice to Independent Activity

The Zinacantec Maya model of teaching and learning has a goal, to train the learner to eventually be able to do the task herself. Paxku' made this an explicit goal in two of the three tasks, weaving and making tortillas, toward the end of the training. She told me that I should buy the weaving tools to take home to the United States in order to weave at home, but where there would be no instructors. In making tortillas, she said, "Now you have learned and you can make tortillas at home." In carrying firewood, it was clear that Paxku' wanted me to chop and carry wood on my own, and I was eventually able to chop and carry firewood as a Zinacantec woman would, with little help. The model incorporates this goal of eventual independence in the procedural features above. The goal that I would eventually be able to do the tasks myself was evident in all of the tasks. After I could make tortillas independently, Paxku' told me on several occasions that I should buy a press to make tortillas at home. She also suggested that I buy a tumpline and a machete to be able to chop and carry wood at home in my land.

Feature 11: Schooling does not Play a Role in Learning to Weave (Those Who have not been to School can Learn to Weave and Those Who have been to School will not be Aided by that Experience in Learning to Weave)

One cannot learn to weave by going to school. Weaving is not taught in the schools. Girls learn to weave at home with their mothers, aunts, grandmothers, cousins, sisters, or neighbors. Paxku' had never been to school and was an experienced weaver. She learned to weave at home. I asked Paxku' if it was possible for her younger sister, Rosy, who was attending school, to learn to weave there.

> AEM: Is it possible for Rosy to learn to weave in school?
> PAXKU': No.
> AEM: Why is it not possible?
> PAXKU': (no answer)
> AEM: How will Rosy learn to weave?
> PAXKU': At home.

Paxku' clearly knew that Rosy would learn to weave at home. She did not answer my question of why Rosy will not learn to weave in school.

There are at least two possible explanations for this. First, she might think that people don't weave in school but she has never been to school herself, so she may not have been certain. However, she did know quite a bit about school from her younger siblings who had gone to school. Paxku' knew that one uses paper and pencil in school. She knew that the children learn songs and games in school. It is likely that Paxku' knows from her siblings who have been to school that there is no weaving in school.

Another explanation for Paxku's reticence when I asked her "Why?" questions is that she was not accustomed to being asked those kinds of questions. In fact when I asked her "Why?" questions without a concrete context, Paxku' did not answer. In an early conversation, I asked Paxku' if it was possible for anybody to learn to weave in school, to which Paxku' answered, "No." I then asked how people learned to weave and Paxku' replied, "They learn from people."

This example of a "Why?" question is abstract and not grounded in immediate experience. Paxku' could have responded that they just don't teach weaving in school. She may have thought that I was asking her why weaving is not taught in school, to which one probable answer is, "Because people do other things there." Paxku' knew that one learns to use paper in school and one learns to weave at home. The issue of asking questions will be further explored in a later section.

Paxku' did not seem to think that going to school changes the way one learns to weave. She knew that I was a student, that my work was going to school, but Paxku' never asked me how many years I had been in school or what I did there. Paxku' may have had some ideas about me as someone who had been to school. We do not know how my occupation as a student influenced Paxku's behavior. We do know that Paxku' taught me to weave as a Zinacantec would be taught, scaffolding the process and giving little verbal instruction.

Feature 12: Schooling can Give one the Ability to Use Paper, in the Pattern Books, to Weave

The Zinacantecs know that going to school can affect one's ability to use paper to weave, although school does not affect one's ability to learn to weave. Pattern books for embroidery are found in some homes in the village, and some of the girls and women use them to weave. The Tzotzil word for school is *chanvun*, literally, "learn paper." One Zinacantec woman said, "to look at paper [use patterns] you have to learn paper" (Greenfield, 1999).

Feature 13: One cannot Learn to Weave from Looking at or Using Paper

The embroidery patterns used for weaving by some girls and women in Nabenchauk must be mentally transformed from a one-to-one correspondence with each square in the cross-stitch pattern, to a one-to-three or four correspondence in the weft dimension to make the pattern appear the same way once woven into a piece of cloth (Greenfield, 2000). I asked Paxku', "Is it possible to learn with paper?" and Paxku' answered, "No." I asked her why and she said, "It's not possible to learn that way." (August 23, 1995). In fact, it was not possible to learn basic weaving from pattern books; they were relevant only to brocade weaving. Indeed, in Paxku's generation, 64% of the 45 learners interviewed said they had learned basic weaving from their mothers (Greenfield, 2004); not one mentioned leaning from "paper." However, even for brocade weaving, only 13% of weaving learners mentioned learning the technique from paper. The dominant response when asked how they learned was "by myself" (49% of 39 girls) (Greenfield, 2004).

Feature 14: The Learner is Ready to Move up to Something New When She "Knows"

Characteristics of the learner influenced the scaffolding process in the weaving lessons and are part of the model of teaching and learning. Paxku' gave new tasks to do when I showed that I could do an old task on my own. In a sense, this is the personal part of scaffolding; it is intrinsic to it.

The following excerpt is an example from a weaving lesson of Paxku' telling me that I was doing something because I "knew." However, the Maya concept of "knowing" requires the knowledge to have become habitual and be part of the knower's character or personality (Zambrano & Greenfield, 2004); the criteria for knowing are usually more stringent than for the English word "know."

The example is about winding the thread to be woven. Thread for weaving can be wound in two ways, on the *komen*, a large device with notches used to select the desired length of cloth, or on the loom itself. Winding on the loom itself requires setting up a "toy loom" (Maynard &

Greenfield, 2003). The toy loom is a part of a pre-weaving stage of weaving, performed common in Nabenchauk. Girls proceed from winding on the loom to winding on the *komen*. Toward the end of the weaving lessons, when I was able to keep the weaving going on my own, Paxku' decided we would use the *komen* to wind the thread. I asked Paxku' why they were winding on the *komen* when before they were winding on the loom. Paxku' replied, "You know well already." Paxku's aunt, Mal, came out of the house to see what they were doing and suggested that I weave a tortilla bag. She brought an example of such a bag. I asked Paxku' if it was possible and she said yes. We went to the store to buy more colors to make the tortilla bag and then returned to unwind the piece we had already started. After winding the large piece on the *komen*, Paxku' decided we should wind the smaller piece on the loom, and we had the following conversation.

AEM: Why are we winding this on the loom now when before we were winding on the *komen*?

PAXKU': For the tortilla bag, it is longer, so we use the *komen*. For the little one, now, we do it this way.

AEM: But why did we use the *komen* for the striped bag?

PAXKU': Because now you know.

There are several other instances of Paxku' saying that I could do some part of the process because "Now you know."

Feature 15: Bodily Experience and Skill Play a Role in Weaving

As part of the loom, the body is central to the weaving process. Knowing how to properly use one's body to weave is crucial to successful weaving (Maynard et al., 1999). Paxku' was aware that I would weave better if I had better bodily skills and she tried to explain that many times while I was attempting to weave. She often had to tell me what to do with her body when she was weaving and she would direct her as to what to do, touching my body and helping me.

Feature 16: Continuity Across Tasks: Conceptual Knowledge of Instruction of Making Tortillas and Gathering Firewood

Though most of the conceptual features of this model reflect the teaching and learning of weaving skill, there was continuity in several conceptual features across the tasks of making tortillas and chopping and carrying firewood. For example, bodily skills such as strength and balance that were so important in weaving (Feature 15) were also important in carrying firewood and in kneeling while pressing tortillas. Features 10, 11, and 14 are also relevant to conceptions of the learner in the acquisition of the other skills.

DISCUSSION

The psychological reality of a person is the world as he or she experiences it, through interaction with it, filtered through his or her own expectations, biases, and mental models. We have attempted to construct a psychologically real model of Zinacantec teaching and learning. By "psychologically real" we mean that the model is a description of Zinacantec teaching processes, which reproduces in an observer the world of meanings of the native users of that culture. The model has been validated in a number of crucial respects by its correspondence to the strategies used by Zinacantecs to teach weaving to other members of their families and by what they say about this process in an interview situation.

In the present ethnographic study, we generalized the model from weaving to two other tasks that are central to women's work: making tortillas, and carrying firewood. We hypothesize that it is a general model of the teaching-learning process of the Zinacantecs. Indeed a major potential implication of this study is that a given group may have a generalized model for cultural apprenticeship. A contrasting case in which pedagogical methods have been studied in different domains would be interesting in this respect.

The model is in agreement with some particular findings elsewhere in the Maya world. For example, it reflects the specific model used to teach and learn tortilla making in a Maya community in Guatemala (Rogoff, 1990). At least one aspect of the model—the importance of following commands—has also been described for Maya children's contributions to their households in the Yucatan (Gaskins, 2003). Finally, the model reflects the general process of Maya teaching and learning described by Arias Sojob (1970, cited in Modiano, 1973):

> Education means to be conscious of the world where fate has placed him and shaped all the possibilities of his life. There is also a connotation of "becoming accustomed" in this concept of education, somewhat akin to the North American concept of training as opposed to problem solving. A situation is repeated as many times as necessary, until the child becomes accustomed and is able to perform as expected ... Learning, then, is intimately tied to the environment, to the community, and to the daily round of activities. Children learn as they participate in the religious, economic, and social life of the community, contributing their share to the family's welfare. They learn to farm by farming, to weave by weaving, to communicate with the supernaturals by communicating.

The process by which Zinacantec children are educated in important cultural knowledge stayed largely the same through the twenty-five years between our first study of weaving apprenticeship in 1970 and Maynard's experience in learning to weave in 1995: they learn to do something by doing it. Maynard learned to perform the Zinacantec tasks of weaving, making tortillas, and carrying firewood by doing them in an apprenticeship process, with help and guidance from a teacher.

The teaching of weaving, cooking, and carrying firewood is part of the education of Zinacantec females. We have constructed a model to build a generalized description of the teaching and learning of these activities. Thus far, we have evaluated it by comparing the model to the empirical findings of Greenfield and Childs (Childs & Greenfield, 1980; Greenfield, 1984, 1999, 2004; Greenfield & Childs, 1991; Greenfield, Maynard, & Childs, 2000, 2003). As we have seen, there are many parallels between the ethnographic data presented here and their cross-sectional database of 72 weavers from two historical periods. For instance, in both sets of data there is scaffolding. In both sets of data, verbalization to beginners consists mainly of commands and is tightly coordinated with action and gesture. We also have independent evidence in our experimental data of the importance of observational learning in acquiring weaving skill (Maynard & Greenfield, 2003). The way in which Paxku' taught Maynard to weave from start to finish reflects the same strategies used by teachers in the Childs and Greenfield (1980) database who were teaching girls of different stages of acquisition. However, Maynard's teacher was able to adapt her strategies to specific differences in Maynard as a learner, compared with Zinacantec girls. For example, she provided more help and guidance concerning the use of her body because she did not have the culturally "trained" body of a Zinacantec learner (Maynard et al., 1999). In this way, she generalized the strategy of a scaffold—providing whatever help the learner needs at her particular stage of development—to a new situation. Her particular moves or behaviors were different because her pupil's bodily knowledge was different from an indigenous learner—but, at the more abstract level, what remained constant was the higher level scaffolding strategy. All indications are that the Zinacantecs generalize their model to different activities and to different kinds of learners, both indigenous and foreign. We therefore predict that it would apply to Zinacantec boys and male tasks as well.

While it might be valuable to do a longitudinal study of one Zinacantec teaching another Zinacantec how to weave, there is a benefit of this longitudinal study involving a non-native learner. To extend the analogy that a cultural model is like the grammar of a language, exposure to another language makes the grammar of one's native language more obvious. For Maynard as an investigator, learning how to do things in Zinacantán made Paxku's cultural models and her own cultural models stand out in relief. Pitted against each other each of their cultural models of teaching and learning became quite obvious. For example, Maynard's model of personal choice in selecting colors for weaving a piece of cloth did not fit with Paxku's model of the teacher choosing for the student.

This model of teaching and learning, the Zinacantec model, is only one of many possible models people in various cultural places use to transmit culture. The model is instantiated in Zinacantec culture and activities, activities influenced by ecocultural features of the place. For example, the general cultural value of obedience to the weaving teacher as authority was instantiated in the apprenticeship process. Although Maynard was Paxku's "boss," in that she paid her for her work, Paxku' was the clear authority on Zinacantec culture, and she expected Maynard to conform to her suggestions. For the Zinacantecs, the cultural education of an individual is a long-term, ongoing process which involves a great deal of teacher attention and teacher-learner interaction at the beginning of the learning process, with decreasing interaction until the learner can perform the task alone. For the weaver to know weaving, the practice must become habitual (Zambrano & Greenfield, 2004).

Other models for learning might look very different. For example, one might imagine a teacher giving her pupil an outline of the entire task before starting to do any one part of a task. A weaving teacher might say, "First we will wind the thread. Then we will make a heddle. Next we will make a bobbin. And then we will finally start to weave," explaining in detail what it means to do each of those steps. Paxku', however, did not explain the tasks she taught Maynard to perform. She just started teaching the tasks in practice, giving some part or another to do. On the other hand, learning might also be more trial-and-error, as in the backstrap loom weaving class observed by Greenfield (Greenfield & Lave, 1982).

One purpose of deriving the model is to have available the kind of ethnographic information which can and should inform any experimental investigation of the same domain in Nabenchauk. More generally, future researchers who wish to study in a particular culture can use ethnographic findings. Further study might also be ethnographic, but might include more subjects, measurement of behaviors or variables in question, and testing the model for its psychological validity with informants. Or, further research might include an experimental paradigm in which the researcher desires to study how the Zinacantec Maya learn a new task. If a researcher wants to explore how it is that Zinacantec Maya people perform a task that involves learning something new, such as a spatial learning task, then this model can be used as a basis for the design of such an investigation. For example, a researcher might combine knowledge about spatial ability and the acquisition of spatial skills with this model of teaching and learning in Nabenchauk to conduct a study involving the education of spatial skills in Nabenchauk, or to use an experimental paradigm that involves teaching and testing a group on spatial ability.

Questioning as a Culturally-Specific Technique

This chapter has brought to light an important methodological issue in the study of another culture: the use of questions to gain information about a cultural practice. Questions, while they are often useful for acquiring information, do not always get at the whole picture. Activities are structural processes embedded within cultures and which reflect organized and systematic culturally shared ideas (D'Andrade, 1995). It is acceptable and perhaps desirable for the researcher to get involved as a participant in the activities of the study culture in order to find out what is important in the other culture. The need to ask questions then becomes unnecessary. By working in a culture in which decontextualized questions are out-of-bounds, Maynard was obliged to take this approach. While there are limitations of ethnographic participant observation, it is the only way to learn certain things. The best way around the limiting nature of asking questions, whether they are open- or closed-ended, contextualized or not, is to invest the time in long-term ethnographic study (Weisner, 1996). The research presented in this chapter reflects just such an ethnographic approach: the long-term exposure to and analysis of the cultural models of another culture.

REFERENCES

Beach, K. (1992). Becoming a bartender: The role of external memory cues in a work-directed educational activity. *Applied Cognitive Psychology* 7:191–204.

Cancian, F. (1992). *The decline of community in Zinacantan: Economy, public life, and social stratification, 1960–1987.* Stanford University Press, Stanford, California.

Carothers, J. C. (1953). *The African mind in health and disease: A study in ethnopsychiatry.* Geneva: World Health Organization.

Chaiklin, S. and Lave, J. (1993). *Understanding practice: Perspectives on activity and context.* Cambridge University Press, New York, NY.

Childs, C. P. and Greenfield, P. M. (1980). Informal modes of teaching and learning: The case of Zinacanteco weaving. In: Warren, N. (ed.), *Studies in cross-cultural psychology, Volume 2.* Academic Press, London, pp. 269–316.

D'Andrade, R. G. (1992). Schemas and motivation. In: D'Andrade, R. G. and Strauss, C. (eds.), *Human motives and cultural models.* Cambridge University Press, New York, NY, pp. 23–44.

D'Andrade, R. G. (1995). *The development of cognitive anthropology.* Cambridge University Press, New York, NY.

D'Andrade, R. G. and Strauss, C. (1992). *Human motives and cultural models.* Cambridge University Press, New York, NY.

Fortes, M. (1937). Social and psychological aspects of education in Taleland. *International Aafrican Institrute Memorandum,* No. 17.

Gaskins, S. (2003). From corn to cash: Change and continuity within Mayan families. *Ethos* 31(2):248–273.

Geertz, C. (1973). *The interpretation of cultures*. Harper Collins, USA.

Goodwin, C. (1994). Professional vision. *American Anthropologist* 96:606–633.

Greenfield, P. M. (1973). Comparing categorization in natural and artificial contexts: A developmental study among the Zinacantecos of Mexico. *Journal of Social Psychology* 93:157–171.

Greenfield, P. M. (1984). A theory of the teacher in the learning activities of everyday life. In: Rogoff, B. and Lave, J. (eds.), *Everyday cognition: Its development in social context* Harvard University Press, Cambridge, MA, pp. 117–138.

Greenfield, P. M. (1994). Independence and interdependence as developmental scripts. In: Greenfield, P. M. and Cocking, R. R. (eds.), *Cross-cultural roots of minority child development*. Mahwah, NJ: Erlbaum.

Greenfield, P. M. (1997a). Culture as process: empirical methodology for cultural psychology. In: Berry, J. W., Poortinga, Y., and Pandey, J. (eds.), *Handbook of cross-cultural psychology*, Volume 1: Theory and method. Allyn & Bacon, Boston, MA, pp. 301–346.

Greenfield, P. M. (1997b). You can't take it with you: Why ability assessments don't cross cultures. *American Psychologist* 52:1115–1124.

Greenfield, P. M. (1998). The cultural evolution of IQ. In: Neisser, U. (ed.), *The rising curve: Long-term gains in IQ and related measures*. American Psychological Association, Washington, DC, pp. 81–123.

Greenfield, P. M. (2000). Culture and universals: Integrating social and cognitive development. In: Nucci, L. P., Saxe, G. B., and Turiel, E. (eds.), *Culture, thought, and development*, Lawrence Erlbaum Associates, Mahwah, NJ, pp. 231–277.

Greenfield, P. M. (2004). *Weaving generations together: Evolving creativity in the Maya of Chiapas.* SAR Press, Santa Fe, NM.

Greenfield, P. M., Brazelton, T. B., and Childs, C. P. (1989). From birth to maturity in Zinacantán: Ontogenesis in cultural context. In: Bricker, V. and Gossen, G. (eds.), *Ethnographic encounters in southern mesoamerica: Celebratory essays in honor of Evon Z. Vogt*. Institute of Mesoamerican Studies, State University of New York, Albany, pp. 177–216.

Greenfield, P. M. and Childs, C. P. (1977). Weaving, color terms and pattern representation: Cultural influences and cognitive development among the Zinacantecos of Southern Mexico. *Inter-American Journal of Psychology* 11:23–48.

Greenfield, P. M. and Childs, C. P. (1991). Developmental continuity in biocultural context. In: Cohen, R., and Siegel, A. W. (eds.), *Context and development*. Hillsdale, NJ: Lawrence Erlbaum Associates, Hillsdale, NJ, pp. 135–159.

Greenfield, P. M. and Cocking, R. R. (1994). Effects of interactive entertainment technologies on development. Special issue of *Journal of Applied Developmental Psychology*, 15(1).

Greenfield, P. M., Keller, H., Fuligni, A., and Maynard, A. (2003). Cultural pathways through universal development. *Annual Review of Psychology* 54:461–90.

Greenfield, P. M. and Lave, J. (1982). Cognitive aspects of informal education. In: Wagner, D., and Stevenson, H. (eds.), *Cultural perspectives on child development*. Freeman, San Francisco, pp. 180–207.

First published in French in 1979: Aspets cognitifs de l'education informelle. *Recherche Pedagogie et Culture* 8:16–25.

Greenfield, P. M., Maynard, A. E., and Childs, C. P. (2000) History, culture, learning, and development. *Cross-Cultural Research* 34:351–374.

Greenfield, P. M., Maynard, A. E., and Childs, C. P. (2003). Historical change, cultural apprenticeship, and cognitive representation in Zinacantec Maya children. *Cognitive Development* 18:455–487.

Greenfield, P. M., Quiroz, B., and Raeff (2000). Cross-Cultural conflict and harmony in the social construction of the child. *New Directions in Child and Adolescent Development*, Jossey-Bass, San Francisco, pp. 93–108.

Guberman, S. (1996). The development of everyday mathematics in Brazilian children with limited formal education. *Child Development* 67:109–1623.

Guberman, S. (1992). Math and money: A comparative study of the arithmetical achievements and out-of-school activities of Latino and Korean American children. Unpublished doctoral dissertation, University of California, Los Angeles.

Guberman, S. and Greenfield, P. M. (1991). Learning and transfer in everyday cognition. *Cognnitive Development* 6:233–260.

Hatano, G. and Inagaki, K. (1986). Two courses of expertise. In: Stevenson, H., Azuma, H., and Hakuta, K. (eds.), *Child development and education in Japan*. W. H. Freeman/Times Books/Henry Holt and Co., New York, NY, pp. 262–272.

Haviland, L. K. M. (1978). The social relations of work in a peasant community. Unpublished doctoral dissertation, Harvard University, Cambridge, MA.

Holland, D. and Quinn, N. (1987). *Cultural models in language and thought*. Cambridge University Press, New York, NY.

Hutchins, E. (1996). Learning to navigate. In: Chaiklin, S., and Lave, J. (eds.), *Understanding practice: Perspectives on activity and context*, Cambridge University Press, Cambridge, pp. 35–63.

Knapen, M.-T. (1962). *L'enfant Mukongo: Orientations de base du systeme educatif et developpement de la personalite*. Louvain: Publications Universitaires.

Laughlin, R. M. (1975). *The great Tzotzil dictionary of San Lorenzo Zinacantán*. Smithsonian Institution Press, Washington, DC.

Lave, J. (1980). Tailored learning: Education and cognitive skills among tribal craftsmen in West Africa. Unpublished manuscript, University of California, Irvine.

Lave, J. (1988a). *Cognition in practice*. Cambridge University Press, New York.

Lave, J. (1988b). *The culture of acquisition and the practice of understanding*. Institute for Research on Learning, Report No. IRL88-007.

Lave, J. and Wenger, E. (1991). *Situated learning: Legitimate peripheral participation*. Cambridge University Press, New York, NY.

Maynard, A. E. and Greenfield, P. M. (2003). Implicit cognitive development in cultural tools and children: Lessons from Mayan Mexico. *Cognitive Development* 18: 489–510.

Maynard, A. E., Greenfield, P. M., and Childs, C. P. (1999). Culture, history, biology, and body: Native and non-native acquisition of technological skill. *Ethos* 27(3):379–402.

Modiano, N. (1973). *Indian education in the Chiapas highlands*. Holt, Rinehart and Winston, Inc., New York, NY.

Nunes, T., Schliemann, A. D., and Carraher, D. W. (1993). *Street mathematics and school mathematics*. Cambridge University Press: Cambridge, England.

Ochs, E. and Jacoby, S. (1997.) Down to the wire: The cultural clock of physicists and the discourse of consensus. *Language in Society* 26(4):479–505.

Rogoff, B. (1990). *Apprenticeship in thinking: Cognitive development in social context*. Oxford University Press, New York, NY.

Rogoff, B., and Lave, J. (1984). *Everyday cognition*. Harvard University Press, Cambridge, MA.

Ruddle, K. and Chesterfield, R. (1978). Traditional skill training and labor in rural societies. *Journal of Developing Areas* 12:389–398.

Scribner, S. (1984). Product assembly: Optimizing strategies and their acquisition. *Quarterly Newsletter of the Laboratory of Comparative Human Cognition* 6:11–19.

Scribner, S. and Cole, M. (1973). Cognitive consequences of formal and informal education. *Science* 182:553–559.

Scribner, S. and Cole, M. (1981). *The psychology of literacy.* Harvard University Press, Cambridge, MA.

Shweder, R. A. (1990). Cultural psychology—what is it? In: Stigler, J. S., Shweder, R. A., and Herdt, G., (eds.), *Cultural psychology: Essays on comparative human development.* Cambridge University Press, New York, NY, pp. 1–46.

Shweder, R. A. and LeVine, R. A. (1984). *Culture theory: Essays on mind, self, and emotion.* Cambridge University Press, New York, NY.

Sternberg, R. J. and Grigorenko, E. L. (eds.) (2004). *Culture and competence: Contexts of life success.* American Psychological Association, Washington, D.C.

Stigler, J. S., Shweder, R. A., and Herdt, G. (1990). *Cultural psychology: Essays on comparative human development.* Cambridge University Press, New York, NY.

Strauss, C. (1992). Models and motives. In: D'Andrade, R. G., and Strauss, C. (eds.), *Human motives and cultural models.* Cambridge University Press, New York, NY, pp. 23–44.

Suchman, L. A. and Trigg, R. H. (1996). Artificial intelligence as craftwork. In: Chaiklin, S. and Lave, J. (eds.), *Understanding practice: Perspectives on activity and context*, Cambridge, University Press, Cambridge, England, pp. 144–178.

Tobin, J., Wu, D., and Davidson, D. (1989). *Preschool in three cultures: Japan, China, and the United States.* Yale Press, New Haven.

Turok, M. (1972). Handicrafts: A case study on weaving in the highlands. Manuscript on file, Harvard Chiapas Project, Department of Anthropology, Harvard University, Cambridge, MA.

Weisner, T. S. (1984). Ecocultural niches of middle childhood: A cross-cultural perspective. In: Collins, W. A. (ed.), *Development during middle childhood: The years from six to twelve.* National Academy of Sciences Press, Washington, DC, pp. 334–369.

Weisner, T. S. (1996). Why ethnography should be the most important method in the study of human development. In: Colby, A., Jessor, R., and Shweder, R., (eds.), *Ethnography and human development.* University of Chicago Press, Chicago, IL, pp. 305–324.

Weisner, T. S. and Gallimore, R. (1985). The convergence of ecocultural and activity theory. Revised version of paper presented at the annual meetings of the American Anthropological Association, Washington, DC.

Vogt, E. Z. (1970). *The Zinacantecos of Mexico: A modern Maya way of life.* Holt, Rinehart, and Wilson, New York, NY.

Zambrano, I. and Greenfield, P. M. (2004). Ethnoepistemologies at home and at school. In: Sternberg, R. J., and .Grigorenko, E. L. (eds.), *Culture and competence: Contexts of life success,* American Psychological Association, Washington, D. C., pp. 251–272.

AUTHOR NOTE

We are indebted to Paxku' Pavlu, Greenfield's assistant in 1991, Maynard's teacher in 1995, and our research assistant in the years since. Thanks also to the Pavlu family for opening their hearts and their homes to us and our research. We are also grateful to the UCLA Center for the Study of Evolution and the Origin of Life (CSEOL), which provided a graduate research fellowship to Maynard to collect the data reported in this chapter.

Section II

Cultural Approaches to Supporting Early Learning in Preschoolers

Section Two examines children's cognitive and social learning in preschool contexts. In the first chapter in this section, Shawn Kana'iaupuni and Iwalani Else help us transition from the everyday contexts of the child's home to the preschool context. They make the link between culture at home and early education outcomes of Hawaiian preschool children. They show that a seemingly mundane and simple variable, a child's knowing his Hawaiian name, how to pronounce it, and what it means, is related his performance in preschool and on standard tests of early childhood development. They review the literature on culture and education, and they answer the call for more research that links identity development and cultural socialization in learning processes. Clearly, the child's knowing his or her Hawaiian name is an important part of identity development, but what Kana'iaupuni and Else demonstrate so elegantly is that the child's knowing his name also relates to verbal ability, widely believed to be a marker of intelligence in young children.

Helen Davis uses an activity settings approach to compare preschool children's play groups and themes in two different communities in Costa Rica, one urban and one rural. She relates children's friendship circles and play to their physical surroundings and to the teacher's beliefs about inclusion at each school. In her innovative research, Davis examines the developmental trajectories of children across socioeconomic strata, noting that each teacher's beliefs about children and about education influenced the physical setup of her classroom, which had a major impact on the ways that children organized themselves in play situations. Davis' research emphasizes the importance of ethnographic observations to support interview data. For example, she finds that one teacher in the urban preschool claimed to support inclusion of everyone in play, but actually did not enforce that standard in actual play time. During actual play, the teacher emphasized each child's choice in deciding whom their play partners would be. Most importantly, Davis shows that learning is influenced by the local cultural practices of inclusion: children at the rural preschool played together more often as a whole class, and play behaviors and themes were well-known to all the children. On the other hand, at the University preschool, children played in small groups, excluding many other children, and play behaviors and themes were particular to each group. In the urban, University setting, children learned to innovate in order to win the seat as "boss" of a play session.

Mary Martini describes effective classroom teaching for preschoolers. She compares classrooms that are effective to varying degrees and shows how conceptual clarity and opportunities for children's experimentation make all the difference in preschoolers' gains in knowledge. Her research is guided by the theoretical principles of "Learning with Understanding," put forth by Bransford, Brown, and Cocking (2000). Learning with understanding happens when students can pay attention to what they are learning and produce products that indicate a high level of understanding. This notion can be compared with the simple memorization of facts that dominate so many textbooks and classroom efforts. Martini finds that more effective preschool teachers attempt to create a depth of understanding by actively engaging them in the process of learning (the attention factor) and by making the knowledge applicable outside of the classroom (the product factor).

DeBaryshe and Gorecki describe a research program designed to promote literacy and mathematics skills in preschool children. Through longitudinal research that involved ethnographic interviews with teachers and parents, and observations of classrooms, the researchers designed a curriculum called "Learning Connections," (LC) with the goal of enriching the focus on math and literacy in the preschool classroom. An additional goal was to reduce home-school barriers to education by involving parents and by emphasizing culture in the curriculum. Though the research was particular to Hawai`i's multicultural preschoolers, the LC curriculum could be adapted to another cultural milieu. The links made between home and school were particularly effective and showed promising results for the children's later adaptation to kindergarten and primary school. The research demonstrates the value of using a sociocultural approach to approach education across domains, such as teachers, parents, and home and school culture. By engaging parents in the research, and by making learning materials using concepts, objects, and words that were familiar to the children, the researchers were able to design and implement a program that worked because it used information and personnel from across socio-cultural domains.

REFERENCE

Bransford, J. D., Brown, A. L., and Cocking, R. R. (2000). *How people learn: Brain, mind, experience, and school.* National Academy Press, Washington, DC.

Chapter 4

Ola Ka Inoa (The Name Lives)
Cultural Inputs, Naming Practices, and Early Education Outcomes of Hawaiian Children

Shawn Malia Kana`iaupuni and Iwalani Else

INTRODUCTION

Educational approaches to culture take a variety of forms. Each answers differently questions about how to integrate culture and school. Cultural education models include specialized schools or programs that teach children cultural traditions and knowledge, such as immersion or other culturally grounded schools found in Hawaiian, Maori, Alaska Native and American Indian communities. Other approaches are culturally-based, adopting culturally compatible methods and/or learning environments as teaching tools for conveying Western ways of knowing (e.g., Jordan, 1992). Most common in education are cultural styles or sensitivity approaches that stress respect and tolerance for other cultures and ways of learning, including staff, student, and faculty training (see Gutierrez & Rogoff, 2003).

Underlying these approaches are several theories about the importance of culture in education. Scholars argue that children's learning is more effective if it occurs in cultural context; that is, with attention to cultural values and behaviors, learning styles, and the context of place and the physical environment (Irvine & York, 1995; Lee, 2001; Gruenewald, 2003; Kawakami, 2003). In addition to its role in the cultural survival of indigenous groups, culturally based education is also believed to increase children's resiliency by creating a strong sense of individual identity and cultural pride, which can lead to positive self-esteem and confidence (Bowman 1989; Phinney & Chavira, 1992; Phinney, Cantu, & Kurtz,

1997). Self-esteem typically is linked to achievement, although disidentification theorists argue that the association is not necessarily automatic (Steele, 1992). Inferiority stereotypes continue to challenge ethnic minority students, especially the high achieving ones, who may eventually disengage from performances where they may be judged against the white norm (Steele, 1997). As a result, education researchers point out the need for more research that integrates cultural socialization and identity development processes into learning (Lee, Spencer, & Harpalani, 2003; Kawakami, 2003).

Despite strong interest, and for some, emotional investment in cultural education, we still struggle to understand the effects of culture and cultural identity on school outcomes such as achievement and to measure the direction of causality. Some studies suggest that the biggest positive effects of culturally-based education are on children's self-esteem and strengthened relationships between schools and their surrounding communities and families. Strong links between home, neighborhoods, and school, for example, are key features of effective educational settings in indigenous communities (Lipka & McCarty, 1994). To date, only weak evidence suggests corollary improvements in achievement stemming from culturally based education in schools (Bacon et al., 1982; Brenner, 1998).

In this paper, we examine early influences of culture on child achievements. We focus on the effects of culture in the home environment on young children's adaptation and school readiness. Specifically, we examine the cultural inputs of parents or primary caregivers—their practices, beliefs and knowledge, on the development of young children. We argue that cultural activities and participation can form an important mechanism for parent-child interaction and learning that enhance the early educational experiences of children.

BACKGROUND

Our analysis relies on a unique data set containing information about indigenous Hawaiian children and their families. Native Hawaiians ("Hawaiians" hereafter) are descendants of the indigenous Polynesians who inhabited the Hawaiian Islands prior to 1778, the date of Captain Cook's arrival to the Hawaiian Islands.

Today's ethnically Hawaiian population stems from a history of a large, isolated, indigenous society turned immigrant plantation society turned major U.S. military and tourist hub (Kana'iaupuni & Liebler, 2004). Following Captain Cook's arrival to the shores of Hawai`i, the first 100 years of western contact decimated the Native Hawaiian population by an estimated 90 per cent. By 1893, at the time of the overthrow of the Hawaiian monarchy, Hawaiians numbered only about 35,000 full-blooded and 9,000 part-Hawaiians (Nordyke, 1989).

As the number of Hawaiians continued to dwindle, the non-Hawaiian population flourished rapidly. A surge in White immigration to Hawai`i occurred in the early 1880s and by 1910, White immigrants outnumbered Hawaiians. Throughout the mid-1800s and early 1900s, the whaling industry and sugar plantations also brought laborer migrants from China, Puerto Rico, Portugal, Japan, the Philippines, Korea and other countries. More recent immigrants added to the mix, including those from Micronesia, Polynesia, and Southeast Asia (Nordyke, 1989).

In today's Hawai`i, about one-fifth to one-quarter of the population is Hawaiian, less than 1 per cent of whom are full-blooded. A minority in their homeland, Hawaiians have taken on the characteristics shared by other racial and ethnic minorities in the United States. As a group, they experience high morbidity and mortality rates, poor educational outcomes, and a marginalized socioeconomic position in U.S. society (Barringer, Gardner, & Levin, 1993; Blaisdell, 1993; Braun et al., 1997; Mokuau, Browne, & Braun, 1998; Humes & McKinnon, 2000; Srinivasan & Guillermo, 2000; Kana'iaupuni & Ishibashi, 2003).

The Hawaiian Culture Scale

Our analysis of cultural inputs among Hawaiians builds on prior analyses of cultural practice and identity conducted by the Native Hawaiian Mental Health Research Development Program (NHMHRDP), a division of the Department of Psychiatry, John A. Burns School of Medicine, at the University of Hawai`i at Mānoa. In their pioneering work on the psychological adjustment of Native Hawaiian adolescents, researchers developed a Hawaiian Culture Scale (Hishinuma et al., 2000) for use in the Hawaiian High Schools Health Survey (HHSHS). Since 1992, over 7,000 students, grades 9 to 12, have participated in the HHSHS cross-sequential study of five high schools on three islands in the state of Hawai`i.

To date, research from this study demonstrates significant gender differences, but negligible differences in self-esteem between those with and without Hawaiian ancestry. Consistent with other studies, higher self-reported grades and education level of the primary wage earner at home were positively associated with adolescent self-esteem (Miyamoto et al., 2000). In addition, analyses showed that anxiety, aggression, substance abuse, and depression indirectly influence self-esteem through family support ties, and that anxiety and depression have direct, independent effects on self-esteem (Miyamoto et al., 2001).

Key to the development of the HHSHS project was the Hawaiian Culture scale, which we adapt for this study. Its purpose was to assess traditional Hawaiian beliefs, values, and practices of individuals and to examine the process of ethnic identification primarily among adolescents (Andrade, et al., 2000). Developed in the early 1990s by Native Hawaiian psychiatric researchers and colleagues over a two-year period, the scale relied on input from *kūpuna* (Hawaiian elders), Native Hawaiian professionals (e.g. school teachers, administrators, professors, ministers), *kua`āina* (those who live off the land and sea), and late adolescents and young adults (Andrade et al., 2000a). Overall, the complete Hawaiian Culture scale includes constructs measuring two principal domains. First is the source of learning a Hawaiian way of life. Second is involvement in specific cultural traditions, as measured by the seven subscales of lifestyles, customs and beliefs, activities and social events, folklore and legends, causes-locations, causes-access, and language proficiency (Hishinuma et al., 2000).

Research by Hishinuma and colleagues (2000) finds that the scale successfully differentiates between Hawaiian and non-Hawaiian groups. Hawaiians scored significantly higher than did non-Hawaiians on all of the ethnic identity variables. Hawaiian students also came from homes where Hawaiian was spoken significantly more often than did students without Hawaiian ancestry. This scale forms the basis of our attempt to measure the effects of parents' cultural inputs on early childhood learning.

Links between Hawaiian Culture and Learning

Our work contributes to a growing body of research on Hawaiian culture in relation to educational, social, and health outcomes. The analysis builds on the argument that cultural processes in Hawaiian families are integral to the survival of Hawaiian culture and identity and provide important benefits to children and other members. Research argues that the cultural practices forming the cornerstones of today's diverse Hawaiian families include genealogy practices, *aloha'āina*, or love of the land, and interdependent families, or *'ohana* (Kana'iaupuni 2004). These cornerstones are an important source of connection and identity to contemporary Hawaiians who have been raised in multiracial families and a Western society, many of whom have lost touch with Hawaiian cultural traditions. A growing number of families, however, are more heavily immersed in Hawaiian traditions and practices, some as a result of regaining cultural identity and ways of knowing, and others to carry on the strong existing cultural foundations of their own family traditions.

Support for Hawaiian culture in education continues to thrive alongside this revival of Hawaiian culture. Some of the reasons include the "development of positive identity and self-esteem, the perpetuation of Hawaiian values, the revitalization of the Hawaiian language and culture, the reclamation and stewardship of endangered natural habitat, and the perpetuation of Hawaiian cultural arts" (Kawakami 2004:3). A key example of this thinking includes the recently published Hawaiʻi guidelines for culturally healthy and responsive learning environments, *Na Honua Mauli Ola*. Through the guiding philosophy of *mauli* as the cultural heart and spirit of a people, the guidelines set out an educational foundation for teaching and learning through Hawaiian language and culture. The objectives are to develop learners to their full potential and to benefit the physical and cultural environment of Hawaiʻi in ways that make visible its host culture and that respect its indigenous people.

Based on these arguments, our specific research question examines whether family environments steeped in Hawaiian cultural tradition also enhance the early learning experiences of children. From our review of the *Nä Honua Mauli Ola* guidelines, we hypothesize that greater cultural embeddedness of parents will yield positive effects on achievement and social skills that can be observed in preschool classrooms. This would occur, we argue, because of the diverse set of opportunities that culture offers parents and/or caregivers to interact with children and in ways that are important to child development.

We examine cultural embeddedness with two key concepts, which we analyze in relation to early child achievements. The first concept is cultural inputs provided by parents or primary caregivers' practice of cultural customs. Through family practice of customs, children become the beneficiaries of cultural knowledge and learning. Examples of these might include hands-on activities like making poi, dancing hula, cultivating taro or other nature-based activities, ocean learning through fishing, surfing, and so on. All of these examples enhance fine and gross motor skills while developing practical problem solving and other experiential learning skills. In addition, Hawaiian cultural customs also offer an important medium to develop oral, academic, and artistic knowledge through activities such as learning genealogy, storytelling and legends, music, history, and possibly even political activism.

Second, because we are considering very young children in the present study, we include a simple measure of whether a child has been taught how to pronounce and/or to know the significance of his or her Hawaiian name. The emphasis on Hawaiian names is best understood as part of the sophisticated oral practices in Hawaiian genealogical tradition. In learning these traditions, listening is an important skill for children to develop.

Johnson (19xx) describes how listening, *ho'olono*, to parents and elders was a very highly valued learning skill in Hawaiian culture and how disobedient children were called "deaf ear" (*pepeiao kuli*).

Moreover, the teaching that goes along with a name reflects the importance of naming practices in Hawaiian culture. Past scholarship describes the deep, symbolic value of names in Hawaiian society (Puku'i et al., 1972; Kame'eleihiwa, 1992). In early Hawai`i, names were perhaps the most precious personal possession, prized far above any tools or material goods, to be given or taken only with permission from the owner. Not only was a name highly valued property, it also carried its own force as a "causative agent" with "potential to benefit or harm" (Puku'i, 1972; 94).

Naming practices in Hawaiian retain their familial and individual significance today, requiring great thought and consultation. This importance reflects the spiritual and practical meaning of a name. As Kame'eleihiwa (1992) relates, names link individuals to their past, while providing the force for the future. In essence, she states, children become the name.

The significance of naming for child development, we argue, creates a cultural mechanism for parent/caregiver-child interaction that stimulates children's learning and growth. It may include exposure to family history and stories, linguistic expression (in English and Hawaiian), and verbal exercises in pronunciation, all of which enhance family communication and interaction. As a significant family event, hearing about the history behind a name and why it was chosen may reinforce children's feelings of family connection, self-esteem, and sense of control, which we expect would positively affect achievement and growth.

DATA AND METHODS

We test this cultural hypothesis using data from the Preschool and Beyond Study (PABS), a study conducted by the Kamehameha Schools' department of Policy Analysis & System Evaluation (PASE). The primary objective of the project is to address the determinants of educational success among children in the state of Hawai`i, with particular focus on early childhood experiences. The PABS is modeled after the Early Childhood Longitudinal Study (ECLS), a national longitudinal study of children, their families, teachers, and schools in the United States (West, 1999). It tracks a group of four-year-olds who entered preschool in 2001 and follows their transition into the formal education system. Like the ECLS, the PABS provides a rich data source that describes children's educational experiences, early learning, developmental stages, and general health at the individual, family/household, school, and community levels.

We use data collected in the first year of the study from over 30 preschool classrooms in rural and urban areas. In total, data from 464 participating families were collected at the beginning and end of the 2001–02 school year. Trained professionals conducted individual child assessments at the beginning and end of the year. Teachers completed a paper survey at the beginning of the year and followed up with an individual child evaluation and information about the school year and their classroom at the end of the year. In addition, a lengthy parent survey was conducted in person or by telephone with primary caregivers of children to gather demographic, health, social, cultural, and other information about home environments.

The analysis examines the effects of our two measures of Hawaiian culture on several child learning outcomes, including both standardized tests and teacher rated skills. The first cultural measure, as reported by the parent or primary caregiver, proxies the family's traditional knowledge of and practice in Hawaiian culture. The second measure, whether the young child has been taught about his or her Hawaiian name, is also reported by the parent or primary caregiver during the parent interview.

Our analytic strategy began with assigning each of the 1,971 variables to a construct: for example, home conditions (e.g., household size and composition, education, age of household members, marital history, employment, occupations, marital history, etc); school conditions (e.g., facilities, equipment, instruction, time spent by activity, teacher experiences and training, support from administrators); child characteristics (e.g., age, sex, ethnicity, health, childcare history, various assessments); adult/child interactions (e.g., home activities, outside of home activities, routines, reading, television time, interactions with other family members, interactions with school); and culture (e.g., knowledge, practices, importance, identity, etc). We then performed factor analyses by construct to reduce the data into several composite variables. Variables with little variance (.90 or more) were excluded from the factor analyses, whereas those with a factor loading of .30 were included. Three of the composite variables generated are used in this analysis, measuring independent learner skills, cultural customs practiced by parents, and what children have been taught about their Hawaiian names.

Dependent Variables

Our key dependent variables include three early learning outcomes for each child in the analysis: achievement, measured by the Peabody Picture Vocabulary Test III, (PPVT-III) which is a standardized test of receptive vocabulary skills; social skills, measured by the Social Skills

Questionnaire, a standardized instrument completed by teachers; and overall language skill, measured by a question on the teacher's child evaluation. Compared to other children of the same grade level, teachers were asked to rate children as: 1) far below average; 2) below average; 3) average; 4) above average; and 5) far above average.

Independent Variables

We regress each of these dependent variables on characteristics of children, their caregivers and households, their schools and teachers, and the two Hawaiian cultural measures. The key cultural measures are based on information collected during the parent interview. Factor analysis of our culture scale (adapted from the Hawaiian Culture scale) resulted in 21 key items used to create the composite variable measuring cultural customs (cronbach's alpha = .92). The items assess knowledge of and practice in several key areas of traditional activities in Hawaiian culture, as displayed in Appendix Table 1. The items in bold are those shared with the NHMHRDP's customs factor in its prior research.

The second cultural factor, unique to the PABS study, was developed to incorporate the significance of naming practices in Hawaiian culture. We derived the factor score from the mean of three questions in our cultural scale dealing with teaching about children's Hawaiian names (cronbach's alpha = .94) : 1) *"Does child know the history/significance of their Hawaiian name?"*; 2) *"Does child know what their Hawaiian name means?"*; and 3) *"Does child know how to pronounce their Hawaiian name?"* The answers are coded 0 for no and 1 for yes. Children who did not have a Hawaiian name are included in the factor and assigned a score of "−1." Note that all models were tested with and without the latter group (not shown). Although some effects lost statistical significance as noted in the text, all were consistent in direction and magnitude.

For other child attributes, in addition to variables for age (in months), sex, and Hawaiian ethnicity, we include controls for the assessment date, which specify dates between April and June. Proficiency in speaking and understanding English is rated in the teacher survey with a four-point scale ranking from not well at all to pretty well. We collapse it into a mean indicator for limited proficiency. Also included is the child's skill level as an independent learner, a composite variable created from factor analysis of seven items from the teacher survey (see Appendix Table 2).

Several variables capture demographic and socioeconomic characteristics of primary caregivers and their households. These include age and marital status (married or not) of the primary caregiver. To estimate socioeconomic status, we added main caregiver's educational attainment;

household income in the past year, which we collapsed into terciles indicating less than \$25,000, between \$25,000 and \$55,000, and more than \$55,000; and monthly rent/mortgage.

We measure parent-child interactions with three variables collected during the parent interview. The first two measure parents' perceptions about interactions with their children. In the absence of actual behavioral data about hours spent in various activities, they provide some indication of what parents view as important to child development. First is a general question about the importance of parent-child interaction, assessed with the statement, *"Parents should read to their children, and play counting games at home, regularly."* Answers were coded from 1, "strongly agree," to 5, "strongly disagree." Another variable specifically targets the importance of reading to the children, captured by a five point scale from 1, "essential," to 5, "not important at all." We also include the presence of routines as a general indicator of a stable home environment for young children. We derived a score from answers to two questions, *"Does child have any regular jobs or chores?"* and *"Does child usually go to bed at about the same time each night?"* where 0 equals no and 1 equals yes. We expect that each will positively influence child learning outcomes.

For classroom characteristics, several indicators collected from school surveys control for differences between preschools, including private or public preschool; length of preschool day (full or half day); location of preschool (schools 1, 3 and 4 are rural schools and 2 is urban); and the number of boys and girls in the classroom. From the latter, we created a difference score by subtracting the number of girls from boys and suspect that classrooms with more girls, who mature more rapidly than boys, may create more advanced learning opportunities. Two teacher-level variables included the number of paid and unpaid preparation hours that teachers dedicate per week, ranging from 2 or less up to 15 or more hours per week, on average. We expect that more preparation hours will also positively influence learning.

With a primary focus on the two cultural constructs, we examine each variable descriptively. We then introduce them into bivariate, stepwise, and finally, multivariate regression models predicting the three early learning outcomes for receptive vocabulary achievement, positive social skills, and language skills. From this analysis, we can examine the associations between Hawaiian cultural measures and early learning skills as an initial step in the testing of our hypothesis.

Two important limits to this analysis deserve note. First, these data do not permit us to examine causal relationships in this analysis. However, we are able to examine the data for statistical associations and patterns that might support our hypotheses. Second, we lack data on detailed behaviors within culturally embedded families that would yield greater insights about what kinds of parent-child interactions are influenced by cultural practices. We are reassured, however, that the longitudinal design of our study will permit future analyses that are more robust and specific about the interplay between culture and child development.

FINDINGS

Descriptive Findings

We display measures of central tendency in Table 1, with a focus on what four-year-old children have been taught about their Hawaiian name. According to primary caregivers, of whom 92% are parents (almost all, mothers), 49 of the 299 children—half of whom are not Hawaiian—have no Hawaiian name. Another 8% have limited knowledge/pronunciation of their Hawaiian name, 38% have some understanding or can pronounce the name (usually more often the latter than the former), and 37% have been taught to fully pronounce and know the significance of their name.

The patterns that emerge in the three learning outcomes are consistent with our hypothesis, and almost in linear fashion. Consecutively higher achievement, social, and language skills are apparent in the descriptive statistics by exposure to cultural inputs about Hawaiian names. Among child attributes, age is fairly constant across groups, whereas boys are more likely than girls to be able to pronounce or know something about their Hawaiian names, as do those ranked higher in English proficiency and independent learning.

Parents' cultural inputs, measured by customs, also increase with each successive name group. Socioeconomic status, however, has no immediately apparent relationship. That is, those with more inputs about their Hawaiian name do not appear to come from wealthier, more educated, or even older families. They are, however, more likely to have parents who are married or caregivers who believe that reading to children is important, to live in higher rent homes, and to have routines at home, all of which would lend greater stability and structure to reinforce their developmental gains. Interestingly, teachers' preparation time generally is higher in each successive name group, except for unpaid preparation time, which is highest in the group without Hawaiian names.

In sum, children who have been taught more about their Hawaiian names appear to have several advantages. They are more often boys, but also tend to come from more stable, culturally rich environments, where

Table 1. Descriptive Table of Study Variables by Understanding of Hawaiian Name

Variables	No Hawaiian Name	Hawaiian Name, No Understanding	Hawaiian Name, Limited Understanding	Hawaiian Name, Solid Understanding	Total
	Mean or %	Mean or %	Mean or %	Mean or %	Mean or %
Dependent Variables (Student Outcomes)					
Spring PPVT (range 43–141)	94.7	97	100	107	100
Positive social skills (range 0–100)	51.2	46.8	52.4	56.7	52.6
Language skills (range 1–5)	3.2	3.09	3.15	3.43	3.22
Independent variables					
Child Attributes					
Child's age (in months)	58	58	57	58	58
Child's gender*					
Male	46%	44%	55%	51%	53%
Female	54%	56%	45%	49%	47%
Child's Ethnicity*					
Native Hawaiian	45%	100%	98%	96%	89%
Non-Hawaiian	55%	0%	2%	5%	11%
English proficiency	2.35	2.4	2.32	2.55	2.42
Independent learner (range .5–3.33)	2.51	2.54	2.57	2.73	2.62
Hawaiian Culture					
Parents' cultural inputs (range 1–3.27)	1.92	2.27	2.35	2.50	2.33
Demographic					
Income*					
$5,000–$25,000	37%	24%	38%	21%	31%
$25,000–$55,000	42%	29%	31%	39%	35%
$55,000+	21%	48%	32%	40%	34%
Age of Primary Caregiver (years)	35	33	32	34	33
Educational Level of Primary Caregiver*					

(continued)

Table 1. (*Continued*)

Variables	No Hawaiian Name	Hawaiian Name, No Understanding	Hawaiian Name, Limited Understanding	Hawaiian Name, Solid Understanding	Total
	Mean or %	Mean or %	Mean or %	Mean or %	Mean or %
Less then high school	8%	4%	4%	7%	6%
High school graduate	59%	40%	53%	35%	47%
Some college	25%	36%	30%	36%	32%
College graduate	8%	20%	12%	21%	15%
Marital Status of Primary Caregiver*					
Married	80%	75%	76%	85%	80%
Not Married	20%	25%	25%	15%	20%
Montly rent/mortgate*					
$200–$500	26%	32%	22%	19%	23%
$500–$1100	41%	36%	51%	42%	45%
>$1100	33%	32%	27%	39%	33%
Parental Interaction & Routine					
Parental interaction	1.37	1.36	1.42	1.25	1.35
Routines at home	1.45	1.64	1.65	1.75	1.65
Importance of reading to child	3.3	3.48	3.47	3.57	3.48
School Information*					
Half day	51%	12%	15%	7%	25%
Full day	49%	88%	85%	93%	75%
Location 1	4%	40%	25%	28%	23%
Location 2	53%	16%	20%	23%	27%
Location 3	40%	32%	43%	38%	39%
Location 4	2%	12%	11%	11%	8%
Classroom Characteristics					
Difference boys-girls	1.09	1.20	0.61	0.91	0.91
Length of program	0.7	0.92	0.96	0.96	0.87
Paid preparation time	3.08	3.38	3.52	3.47	3.32
Unpaid preparation time	3.34	2.92	3.21	3.03	3.14

*Categorical variable

education is valued by parents. They are somewhat more proficient in English, able to learn independently, and more likely to be enrolled in full-day preschools with teachers who spend more time preparing for class.

Multivariate Findings

The next step in the analysis is to examine these outcomes with a multivariate analysis that permits us to disentangle some of the multiple relationships noted above. We set up the multivariate analysis with an overview of the bivariate relationships for each independent variable and the three key learning outcomes, shown in Table 2. Across the three panels, cultural customs practiced by parents appear to have little relationship to educational outcomes. Consistent with our hypothesis, however, children who know and understand their Hawaiian names have higher achievement scores. Although not shown here, when we examined this relationship excluding children without a Hawaiian name, we found a similar significant positive relationship with language skills. Once adding those children to the model, however, the effect lost significance (see Table 2). We include all children to maximize our sample size.

Among the remaining explanatory variables, girls do better in social and language skills than do boys, whereas gender is unrelated to PPVT-III scores. English proficiency, independent learning, and education of the primary caregiver are consistently related to most early educational outcomes. Higher income and routines at home are also related to higher language and PPVT-III outcomes, whereas parental interaction (negative relationship) and importance of reading are especially important to only the latter outcome. Private preschools tend to produce higher teacher rated skills (social and language). Finally, both boys and girls in classrooms with more girls appear to have significantly lower academic skills in achievement and language, but greater positive social skills.

Table 3 displays the first set of multivariate analyses predicting the end-of-year achievement test scores. We find, surprisingly, that higher scores in cultural customs and tradition are negatively related to achievement in the full model. On the other hand, the child's knowledge of his or her Hawaiian name operates in the fashion hypothesized and is positively associated with higher end-of-year achievement outcomes. Note that this effect remains significant even after adding a control for overall language skills of the child to the model (not shown).

As we might expect, we find that English proficiency increases achievement, holding constant other factors. Independent learner skills also achieve moderate statistical significance and are positively related to achievement scores. Primary caregivers' household income and

Table 2. PABS—Bivariate regression—Achievement—(Spring PPVT-III), Positive Social Skills (Teacher Evaluation), and Language Skills (Teacher Evaluation)

Predictor Variables	Respondent	Achievement					Positive social skills					Language skills				
		N	F	R^2	β	p	N	F	R^2	β	p	N	F	R^2	β	p
Child Attributes																
Child's age	PPVT	433	7.78 (1,431)	0.018	−0.54	0.0055	423	9.48 (1,421)	0.022	1.21	0.1484	405	24.64 (1,403)	0.058	0.06	0.24
Child's gender (0 = male, 1 = female)	Parent	430	.00 (1,428)	0.000	0.02	0.9904	433	20.18 (1,431)	0.045	12.11	<.0001	417	7.38 (1,415)	0.018	0.23	0.0069
Child's ethnicity (0 = Native Hawaiian 1 = Non-Hawaiian)	Parent	278	26.07 (1,276)	0.086	−13.03	<.0001	280	.05 (1,278)	0.000	−1.25	0.8177	277	.66 (1,275)	0.002	−0.14	0.4176
English proficiency*	Teacher	279	14.66 (2,276)	0.096		<.0001	281	2.19 (2,278)	0.016		0.1136	278	8.11 (2,275)	0.056		0.0004
Independent learner	Parent	279	20.88 (1,277)	0.070	8.20	<.0001	281	32.95 (1,279)	0.106	21.37	<.0001	278	15.0 (1,276)	0.052	0.46	0.0001
Hawaiian Culture Domains	Construct															
Parents' Cultural Inputs	Parent	277	.66 (1,275)	0.002	1.40	0.4172	280	.02 (1,278)	0.000	0.57	0.8764	277	.07 (1,275)	0.000	0.03	0.7986
Hawaiian name**	Parent	279	32.83 (1,277)	0.106	6.41	<.0001	281	1.22 (1,279)	0.004	2.73	0.271	278	2.43 (1,276)	0.009	0.12	0.1201
Demographic																
Income*	Parent	260	6.20 (2,257)	0.046		0.0023	263	.67 (2,260)	0.005		0.5138	260	5.37 (2,257)	0.040		0.0052
Age of caregiver (PCG)	Parent	279	.72 (1,277)	0.003	0.08	0.3966	281	.01 (1,279)	0.000	0.02	0.9396	278	.03 (1,276)	0.000	0.00	0.8728
Educational level of PCG*	Parent	279	7.75 (3,275)	0.078		<.0001	281	3.48 (2,277)	0.036		0.0164	278	2.87 (3,274)	0.030		0.037
Marital Status of PCG	Parent	252	4.38 (1,250)	0.017	4.41	0.0373	251	.20 (1,249)	0.001	2.02	0.6555	248	.33 (1,246)	0.001	0.08	0.5685
Monthly rent/mortage*	Parent	267	1.45 (1,265)	0.005	0.50	0.2297	270	6.26 (1,268)	0.023	2.24	0.013	267	.50 (1,265)	0.002	0.02	0.4815
Assessment date	Fieldworkr	433	8.91 (1,431)	0.020	14.19	0.0030						419	2.14 (1,417)	0.005	0.10	0.1439
Parental Interaction & Routine																
Parental Interaction	Parent	277	3.94 (1,275)	0.014	−3.05	0.0481	280	.81 (1,278)	0.003	−2.97	0.3689	277	.32 (1,275)	0.001	−0.06	0.5729
Routines at home	Parent	279	8.00 (1,277)	0.028	7.75	0.0050	281	.00 (1,279)	0.000	−0.26	0.9657	278	5.80 (1,276)	0.021	0.44	0.0167
Importance of reading to child	Parent	278	7.65 (1,276)	0.027	4.38	0.0061	281	.00 (1,279)	0.000	−0.14	0.9665	278	.00 (1,276)	0.000	0.00	0.9742

School Information

Location*	Fieldworkr	433	9.49 (3,429)	0.062		<.0001			0.029		0.005	419	1.91 (3,415)	0.014		0.1278
Type of preschool	Fieldworkr	433	163.40 (1,431)	0.275	17.95	<.0001	438	.14 (1,437)	0.000	1.17	0.7101	419	4.84 (1,417)	0.012	0.23	0.0283
Classroom characteristics																
Number of boys	Teacher	433	6.96 (1,431)	0.016	−0.73	0.0087	439	.01 (1,437)	0.000	−0.17	0.7469	419	1.27 (1,417)	0.003	0.02	0.2601
Numbers of girls	Teacher	433	14.68 (1,431)	0.033	−0.76	0.0001	439	4.57 (1,437)	0.010	0.84	0.0330	419	7.15 (1,417)	0.017	−0.03	0.0078
Difference boys–girls	Teacher	433	2.90 (1,431)	0.007	0.31	0.896	439	4.84 (1,437)	0.011	−0.80	0.0284	419	11.57 (1,417)	0.027	0.04	0.0007
Length of program	Teacher	433	80.05 (1,431)	0.157	17.77	<.0001	439	.01 (1,437)	0.000	−0.46	0.9115	419	1.78 (1,417)	0.004	0.19	0.1833
Paid preparation time	Teacher	414	15.64 (1,412)	0.037	2.83	<.0001	420	2.08 (1,418)	0.005	2.01	0.1498	401	1.06 (1,399)	0.003	0.04	0.3046
Unpaid preparation time	Teacher	433	1.08 (1,431)	0.003	0.61	0.3001	439	8.20 (1,437)	0.018	−3.30	0.0044	419	.08 (1,417)	0.000	0.01	0.7834

Note: PCG = primary care giver

*categorical variable

Income: 1) $5,000–$25,000; 2) $25,000–$55,000; 3) $55,000+
Spring PPVT: 3, 2 > 1; Positive social skills: None; Language skills: 2, 3 > 1
Education: 1) Less than high school; 2) High school graduate; 3) Some college; 4) College graduate
Spring PPVT: 4 > 3, 1, 2; Positive social skills: none; Language skills: none
English Proficiency: 1) limited, 2) pretty well, 3) well
Spring PPVT: 3, 2 > 1; Positive social skills: None; Language skills: 3, 2 > 1
Location: 1, 2, 3, 4
Spring PPVT: 1, 4 > 3, 2; Positive social skills: None; Language skills: None

Table 3. PABS—Multiple Regression Predicting End-of-Year Achievement

Predictor Variables	Stepwise				Full Model (N = 213)			
	F	R^2	β	p	F (28,184)	R^2	β	p
Child Attributes								
Child's age	0.17	0.000	0.09	0.6832	2.19	0.007	0.30	0.1408
Child's gender (0 = male, 1 = female)	2.64	0.008	−2.36	0.1051	0.39	0.001	−1.05	0.5332
Child's ethnicity (0 = Native Hawaiian 1 = Non-Hawaiian)	24.65	0.072	−12.00	<.0001	0.74	0.002	−2.97	0.3900
English proficiency*	9.85	0.057	- -	<.0001	10.20	0.061	- -	<.0001
Independent learner	10.87	0.032	5.82	0.0011	2.69	0.008	3.45	0.1029
Child attributes model, N = 278, F (6,271)	12.24	0.213		<.0001				
Hawaiian Culture Domains								
Parents' cultural inputs	2.27	0.007	−2.67	0.1331	5.87	0.018	−5.22	0.0164
Hawaiian name	34.32	0.111	7.12	<.0001	5.47	0.016	3.84	0.0204
Hawaiian culture domains model, N = 277, F (2,274)	17.53	0.113		<.0001				
Demographic								
Income*	2.39	0.020	- -	0.0942	3.13	0.019	- -	0.0462
Age of primary caregive (PCG)	0.00	0.000	−0.01	0.9547	0.02	0.000	0.05	0.8808
Educational level of PCG*	4.31	0.053	- -	0.0056	1.58	0.014	- -	0.1951
Marital status of PCG	0.97	0.004	2.26	0.3257	0.38	0.001	−1.44	0.5393
Monthly rent/mortgage*	1.38	0.006	−0.58	0.2422	1.27	0.004	−0.34	0.2619
Assessment date	4.58	0.019	16.21	0.0334	1.04	0.003	6.21	0.3086
Demographic model, N = 225, F (9,215)	3.05	0.113		0.0019				
Parental interaction & routine								
Parental interaction	1.81	0.006	−2.07	0.1793	2.74	0.008	−2.47	0.0996
Routines at home	5.71	0.020	3.29	0.0175	0.32	0.001	−0.89	0.5738
Importance of reading to child	4.77	0.016	3.52	0.0299	0.17	0.001	0.70	0.6828
Parent interaction & routine model, N = 277, F (3,273)	5.37	0.056		0.0013				
School information								
Type of preschool	133.17	0.223	17.65	<.0001	1.84	0.006	4.65	0.1761
Location*	1.97	0.010	- -	0.1177	1.37	0.012	- -	0.2541
School information model, N = 433, F (1,431)	42.60	0.285		<.0001				
Classroom characteristics								
Difference (boys-girls)	8.07	0.016	0.63	0.0047	0.14	0.000	0.19	0.7064
Length of program	78.78	0.155	18.61	<.0001	2.59	0.008	10.48	0.1091
Paid preparation time	1.19	0.002	0.83	0.2760	0.93	0.003	−1.12	0.3353
Unpaid preparation time	0.12	0.000	0.20	0.7302	8.97	0.027	2.61	0.0031
Classroom characteristics model, N = 414, F (4,409)	24.42	0.193		<.001	5.34	0.448		<.0001

Note: PCG = primary care giver

*categorical variable:

Income: 1) $5,000–$25,000; 2) $25,000–$55,000; 3) $55,000+
Stepwise: 3, 2 > 1
Full: 3, 2 > 1
Education: 1) Less than high school; 2) High school graduate; 3) Some college; 4) College graduate
Stepwise: 4 > 1, 3, 2
Full: 4 > 1, 3, 2
English Proficiency: 1) limited, 2) pretty well, 3) well
Stepwise: 3, 2 > 1
Full: 3, 2 > 1
Location: 1, 2, 3, 4
Stepwise: 1, 4 > 3, 2
Full: 1 > 2, 3

educational attainment increase the achievement of young preschoolers, consistent with well-established findings in the early childhood literature. End-of-year achievement rises with each additional unpaid hour that teachers devote to preparing to teach the children.

The next analysis in Table 4 examines the same model to predict children's positive social skills. For this outcome, we find little support for an independent positive effect of cultural inputs on social skills, net of other controls. However, girls, child's age, and independent learner skills are positively associated with teacher evaluations of social skills. Primary caregivers' education also has a positive impact on social skills, whereas caregivers' age is negatively related to this outcome. In addition, children with teachers who have greater paid preparation time are more socially skilled, whereas teachers' unpaid preparation time is inversely associated with positive social skills.

The final analysis in Table 5 predicts language skills of students based on the teacher evaluation relative to other children. For this outcome, we find little support for our cultural hypothesis. Cultural customs practiced by parents and Hawaiian naming are unrelated to this outcome. As with social skills, child's age and gender, as well as household income, are positively related to language skills. Independent learner skills are associated with stronger language achievement.

DISCUSSION

Our analysis has woven together a complicated ecological model of early childhood learning, integrating multiple processes that affect children's learning, including their own attributes, their home environment, their school environment, and family cultural context. We started out with the premise that traditional cultural activities at home offer potential mechanisms for early childhood learning by promoting parent-child interactions and by diversifying the types of experiences to which children are exposed. We tested these hypotheses through information on cultural activities and knowledge of primary caregivers and by addressing an important step through which young children can internalize cultural teachings; that is, by knowing and understanding the significance of their Hawaiian name.

Our analysis controlled for various factors that might influence the relationship between culture and early learning outcomes, such as parent-child interactions, the independent learning skills of children, and characteristics of the schools they attend. We found that cultural customs associated with naming practices appear to be more important to educational

Table 4. PABS—Multiple Regression Predicting End-of-Year Positive Social Skills

Predictor Variables	Stepwise				Full Model (N = 208)			
	F	R^2	β	p	F (27,180)	R^2	β	p
Child Attributes								
Child's age	4.03	0.013	0.96	0.0458	5.61	0.022	1.38	0.0190
Child's gender (0 = male, 1 = female)	11.16	0.036	10.90	0.0010	6.33	0.025	9.54	0.0127
Child's ethnicity (0 = Native Hawaiian 1 = Non-Hawaiian)	0.02	0.000	0.73	0.8921	0.07	0.000	2.34	0.7924
English proficiency*	0.20	0.001	- -	0.8194	0.14	0.001	- -	0.8651
Independent learner	24.52	0.078	19.51	<.0001	10.57	0.041	14.71	0.0014
Child Attributes model, N = 270, F (6,263)	8.35	0.160		<.0001				
Hawaiian Culture Domains								
Parents' Cultural Inputs	0.09	0.000	−1.18	0.7649	0.04	0.000	−1.00	0.8412
Hawaiian name	1.28	0.005	3.05	0.2597	0.32	0.000	−2.07	0.5704
Hawaiian Culture Domains model, N = 280, F (2,277)	0.65	0.005		0.5229				
Demographic								
Income*	0.15	0.001	- -	0.8604	0.24	0.002	- -	0.7833
Age of primary caregiver (PCG)	2.91	0.013	−0.46	0.0894	3.43	0.013	−1.85	0.0657
Educational level of PCG*	3.67	0.047	- -	0.0131	2.41	0.028	- -	0.0688
Marital status of PCG	0.01	0.000	0.60	0.9057	1.42	0.006	−6.28	0.2352
Monthly rent/mortgage	1.16	0.005	1.18	0.2835	2.02	0.002	1.57	0.1570
Demographic model, N = 225, F (8,216)	2.08	0.071		0.0394				
Parental Interaction & Routine								
Parental interaction	0.88	0.003	−3.18	0.3489	0.37	0.001	−2.34	0.5420
Routines at home	0.03	0.000	−0.53	0.8627	0.00	0.000	0.14	0.9683
Importance of reading to child	0.05	0.000	−0.77	0.8278	0.19	0.001	−1.80	0.6645
Parent Interaction & Routine model, N = 280, F (3,276)	0.30	0.003		0.8273				
School information								
Type of preschool	1.52	0.003	4.24	0.2179	0.81	0.003	8.01	0.3705
Location*	4.80	0.032	- -	0.0027	2.11	0.025	- -	0.1002
School information model, N = 439, F (4,434)	3.64	0.032		0.0063				
Classroom characteristics								
Difference (boys-girls)	0.18	0.000	−0.20	0.6744	0.05	0.000	0.19	0.8212
Length of program	0.71	0.002	−3.62	0.3993	0.01	0.000	−1.31	0.9073
Paid preparation time	8.57	0.020	4.60	0.0036	5.14	0.020	5.99	0.0246
Unpaid preparation time	19.17	0.044	−5.55	<.0001	5.83	0.023	−4.72	0.0167
Classroom characteristics model, N = 420, F (4,415)	5.66	0.035		0.0002	2.78	0.294		<.0001

Note: PCG = primary care giver
*categorical variable
  Income: 1) $5,000–$25,000; 2) $25,000–$55,000; 3) $55,000+
    Stepwise/Full: None
  Education: 1) Less than high school; 2) High school graduate; 3) Some college; 4) College graduate
    Stepwise: None
    Full: 4 > 2
  English Proficiency: 1) limited, 2) pretty well, 3) well
    Stepwise/Full: None
  Location: 1, 2, 3, 4
    Stepwise: None
    Full: 2 > 3

Table 5. PABS—Multiple Regression—Language skills (Teacher)

Predictor Variables	Stepwise				Full Model (N = 207)			
	F	R^2	β	p	F (28,178)	R^2	β	p
Child Attributes								
Child's age	27.40	0.086	0.08	<.0001	15.90	0.063	0.07	<.0001
Child's gender (0 = male, 1 = female)	4.14	0.019	0.20	0.0429	5.24	0.021	0.27	0.0232
Child's ethnicity (0 = Native Hawaiian 1 = Non-Hawaiian)	0.26	0.002	−0.08	0.6132	0.22	0.001	0.14	0.6419
English proficiency*	3.84	0.023	- -	0.0228	1.82	0.014	- -	0.1647
Independent learner	5.64	0.018	0.28	0.182	4.38	0.017	0.30	0.0378
Child Attributes Model, N = 269, F (6,262)	9.16	0.173		<.0001				
Hawaiian Culture Domains								
Parents' Cultural Inputs	0.13	0.000	−0.04	0.7163	0.56	0.002	−0.12	0.4542
Hawaiian name	2.48	0.009	0.13	0.1167	0.56	0.002	0.09	0.4540
Hawaiian Culture Domains model, N = 277, F (2,274)	1.27	0.009		0.2821				
Demographic								
Income*	4.26	0.036	- -	0.0154	4.99	0.041	- -	0.0078
Age of primary caregiver (PCG)	0.55	0.002	−0.01	0.4587	0.12	0.001	−.00	0.7276
Educational level of PCG*	3.90	0.050	- -	0.0097	2.04	0.024	- -	0.1095
Marital status of PCG	0.00	0.000	−0.01	0.9732	0.60	0.002	−0.13	0.4378
Monthly rent/mortgage*	0.01	0.000	−.00	0.9150	0.80	0.001	0.01	0.7775
Assessment date	1.25	0.005	0.10	0.2646	0.39	0.002	0.07	0.5310
Demographic Model, N = 218, F (12,205)	2.60	0.100		0.0072				
Parental Interaction & Routine								
Parental interaction	0.16	0.001	−0.04	0.6857	0.67	0.002	−0.10	0.4147
Routines at Home	4.75	0.017	0.20	0.0302	0.63	0.002	0.09	0.4280
Importance of reading to child	0.14	0.001	−0.04	0.7050	0.95	0.004	−0.12	0.3322
Parental Interaction & Routine model, N = 277, F (3,273)	1.69	0.018		0.1685				
School information								
Type of preschool	4.96	0.012	0.25	0.0265	0.19	0.001	−0.13	0.6596
Location*	1.95	0.014	- -	0.1204	0.53	0.006	- -	0.6637
School information model, N = 419, F (4,417)	2.68	0.025		0.0311				
Classroom characteristics								
Difference (boys-girls)	12.25	0.030	0.06	0.0005	1.89	0.007	0.04	0.1708
Length of program	1.59	0.004	0.19	0.2074	0.41	0.002	0.25	0.5213
Paid preparation time	0.24	0.001	−0.02	0.6218	0.63	0.002	−0.07	0.4300
Unpaid preparation time	0.20	0.000	−0.02	0.6560	1.63	0.006	0.08	0.2039
Classroom characteristics model, N = 414, F (4,409)	3.61	0.035		0.0066	2.68	0.296		<.0001

Note: PCG = primary care giver
*categorical variable:
  Income: 1) $5,000–$25,000; 2) $25,000–$55,000; 3) $55,000+
    Stepwise: 2, 3 > 1 Full: 2, 3 > 1
  Education: 1) Less than high school; 2) High school graduate; 3) Some college; 4) College graduate
    Stepwise: None
    Full: 4 > 2
  English Proficiency: 1) limited, 2) pretty well, 3) well
    Stepwise: 3, 2 > 1 Full: 3 > 1
  Location: 1, 2, 3, 4
    Stepwise/Full: None

outcomes observed in preschool than other kinds of customs practiced by parents or primary caregivers. Most significantly, being taught about their Hawaiian name was positively associated with children's achievement scores, but not language or social skills.

That we found inconsistent associations across the three outcomes may be more a result of the types of outcomes explored in this analysis than lack of support for our hypothesis. To begin with, the PPVT-III is a standardized test developed by national standards of knowledge, asking about items and words that may be foreign to islander or indigenous children (i.e., snow, sleds, etc.). Moreover, the social skills test rates positively those behaviors that represent more individualistic, Westernized notions of behavior in children, compared to the collective emphasis that might be more normative in Hawaiian families. And finally, prior research suggests that promoting one's self through language, especially with adults, is not necessarily a valued behavior for children in many Hawaiian families (e.g., see Gallimore, Boggs, and Jordan 1974).

What did matter in these early education experiences, however, were cultural practices associated with children knowing and pronouncing their Hawaiian names. The significance of this finding, we argue, is best understood within the context of naming in Hawaiian culture, which continues to be an important cultural tradition in families. Even for young children, it is a beginning of the genealogy and identity that accompanies children through their lifetimes and connects them to the next generation. Within this context, naming may provide an important, culturally relevant teaching vehicle for parents and children to interact through storytelling, history, oral pronunciation, and verbal reasoning. The end result suggested in this analysis is enhanced parental involvement and early learning opportunities for children through culture.

REFERENCES

Andrade, N.N., Hishinuma, E.S., Miyamoto, R.H., Johnson, R.C., Nahulu, L.B., Yuen, N.Y.C., Makini, G.K., Nishimura, S.T., McArdle, J.J., McDermott, J.F., Waldron, J.A., and Yates, A. (2000). *Development and factor structure of the Hawaiian culture scale—adolescent version.* Unpublished manuscript. University of Hawai`i: Honolulu, HI.

Bacon, H.L., Kidd, G., and Seaberg, J. (1982). The effectiveness of bilingual instruction with Cherokee Indian students. *Journal of American Indian Education* 21(2): 34–43.

Barringer, H. R., Gardner, R. W., and Levin, M. (1993). *Asians and Pacific Islanders in the United States,* New York: Russell Sage Foundation.

Braun, K. L., Yang, H. Onaka, A. T., and Horiuchi, B. Y. (1997). Asian and Pacific Islander mortality differences in Hawaii. *Social Biology* 44(3–4):213–226.

Bowman, P. (1989). Research perspectives on Black men: Role strain and adaptation across the adult life cycle. In: Jones, R. L. (ed.) *Black adult development and aging.* Cobbs and Henry, Berkeley, CA, pp. 117–150.

Brenner, M.E. (1998). Adding cognition to the formula for culturally relevant instruction in mathematics. *Anthropology & Education Quarterly* 29(2): 314–244.

Cotton, K. (1995). Effective Schooling Practices: A research synthesis. Portland, OR: Northwest Regional Laboratory.

Gallimore, R., Boggs, J.W., and Jordan, C. (1974). *Culture, Behavior, and Education: A study of Hawaiian-Americans.* Beverly Hills, CA: Sage Publications.

Gruenewald, D. (2003). The best of both worlds: A critical pedagogy of place. *Educational Researcher* 32(4):3–12.

Gutierrez, K.D., and Rogoff, B. (2003). Cultural ways of learning: Individual traits or repertoires of practice. *Educational Researcher* 32(5): 19–25.

Hishinuma, E. S., Andrade, N. N., Johnson, R. C., McArdle, J. J., Miyamoto, R. H., Nahulu, L. B., Makini, J., G.K., Yuen, N. Y. C., Nishimura, S. T., McDermott, J.F., Waldron, J. A., Luke, K.N., and Yates, A. (2000). Psychometric properties of the Hawaiian Culture Scale—Adolescent version. *Psychological Assessment* 12(2):140–157.

Johnson, R. (19xx). Essays in Hawaiian Literature: Essay #1 A Hawaiian Perspective on Alternative Rationalities. *Alternative Rationalities.* Society for Asian & Pacific Islanders.

Jordan, C. (1992). The Role of Culture in Minority School Achievement. *The Kamehameha Journal of Education* 3(2): 53–68.

Kame'eleihiwa, Lilikalā. (1992). *Native Lands and Foreign Desires: Pehea La E Pono Ai?* Bishop Museum Press, Honolulu.

Kana'iaupuni, S. M., and Ishibashi, K. (2003). Left Behind: The status of Hawaiian students in Hawai`i's public schools, Policy Analysis & System Evaluation Report 02–03:13, Honolulu, Kamehameha Schools.

Kana'iaupuni, S. M. (2004). Amidst Change and Controversy: Identity and Hawaiian families. *Hulili* volume 1. Honolulu, HI: Pauahi Publications, Kamehameha Schools.

Kana'iaupuni, S. M., and Liebler, C. (in press). Pondering Poi Dog: Place and identity of multiracial Hawaiians. To appear in *Ethnic & Racial Studies.*

Kawakami, A. (2003). Where I live, there are rainbows: Cultural identity and sense of place. *Amerasia Journal* 29(2): 67–79.

Kawakami, A. (in press). Issues central to the inclusion of Hawaiian culture in K-12 education. *Hulili,* volume 1, Honolulu, HI: Pauahi Publications, Kamehameha Schools.

Lee, C.C. (2001). Is October Brown Chinese? A cultural modeling activity system for underachieving students. *American Educational Research Journal* 38(1): 97–142.

Lee, C.D., Spencer, M.B., and Harpalani, V. (2003). "Every shut eye ain't sleep": Studying how people live culturally. *Educational Researcher* 32(5): 6–13.

Lipka, J. and McCarty, T.L. (1994). Changing the culture of schooling: Navajo and Yup'ik cases, *Anthropology & Education Quarterly* 25(3): 266–284.

Miyamoto, R. H., Hishinuma, E. S., Nishimura, S. T., Nahulu, L. B., Andrade, N. N., Goebert, D. A., and Carlton, B. S. (2001). Path models linking correlates of self-esteem in a multiethnic adolescent sample. *Personality and Individual Differences* 31:701–712.

Miyamoto, R. H., Hishinuma, E. S., Nishimura, S. T., Nahulu, L. B., Andrade, N. N., and Goebert, D. (2000). Variation in self-esteem among adolescents in an Asian/Pacific Islander sample. *Personality and Individual Differences* 29(1), 13–25.

Mokuau, N., Browne, C., and Braun, K. (1998). NāKupuna in Hawai`i: A review of social and health status, service use and the importance of value-based interventions, *Pacific Health Dialog* 5(2): 282–289.

Nä Honua Mauli Ola: Hawai`i guidelines for culturally healthy and responsive learning environments. 2002. Developed by the Native Hawaiian Education Council in partnership with Ka Haka 'Ula O Ke'elikolani College of Hawaiian Language, University of Hawaii-Hilo.

Nordyke, E. 1989 *The Peopling of Hawaii*, 2nd edn, Honolulu, HI: University of Hawai`i Press.

Phinney, J.S., Cantu, C.L., and Kurtz, D.a. 1997. Ethnic and American identity as predictors of self-esteem among African American, Latino and White adolescents. *Journal of Youth and Adolescence* 26(2): 165–185.

Phinney, J.S., and Chavira, V. (1992). Ethnic identity and self-esteem: An exploratory longitudinal study. *Journal of Adolescence* 15: 271–281.

Pūku`i, M.K., and Elbert, S.H. (1986). *Hawaiian Dictionary: Hawaiian-English, English-Hawaiian.* University of Hawai`i Press: Honolulu, HI.

Pūku`i, M. K., Haertig, E.W., and Lee, C.A. (1972). *Nānā I Ke Kumu (Look to the Source), Volume I.* Honolulu, Hawaii: Queen Liliuokalani Children's Center.

Srinivasan, S., and Guillermo, T. (2000). Toward improved health: Disaggregating Asian American and Native Hawaiian/Pacific Islander data. *American Journal of Public Health* 90(11): 1731–1734.

AUTHOR NOTE

We gratefully acknowledge input and comments from Earl Hishinuma, technical assistance from Stephanie Nishimura and Janice Chang, and project assistance from Alma Trinidad.

GLOSSARY

'aumakua	Family or personal gods, often an ancestor who assumes the shape of an animal, plant or things. 'Aumākua communicated with morals through dreams and visions.
heiau	Place of worship or shrine before Christian times (pre 1778), ranging from earth terraces to elaborately constructed stone platforms.
hō'ailona	As used in the culture scale—signs of nature, omen or portent.
kahuna	Usually refers to a Hawaiian priest, but also a group of professionals, regardless of gender, such as doctors, and sorcerers.
kupuna	An elder, usually a grandparent, ancestor, close friend or relative of a grandparent's generation.
kapu	Taboo, sacred, prohibited, consecrated, or forbidden.
lōkahi	Harmony, unity and agreement.
makahiki	Ancient festival starting the middle of October lasting about four months with religious and sports activities and a ban on war. Today, it has been replaced by "Aloha Week," with Hawaiian cultural activities.
mälama`ōina	Caring for the land.
mālama Makua	Caring for the Makua (a valley with historical significance on the leeward coast of O'ahu).

Source: Pūku`i Elbert, 1986 and Pūku`i, Haertig, & Lee, 1972.

Appendix Table 1. Cultural Customs Domain Items and Factor Loading Score

Cultural Customs Domain Items	Eigenvalue
Respondent learned about Native Hawaiian Way of Life from Family	0.49
How much do you value Hawaiian beliefs, behaviors, and attitudes?	0.57
How important is it to you to maintain Hawaiian cultural traditions?	0.52
Know/Practice: Talking to Kupuna	0.56
Know/Practice: Having Family Home Blessed by Kahuna	0.47
Know/Practice: Hawaiian Healing Practices	0.60
Know/Practice: Offerings at Heiau	0.41
Know/Practice: Telling of Family Stories/Traditions	0.59
Know/Practice: Aumākua	0.61
Know/Practice: Kapu System	0.60
Know/Practice: Learning Genealogy	0.59
Know/Practice: Formal Passing of Knowledge over Generations	0.69
Know/Practice: Mālama`Āina	0.70
Know/Practice: Hō'ailona	0.53
Know/Support: Sovereignty	0.47
Know/Support: Return of Ceded Lands	0.53
Know/Support: Mālama Makua	0.60
Know/Support: Access Rights	0.57
Know/Practice: Makahiki Celebration	0.54
Know/Practice: Hawaiian Civic Clubs	0.38
Know/Practice: Playing Hawaiian Games	0.43

Appendix Table 2. Independent Learner Domain Items and Factor Loading Score

Independent Learner Domain Items	Eigenvalue
T/F: Child can be diverted and calmed when upset	0.41
T/F: Child can adapt to transitions and change	0.34
T/F: Child becomes frustrated with obstacles/limits	−0.38
Comparing Child to Peers: Being independent and taking care of self	0.32
Comparing Child to Peers: Paying attention	0.62
Comparing Child to Peers: Learning, thinking, and solving problems	0.54
Comparing Child to Peers: Saying words and talking with/understanding others	0.50

Chapter 5

Cultural Transmission of Social Knowledge in Preschool

A Costa Rican Perspective

Helen M. Davis

INTRODUCTION

"You can't play" is heard frequently at an urban University preschool in Costa Rica but rarely heard at a Costa Rican rural preschool. Rules of inclusion differed in these preschools and were socialized on two levels in the classroom: from teacher to child and from child to child. In this chapter, I examine two teachers' implicit and explicit socialization models, and the differential effects each has on the transmission of play behaviors among the children.

Cultural norms and knowledge, such as rules of inclusion, are transmitted through intentional instruction, but they are also often transmitted implicitly (Maynard & Greenfield, 2003) and without the awareness of the teacher. An activity settings' approach can unpack how communities arrange children's settings and socialize children. This approach frames development as a cognitive trajectory that is structured by a child's experience with the activities that are meaningful in his or her community (Rogoff, 1993; Rogoff, Mistry, Göncü, & Mosier, 1991; Rogoff, Mosier, Mistry, & Göncü, 1993). The child develops cognitive and social skill sets that are dependent on the available cultural knowledge. The extent to which cultural knowledge is shared throughout the group depends on how members of a group are included in cultural activities. The more activities a child is included in and exposed to, the more cultural norms the child knows.

The role of play in development has frequently been considered independent of its context, but more recently, cultural variation in play has been shown through activity settings' approaches (Gaskins, 1996; Göncü, 1999; Lancy, 1996; Rogoff, 1990; Roopnarine, Johnson, & Hooper, 1994). Play is a cultural activity like any other activity (Göncü, 1999), and the same rules about exposure, transmission, and development apply. While these processes have been explored in various community settings, very few studies have been conducted on the transmission of knowledge within children's peer groups. In a notable exception, Musatti & Mayer (1990/93) found that play themes were indeed propagated throughout a group of young children. We still need to know the mechanisms of propagation for different socio-cultural groups.

A community determines inclusion in activities in various ways, such as by gender or by age (Whiting & Whiting, 1975). Developmentally, infants, young children, children in middle-childhood, and adolescents are exposed to more and more cultural activities depending on the appropriateness of the activity for their age, (Barker & Wright, 1954; Lancy,1996; Whiting & Edwards, 1988). In Costa Rica, preschool-aged children have had contact with community life through inclusion in family gatherings and excursions out of the house for routine, family-related activities, such as grocery shopping and soccer games. Young children observed the activities, but children's inclusion and levels of participation were monitored by adults and older children. Up until pre-Kindergarten, children were generally in family-based care settings. For most four- and five-year-old children, preschool was the first time they experienced a group setting with same-aged peers. School is the first setting where young children are active participants in determining others' inclusion in group activities, such as play, where children have a role in determining who gets to play and who decides who gets to play.

I selected two preschool sites for economic and social diversity within Costa Rica on the hypothesis that a rural, agrarian community would emphasize more interdependent (Greenfield, 1994; Markus & Kitayama, 1991) and cooperative (Madsen, 1967, 1971, 1981) social practices while a professional, urban community would emphasize a more independent and competitive approach to social structures. Are there differences in socialization practices that lead to differences in inclusion and in other play patterns in the preschools? How widely is local cultural knowledge shared within the preschool classroom? Do the local cultural practices of inclusion at each preschool have an impact on the transmission of social knowledge—such as play behaviors—throughout the group?

While there are clear differences in preschool practices at these two sites, it is important to note that within the larger context of early childhood schooling around the world, the sites were remarkably alike. Both teachers believed play was developmentally appropriate and valuable, and they structured the school day and materials to encourage spontaneous play among children. Unlike most preschool environments in the U.S., however, neither teacher directly scaffolded play through their own involvement in it because they believed play would just happen, without adult support.

Like preschools in the United States, in these Costa Rican preschools, children and teachers co-constructed the social rules of inclusion for play. Children chose their own playmates, including some and excluding others. However, playmate selections were not pure free choice; they were bounded by teachers' socialization practices and the structure of the classroom, such as the physical layout and the routines and activities (Davis, 2003). Through her practices in the classroom, the teacher imparted specific cultural choices about managing social inclusion in play. The lessons of inclusion are in large part an underground curriculum: many of them are implicit and often invisible to the teacher herself.

In this study of two Costa Rican preschool classrooms, I trace children's and teachers' behaviors and beliefs around social inclusion. In these two classrooms, the teachers' practices affected children's inclusion practices, for example, in work and play group sizes or in patterns of leadership. I also explore some of the ways that play knowledge is transmitted throughout the group of children. The teacher indirectly played a large role in determining the extent to which play knowledge was shared. The social organization of each preschool group was heavily defined by the local rules of inclusion. In turn, inclusion patterns affected aspects of play, such as propagation of themes. Through analysis of classroom practices and children's social play, I show how local patterns of inclusion affect the transmission of play knowledge throughout the group.

For each classroom, I describe the teachers' socialization practices, the physical structure of the room, and the routines. I show that the classroom context of the urban, preschool for professional families is oriented towards small groups whereas the rural, primarily agrarian community preschool is oriented towards larger and whole-group or whole-gender-group activities. The children's patterns of inclusion mirror their classroom's orientation towards larger or smaller groups. The socio-cultural rules and patterns of inclusion in play in each classroom produced a different model of transmitting cultural knowledge. Rules of play and the repertoire of play activities constituted cultural knowledge for the children. The trends towards larger or smaller groups either exposed most members of the group to common cultural knowledge (large groups) or limited exposure to shared knowledge (small groups).

METHODS

Costa Rica's national culture is relatively homogenous ethnically and religiously, which allows for a comparison of cultural practices across communities that differ economically, with only limited confounds. Costa Rica does have ethnic and religious diversity, but the majority of the population is *mestizo* (native and Spanish) and Catholic. Within Costa Rica, however, economic and political changes, such as globalization, have affected communities in differing ways, altering some cultural practices. The rural, agrarian community in this study was economically quite different from the community of professionals who sent their children to a laboratory preschool at an urban University.

Costa Rica is one of the few developing countries with a national preschool program for lower-income children. In 1994, the Centers of Education and Nutrition were funded by the Department of Health (*Centro de Educación y Nutrición and Centro Infantíl Nutrición y Atención Integral*—CEN-CINAI). The CEN-CINAI program provided the opportunity for lower-income families to send their children to preschool. As part of its mission, this program extended into the rural communities. The sites for this paper are a CEN preschool in a rural, coffee-farming community, and an urban, private, preschool that served a University community. (A third site was part of the study, but is out of the scope of the current discussion.)

Both preschool classrooms served pre-kindergarten (pre-K) children (age 4 at the start of the year). They had at least a half day program every day of the week, and the children attended regularly. The rural preschool had one classroom with two sessions: one for four- to five-year-olds and the other for children one year younger. The school room was housed upstairs from the health and nutrition center, which had additional programs for mothers and infants. The preschool used the lunchroom for meals and for an indoor play structure. A small grassy area surrounded the building for outdoor play. The University preschool had four full-day groups, from infants to pre-K children. They were divided by age. Each age group had its own classroom and play yard with one additional, large play yard for the three older groups to share. Each lead teacher had grown up and settled in the community where they taught. Coincidentally, both teachers had attended the same University for their education training.

There were one teacher and 18 children in the rural classroom: 12 boys and 6 girls. Priority was given to needy families, whose fees were subsidized. There were a lead teacher, a part-time assistant teacher, two student teachers, and 25 children in the University preschool classroom: 13 boys and 12 girls.

I collected ethnographic data for a contextual description of each preschool classroom and for a description of children's spontaneous play (see Davis, 2003 for a full description of methods). I observed four hours per day for a minimum of 25 school days over seven weeks at each site. I took field notes, shot videotape (often simultaneously with the field notes), and talked to teachers and children, formally and informally.

For the context analysis of the classroom, I followed Harkness and Super's (1986) "developmental niche" model for studying the socialization mechanisms of cultural activity settings. This model focuses on 1) the physical and social *setting*, such as the layout of the classroom, the schedule and daily routines, where children go and with whom they interact throughout the morning; 2) the customs and *practices* of child care, such as the teacher's practices for keeping the children safe, for educating and for socializing them; and 3) the teachers' *ethnotheories and values*, such as the teachers' values behind how they arrange the setting and behind teacher practices. Through formal and informal interviews, the teachers articulated their values. Teachers' ethnotheories were more implicit and became clear through analysis of field notes and videotape.

To collect the play data, I developed a sampling strategy that targeted each of the children and all the places children play (e.g. outside play, block area, etc.). I tracked how many times and for how long each child and each location was taped. Children and locations were tracked separately because the children had their favorite places to play and tended to stick to them. All children and all locations were equally sampled on the videotape. To maximize the thematic continuity in play, I taped each child from beginning to end of a meaningful play episode and followed the target child over a period of days.

I conducted three analyses on the play data: a MANOVA comparison of play group sizes and of numbers of friends and a qualitative microanalysis of a large-group play episode from each site. The number of children in each play episode was calculated from the videotape library of 289 episodes of less than the whole class participating in the play episode. There are 124 play episodes for the rural site and 165 episodes for the urban, University site. The difference in number of episodes available for each site is a function of the nature of play at each setting (e.g. length of episodes) rather than of sampling. For determining the number of friends each child had, I adapted a standard play rating scale used for preschool children (Asher, Singleton, & Tinsley, 1981) to make a friendship interview. The adapted interview measures the extent of a child's social network, in other words, how many children were considered "friends." I interviewed each child separately, using pictures or within sight of all

the children in the class for identification. For each classmate, the interviewee was asked if that child was a friend. For the micro-analysis of play
episodes, I selected episodes with the largest number of children involved.
I used videotape and field note data to understand the social context of
play and the children's play patterns.

In order to compare across sites how children's knowledge of play
behaviors and play patterns were transmitted throughout the group, I
developed the concept of non-divisible, *meaningful* play behaviors—akin
to a schema (Piaget, 1962)—that are also mutually accepted by others
(Davis, 2003). For example, in playing doctor, giving a shot can be parsed
out as a small meaningful behavior whose smaller parts have no meaning. In the preschool rooms, these small play behaviors came into being
in a negotiation between participants and evolved into the play repertoire of the group. A subset of them were imitated by participants, like
a clawing motion that several children made when playing lions. Using
the idea that each group would have its own set of non-divisible, meaningful, imitative and shared play behaviors, I tracked their use throughout the group to find out how universally shared the play repertoires
were.

RESULTS

Physical settings

On walking into each of the classrooms, the physical use of space
was strikingly different. The University preschool classroom was based on
a High Scope model (Hohmann, Banet, & Weikart, 1979). The room was
subdivided into "areas" dedicated to social or cognitive activities, such as
water play, dramatic play, the block area, discovery-science, a book corner,
etc. The small group work areas were separated by furniture walls. For
example, the art table area had an art supplies shelf that separated it from
the adjacent science table. Except for circle time, when the whole group
met together once a day, the teacher structured activities in small groups
and instituted limits of three children in each "area" to keep noise and
disruption levels low.

The physical arrangement of the rural classroom, on the other hand,
maximized the largest work and play space possible by storing the toy
cartons around the edges of the room and the six-seat table in a corner.
In this classroom, children played together or in overlapping spaces. For
example, the children playing airplanes sat on the floor next to the children
playing fisher-price school. The play groups were so close to each other that

the children sitting in the overlapping zone often ended up playing in both games, and the toy people would end up on the planes and in the schools. Beyond circle time, the teacher led activities with the whole group. She also supported whole-group spontaneous play, even when it was noisy and unruly.

The physical arrangement in each room was conducive to a particular kind of group work time and play time. The University children spent most of their teacher-structured time in groups of three, while the rural children spent their structured play and work time in larger groups of children or in groups that overlapped and became large groups. Implicitly, each teacher communicated to the children the value of small group or large group play. The University teacher talked about the work areas in her room as an opportunity for children to work constructively and engage at a deep level with materials. She explained that this was the reason she had limits on how many children could be in each area. The rural teacher talked about the value of interacting socially with many children. The rural teacher explained to me that it was important for the children to hear others' experiences. While each teacher talked at length about both academic preparation and social development, the University teacher embedded social development within academic and creative activities whereas the rural teacher arranged academic activities within the context of whole-group social experiences.

Inclusion Practices

Urban, University Preschool

The two teachers had different philosophies about inclusion in play as well. The University preschool teacher's perspective on inclusion was based on friendship, choice, and respect for others. The children at the University preschool spent a great deal of their time trying to figure out what friendship meant. They knew that when you played together, you were friends, but what about the times you played with someone else? Were you no longer friends? Was your friendship at risk when faced with this competition? The children would check in with other friends they weren't playing with by saying, "We're friends, right?" Since doing the same thing meant friendship to these children, they would also refuse to let a child they *weren't* friends with do what they were doing, such as swinging on the extra swing next to them. Children justified their actions by explaining that they weren't friends. They even allowed and disallowed inclusion based on being a friend's friend or not. For example, one girl said, "I'm not going to make friends with *her* [*your* friend], so I'm not your friend, either."

One day during circle time, the teacher tried to address the problem of excluding others—rather unsuccessfully. She told the children that "we are all friends in this class." It wasn't true, though: the children were *not* all friends with each other. She continued, "We can't be telling our classmates' they can't play. There are children in this class who feel they don't have friends; if you see a classmate alone, we can all ask him or her to play." The teacher's discourse to the whole group conflicted with her regular responses to social conflicts. Normally, she allowed children to choose their playmates themselves and was rarely directly involved in the children's social arrangements. When a child came to her to complain the she or he was being left out, the teacher would say that the child had to respect the other children's choices. The difficulty for the teacher arose when one or two children were consistently isolated. The teacher wanted to increase the children's awareness and sympathy. Even under these circumstances, she continued to present inclusion as a question of choice, by suggesting that children *should* invite the isolated child to play, but not by demanding it.

Rural Preschool

The rural teacher's perspective was quite different. Her inclusion principles were based on obligation and responsibility towards either the child's own gender group or towards the whole class. The teacher explicitly encouraged—and often required—children to include other children, invoking the weighty justification that, "she is your classmate." Inclusion was expected. The children did not have a choice in whether to include another child. When a girl who was difficult to play with was excluded by other girls, the teacher told them firmly that they *had* to let her play. And they did. The exception to full-inclusion was when a child of the opposite gender wanted to play in a single-gender play group. For example, three girls were playing house, and a boy wanted to be a baby lion in the family. When the lion started to get rough, and the girls complained to the teacher, the teacher told him to find some boys to play with. These rules were consistently held and presented by the teacher, and the children abided by them. The rural teacher valued group participation so much that she became concerned with a child who preferred to be "solitary."

Play Patterns

The teachers' socialization practices were reflected in the children's play patterns, specifically, the number of children who played together, the number of friends children had, and children's play rules and practices (Davis 2003).

Spontaneous Play Group Sizes

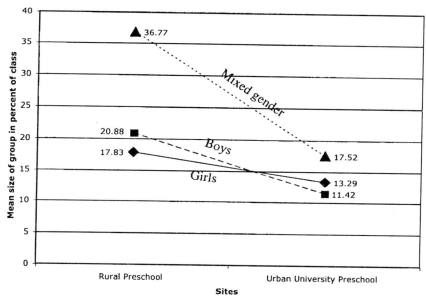

Figure 1. Spontaneous mean play group sizes in percent of class.

Play Group Sizes

The children at both sites often played in pairs and trios. The University preschool children however, played in groups of two, three, and four more frequently than did the rural children. The rural children played in larger groups far more often than the urban, University children. The rural children spontaneously played in groups of eight or more on a regular basis and often played as a whole class. The rural children split their play time between smaller and larger groups (57% time with <5 children; 43% time ≥ 5), while the urban, University children spent three quarters of their time in smaller groups (76% time with <5 children; 24% time ≥ 5).

Among the play episodes in the video database (group sizes less than the whole class), the mean play group size at the University site was 14.7% of the class (3.7 children; SD 6.9%) and at the rural site was 25.7% (4.6 children; SD 14.9%). A MANOVA of spontaneous, single gender and mixed gender play group sizes, when size is calculated as a percentage of children in the class, shows significant differences in the overall model where gender and site are independent variables ($F(5, 288) = 38.43$, $p < .000$). There are significant main effects of site ($F(1, 288) = 81.86$, $p < .000$) and of gender ($F(2, 288) = 44.79$, $p < .000$) and a significant interaction effect between site and gender ($F(2, 288) = 12.78$, $p < .000$).

The average play group size for boys, girls, and for mixed gender groups was smaller for all groups at the urban, University preschool than at the rural preschool. The girls had very similar mean play group sizes across sites: three girls to a group. (University: 13.3% of class/3.3 girls and rural: 17.8% of class/3.2 girls). The boys' groups, on the other hand, were quite different in their average sizes. University preschool boys played in an average group of three whereas the rural boys played in an average group of four (University: 11.4% of class/2.9 boys and rural: 20.9% of class/3.8 boys).

Mixed gender play group sizes were bigger, on average, than single-gender groups in both classrooms. This suggests that mixed-gender play was somehow different from single gender play and that gender was relevant in the type of play that children engaged in. The mean difference across sites in mixed gender play groups is quite striking, considering the skills involved in maintaining a larger group. The mean mixed-gender play group size at the rural site was bigger by two children than the mean play group size at the University site (University: 17.5% of class/4.4 children, SD = 3.9%; rural: 36.8% of class/6.6 children, SD = 11.9%). Further, the University boys did not tend to have a wide range of play group sizes, whereas the rural boys' regularly included most or all of the boys in the class.

Friendship Circles

The friendship data provide further evidence of differences in social inclusiveness across sites and genders. I analyzed the friendship interview data in two ways: MANOVAs of the average number of children who chose someone as a friend 1) within the whole class and 2) within the child's own gender group. There are similar patterns in both analyses, and the differences among the means are significant. In both cases the urban, University children claimed to have fewer friends than the rural children (within whole class $F(1, 42) = 66.76$, $p < .000$ and within own gender group $F(1, 42) = 42.05$, $p < .000$). Also in both cases, the percentages of girls' friends were not as different across sites as the boys' patterns, with the University boys claiming significantly fewer friends than their rural counterparts (within whole class $F(1, 42) = 13.01$, $p < .001$ and within own gender group $F(1, 42) = 4.18$, $p < .05$).

When identifying friends from both genders in the class, boys and girls in Costa Rica are not so different from each other; the MANOVA main effect of gender did not attain statistical significance. However, when identifying friends from within their own gender group, the boys from

Friendship Votes from the Whole Class

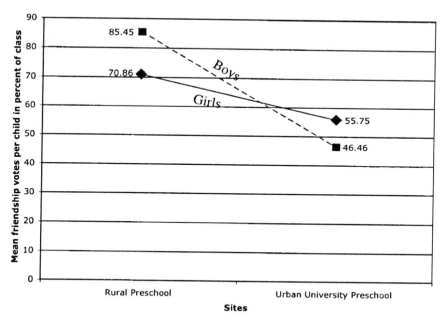

Figure 2. Mean friendship votes for each child in percent of class.

both sites combined chose fewer friends than the girls ($F(1, 42) = 40.85$, $p < .000$). While the boys as a group appear different from the girls as a group in choosing same-gender friends, a closer look reveals that the University boys chose far fewer friends than the rural boys or either of the girls' groups. In contrast to the University boys (43% of votes/5.6 boys), the other three groups are quite similar (rural girls 100% of votes/6 girls; rural boys 81% of votes/9.7 boys; University girls 81% of votes/9.6 girls). The University preschool boys drive the differences in the interaction effect of site by gender when children claim friends within their own gender group.

The rural girls had similar or only slightly larger friendship circles than the University girls on both measures (whole class and own gender group). In the analysis of friendship votes from the whole class, the average number of children voting for a girl was 13 in the rural class and 14 in the University class. The mean percentage of rural children voting for a girl was higher in the rural class because of a smaller class size. There was a possible ceiling effect among the rural girls' votes within their own gender group because there were only six girls in the class and every girl chose

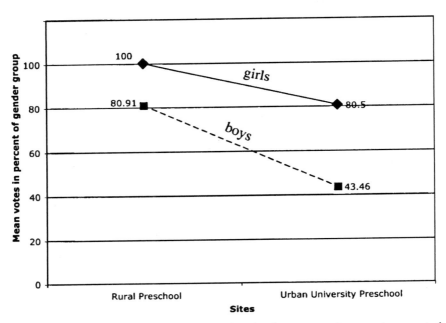

Figure 3. Mean friendship votes for each child from his/her own gender group in percent of gender group.

every other girl as a friend. This pattern is difficult to interpret because a ceiling effect and the theoretical hypothesis of interdependence would both result in a high friendship mean for the rural girls.

In sum, the urban, University preschool boys are the least inclusive socially, particularly when choosing friends from among the other boys in their class. The rural boys and girls are highly inclusive of their classmates, whether they are choosing friends from within their own gender or from among both genders. The girls across sites have some common patterns that may transcend site-specific inclusion rules.

Play Rules and Practices

The differences in play group sizes and in friendship circles determined other characteristics of play, these being the number of children who were leaders; how many children recognized a particular play behavior; and whether invention or elaboration of play scripts was more valued.

The teacher at the urban, University preschool encouraged free choice for including children in play. As a result, play partners revolved around specific friendships. Excluding children who were not your friend at that moment was an important counter-skill in establishing friendships and playmates. These social strategies resulted in smaller and more intimate play experiences. Many small groups of children—and the possibility that some children never played together—limited how many children would be exposed to a particular play behavior. This social structure, of many, small groups, made it necessary for most children to be capable of leading a play group. Leaders needed to have gatekeeping skills and the creative skills to invent new play behaviors in order to maintain the play and to keep their leadership status.

The rural teacher's principles of inclusion contributed to socializing the children to have a more extensive social focus. The skills required of the children to initiate and maintain larger groups are quite different from those needed to sustain small-group play. The rural children had the ability to coordinate more children in play. Larger play groups cannot be sustained when children are competing for leadership. The wider social organization of the rural children was, by necessity, hierarchical. Here, a small number of permanent leaders was established within the group. The leaders were skilful in assigning new roles to children joining ongoing play. The children also used a small number of play scripts that were recognized by most of the group. The characteristics of fewer leaders and less scripts enabled the children to pick up play themes quickly. Most children in the group recognized what was being played, what their role was, and how to join in. This social arrangement provided an advantage in role and thematic complexity through elaboration on re-visited play.

The following vignettes describe one play episode from the University preschool and one from the rural school. These vignettes reflect differences in the initiation and transmission of shared play behaviors as a function of local inclusion practices.

Playing Doctor at the University Preschool.   The Doctor episode took place in the University preschool. The University preschool children only rarely engaged in whole-group play. The Doctor episode was one of the largest spontaneous play episodes (out of 165 in the data library) with 10 children involved, out of 25 in the class[1]. Stefy told everyone what to do and who got to play. With nurturing ideas in mind, Stefy, her best friend German, and another girl tried to squeeze through the fence from their

[1] There was one play episode with 11 children involved without corresponding field notes to use for analysis. It was shorter (6 *min* vs. 12).

outside play yard into the baby yard. They couldn't, so they sat on a ring of half-buried tires, with Stefy nurturing the others and fixing their injuries and illnesses. Other children came over and sat on tires. As the initiator of the play theme (i.e., doctor), Stefy was "boss." As boss, she was responsible for saying who could play and for keeping the play going. Stefy agreed to let another child be a doctor, because there were too many patients for her to care for. She turned children away from the pretend play, saying that there were no more tires for sick people. Stefy kept the play going by assigning or accepting proposed character roles and limiting the participants to the children she wanted and could manage. When new children wanted to join, they asked, *"quien manda?"* (Who's the boss?) to find out with whom they had to negotiate their entry. Of course, all Stefy's friends got to play. Stefy invented new play behaviors, such as pretend-feeding pills to patients, and she fielded suggestions for changing the play and for adding new play behaviors.

By the established social rules in the University preschool class, if the play changed themes, the child who initiated the new theme got to be boss, deposing the previous boss. This practice placed a premium on the *invention* of new themes and new play behaviors. Being boss came with a set of leadership challenges that the majority of children in the class had the skills to manage. The leader had to maintain his or her position through innovation to keep participants involved and to entice others to play. Children would splinter off when someone thought up a different, more interesting, play idea. These social arrangements led to multiple, small groups of children at play, each with a leader competing with others who wanted to be the boss.

The children at the University preschool had developed leadership skills; they had also developed the ability to shift into other roles that did not involve leadership. An individual child's roles potentially changed with every new theme or set of play partners, requiring children to quickly assess their positions in the new play theme. Although girls and boys sometimes excluded each other from playing based on gender, children were rarely limited by gender in what roles they could take.

The Doctor play lasted almost 15 minutes, which was a very long time for these children to maintain large group play. This coherent, creative play dissolved when the children were called to go in. The children left the pretend play reluctantly. Even as the children took care of the last wounds, the children were scolded by the student teacher. In two months of observations, I never saw the Doctor theme revived or the play behaviors used again.

Playing Lion King at the Rural Preschool.   The Lion King episode took place in the rural group. The entire class participated at one time or another.

Unlike the rare whole-group play at the University preschool, the rural children regularly played together as a class. The Lion King episode was one of the three largest spontaneous play episodes (out of 124 in the data library), with 12 children involved. This play episode lasted 9.5 minutes. The Lion King theme was familiar to every child in the class, because they had been playing it in large and small groups for about a month. Adrian, who was the originator of the Lion King theme, started growling at the other children. This play behavior was recognized by everyone around as an invitation to play Lion King. The other boys started growling and crawling, two familiar behaviors that had long formed the basis to this pretend play theme. The number of play behaviors in Lion King, as in other pretend play themes, was limited—usually to six or less. In the Lion King, the play behaviors were growling, clawing, chasing, running away, screaming, and catching.

The girls were not allowed to be lions or to use lion play behaviors, because play roles didn't readily cross gender boundaries in this group. The girls' established role was to run away and scream, which they did. Differentiated play roles, such as who played Simba (the baby lion king), were not readily interchangeable to other children even within the gender group. Adrian was always Simba. Often, individuals took the same roles over and over again. The children didn't talk about who was boss because the group had three or four established, regular leaders, accepted and supported by the rest of the group. These children had the skills to include other children by making up roles for them or by playing something like Lion King that has built-in roles for everyone. The Lion King episodes could easily last 45 minutes with most of the class included.

The complexity of the rural children's play could be seen not in innovation, as seen at the University preschool, but rather in elaboration and theme development over time. The basic play behaviors from the Lion King were recognized by everyone in the group and were used in other thematic play. For example, three children played house and Lion King at the same time because the two play events overlapped in physical space. There was a mommy lion and two baby (boy) lions, and the play behaviors from both separate play themes were combined. This elaboration of the Lion King and house themes was a turning point for children's roles in both play themes. The combined play made it acceptable for boys to play house because they were actually lions and playing Lion King. The combined play also opened the way for the girls to be lions.

These two episodes reflect differences in the initiation and transmission of shared play behaviors as a function of local inclusion practices.

DISCUSSION

In this study, I have presented an activity settings' approach to under-standing cultural transmission of social knowledge within the context of Costa Rican preschool children's play. The activity settings' approach pro-vided the analytical tools to link classroom context and inclusion prac-tices with patterns of transmitting play knowledge. The structure of the classroom settings, teachers' practices concerning social interaction, and teachers' ethnotheories about inclusion socialized the children into dis-tinct patterns of inclusion in play. The children's inclusion practices, in turn, shaped the nature of their social organizations and, subsequently, the patterns of transmission of social knowledge.

Each classroom context produced a different model for the transmis-sion of children's play behaviors based on practices of inclusion. The differ-ences in play group sizes and in friendship circles determined other char-acteristics of play, these being the number of children who were leaders; how many children recognized a particular play behavior; and whether invention or elaboration of play scripts was more valued. Rural patterns of gender group or whole group inclusion requirements supported large group, elaborated and complex play with few leaders. Inclusion at the urban, University site was more intimate, and inclusion by choice rather than obligation was encouraged. As a result, children tended towards small group, inventive play with many leaders. With many small play groups that didn't overlap, many more play behaviors were invented, but they were introduced to a smaller number of children and didn't become as widely shared as at the rural preschool.

Conversely, the larger play groups and limited number of leaders at the rural site made it unnecessary—or not of value—to innovate play be-haviors. However, the more limited number of play behaviors at the rural site were universally shared and became part of the repertoire of the whole group. As the play behaviors were re-visited over time, the children elab-orated on them, creating more complex roles and themes. These charac-teristics determined the transmission of local, play knowledge throughout the group. The rural, coordinated, large-group play widely propagated cultural knowledge whereas the urban, creative, small group play limited exposure of play behaviors and themes.

The quantitative analyses provided three clear findings. First, the rural and urban, University sites are quite different in children's social organi-zations. The rural children have wider friendship circles and play in larger groups than the University children. Second, girls are similar to each other, even across sites. The girls' play size percentages were farther apart than the girls' raw numbers: on average, the girls at both sites played in groups of three. The girls' data on all measures suggests there may be a maximum social circle for children of this age. I can speculate that it may vary slightly across genders, but perhaps not across sites, suggesting developmental anchors to the cultural differences. And third, the rural boys tend towards even wider social networks than the girls, and the urban, University boys tend towards even narrower ones.

Despite having attended the same teacher training program, the two lead teachers structured very different preschool programs. Each teacher came from the community where she taught, which may have a stronger influence on her teaching practices than her training. Without explicitly articulating her rationale beyond the importance of social experiences, the rural teacher organized her classroom to encourage social interactions and demanded full inclusion, by gender group or by whole class, from the children. On the other hand, the University preschool teacher intentionally organized small work and play spaces to prevent children from distracting each other while they are engaged with an academic activity.

The specific practices of social inclusion and transmission of social knowledge within each preschool classroom guided children's development into two different trajectories. The rules of inclusion structured the social arrangements within the group, affecting play group sizes, friendship, cultural transmission patterns, leadership, gender roles, and the relative importance of innovation vs. elaboration. The rural children's spontaneous play showed clear evidence of a more extensive and interdependent approach towards their classmates while the urban children tended to have a narrower social focus and to be more independent in their social choices. These patterns were particularly evident for the boys. The differences in child outcomes around play patterns can be traced back to the teacher's beliefs and practices in setting up her classroom and the daily routines.

The boys and girls at each site developed play skills that suited a particular micro-culture. It is tempting to speculate on how these skills will affect their developmental trajectories. We saw that the children developed cognitive skill sets that were adaptive to the social setting around them. For example, knowing one's place within a hierarchy of people better serves a farming community than an industrial or technological one (in which invention and personal advancement are valued). The children in each group are well-prepared for their own communities. Given globalization and a current need for internal migration of nuclear families towards city centers without their extended family supports, the rural children may find themselves at an immediate disadvantage. On the other hand, the complex and non-competitive social thinking of the rural children may ultimately be extremely valuable.

REFERENCES

Asher, S. R., Singleton, L. C., & Tinsley, B. R. (1981). A reliable sociometric measure for preschool children. *Developmental Psychology*, 15:443–444.

Barker, R. G., and Wright, H. F. (1954). Midwest and its children; The psychological ecology of an American town. Row, Peterson, Evanston, IL.

Davis, H. (2003). Play and culture: Peer social organizations in three Costa Rican preschools. *Dissertation Abstracts International*.

Gaskins, S. (1996). How Mayan parental theories come into play. In: Harkness, S. and Super, C. M. (eds.), *Parents' cultural belief systems: Their origins, expressions, and consequences*. The Guilford Press, New York, pp. 345–363.

Göncü, A, Tuermer, U., Jyoti, J. & Johnson, D. (1999). Children's play as cultural activity. In: Göncü, A. (ed.). *Children's Engagement in the World: Sociocultural perspectives*. Cambridge University Press, New York, pp. 148–171.

Göncü, Artin (ed). (1999). *Children's engagement in the world: Sociocultural perspectives*. Cambridge University Press, New York.

Greenfield, P. M. (1994). Independence and interdependence as developmental scripts: Implications for theory, research, and practice. In: Greenfield, P. M. and Cocking, R. R. (eds.), *Cross-Cultural Roots of Minority Child Development*. Lawrence Erlbaum Association, Hillsdale, N. J, pp. 1–37.

Harkness, S. and Super, C. M. (eds.). (1986). The cultural structuring of children's play in a rural African community. In: Blanchard, K. (ed.), *The many faces of play*. Association for the Anthropological Study of Play Meeting, Volume 9. Human Kinetics Publishers, Champaign, IL, pp. 96–103.

Hohmann, M., Bernard B., and Weikart, D. P. (1979). *Young children in action : a manual for preschool educators: the cognitively oriented preschool curriculum*. High/Scope Press, Ypsilanti, Michigan.

Lancy, D. (1996). *Playing on the Mother Ground: Cultural routines for children's development*. The Guilford Press, New York, NY.

Madsen, M. and Lancy, D. (1981). Cooperative and competitive behavior: Experiments related to ethnic identity and urbanization in Papua New Guinea. *Journal of Cross-Cultural Psychology*. 12(4):389–408.

Madsen, M. C. (1967). Cooperative and competitive motivation of children in three Mexican subcultures. *Psychological Reports* 20:1307–1320.

Madsen, M. C. (1971). Developmental and cross-cultural differences in the cooperative and competition behavior of young children. *Journal of Cross-Cultural Psychology* 2:365–371.

Markus, H. R. and Kitayama, S. (1991). Culture and the self. Implications for cognition, emotion, and motivation. *Psychological Review* 98:224–253.

Maynard A. and Greenfield, P. M. (2003). Implicit cognitive development in cultural tools and children: lessons from Maya Mexico. *Cognitive Development* 18(4):489–510.

Musatti, T. and Mayer, S. (1990/93). Pretend play in the schoolyard: Propagation of play themes among a group of young children. In Mira Stamback & Hermina Sinclair (eds.), *Pretend Play Among Three Year Olds*. Lawrence Erlbaum Association, New Jersey, pp. 31–54.

Piaget, J. (1962). *Play, Dreams And Imitation*. W. W. Norton & Co. Inc., New York.

Rogoff, B. (1990). *Apprenticeship in thinking: Cognitive development in social context*. Oxford University Press, New York.

Rogoff, B. (1993). Guided participation in cultural activity by toddlers and caregivers. *Monographs of the Society for Research in Child Development*, 58(8, Serial No. 236).

Rogoff, B., Mistry, J., Göncü, A. and Mosier, C. (1991). Cultural variation in the role relations of toddlers and their families. In: Bornstein, M. H. (ed.), *Cultural approaches to parenting.* Erlbaum, Hillsdale, NJ.

Rogoff, B., Mosier, C., Mistry, J., and Göncü, A. (1993). Toddlers guided participation with their caregivers in cultural activity. In: Forman, E. A., Minick, N., and Stone, C. A. (eds.), *Contexts for learning: Sociocultural dynamics in children's development.* Oxford University Press, New York.

Roopnarine, J. L., Johnson, J. E., and Hooper, F. H. (1994). *Children's Play in Diverse Cultures.* State University of New York Press, Albany, N.Y.

Whiting, B. B. and Whiting, J. W. M. (1975). *Children of six cultures: A psycho-cultural analysis.* Harvard University Press, Cambridge, MA.

Whiting, B. and Edwards, C. (1988). *Children Of Different Worlds: The Formation Of Social Behavior.* Harvard University Press, Cambridge, MA.

AUTHOR NOTE

This chapter has been adapted from a presentation entitled *Play and Culture: Rules of inclusion in two Costa Rican preschools* at the Jean Piaget Society, June 2003, Chicago. I am indebted to William J. Fulbright Foundation for their support of this research and to Patricia Greenfield for her help in developing the concept of innovation versus elaboration.

Chapter 6

Features of Teaching Associated with Significant Gains in Language Test Scores by Hawaiian Preschool Children

Mary Martini

INTRODUCTION

Problem: How Can Teachers Best Facilitate Learning in Young Children?

Several instructional processes are needed to make significant impacts on learning (Bransford, Brown & Cocking, 2000). To learn effectively, people need: a) new information, models, and skills that are presented clearly and in depth; b) opportunities to practice these new ways; c) opportunities to use new learning to pursue personally relevant goals; and d) guidance in how to integrate new models with previous ways of thinking and how to solve problems with these new methods.

In view of this, effective teachers perform at least four functions. They present new information; structure tasks and learning settings; help learners recognize what *they* want to learn and do; and guide learners in using new models to solve problems that are important to them. A major problem for teachers is how to balance their efforts, day to day, to perform each of these four functions.

This chapter describes how some successful preschool teachers balanced instructional processes day-to-day. It addresses a key question in curriculum design and the study of learning: Are teachers more successful if they provide thematic integration of skills and knowledge or if they insist on children practicing skills at the expense of such integration?

This chapter examines the day-to-day practices of a group of teachers whose children improved significantly on language tests from the beginning to end of the preschool year. Their practices are compared to teachers in the same schools whose children made little progress across the year. The sample consists of the preschool classes in the Preschool and Beyond Study developed by the Kamehameha Schools, that showed the highest and lowest gains in language test scores across the year. It draws on classroom observations conducted by independent fieldworkers.

National and state associations for the education of young children express concern that preschool teaching in the United States has become overly oriented toward presenting new information and building discrete skills in the three "R's" at the expense of developing habits of learning in children (Cotton & Conklin, 2000; HAEYC, 2001; NAEYC, 2002). One concern is that young children may not be provided adequate opportunities to practice, apply, and create with their new abilities. The push to teach discrete skills stems from societal pressures to prepare children at an earlier and earlier age for skill-oriented testing and formal schooling. But, these practices may have the opposite effect on readiness to learn, which is a more nuanced process.

In the Harvard longitudinal Home-School Study, Snow, Beal, Dickinson, Tabors and others (1994, 2001) studied a wide range of preschool activities and related these to later school success. They found that "having many opportunities to engage in interesting conversations with adults" was the variable with the greatest effect on language test scores. Dickinson and Tabors (2001) concluded that "unrushed conversations with adults give children the chance to develop and practice oral language skills such as describing events beyond the here and now and learning new vocabulary." They also found that "teachers' availability, their responsiveness, the complexity of their vocabulary in talking to children, and their tendency to elaborate the children's inputs" correlated strongly with high scores as children went on to further schooling. The present study generalizes from the Harvard group's focus on conversational interaction. A main question is whether significantly more High Gain teachers integrate skill development around conceptual themes and provide time for exploration, rather than stressing practice of discrete skills.

Key Findings of Preschool Studies

Language-Rich Home and School Environments are Key to Reading Success

In the Harvard longitudinal project (the Home-School Study), Snow, Beal, Dickinson, Tabors and other researchers (2001) found that children who had many opportunities to engage in interesting conversations with adults had significantly higher language test scores—particularly in vocabulary.

The Home-School Study shows that these quiet conversations are strongly related to child outcomes. The conversations give children the chance to develop and practice oral language skills such as describing events beyond the here and now and learning new vocabulary.

Teachers of high performing children spoke in long sentences significantly more than did teachers of low performing children. They concluded that "teachers' availability, their responsiveness, the complexity of their vocabulary in talking to children, and their tendency to elaborate the children's inputs" correlated with high scores as children went on to further schooling (Dickinson and Tabors, 2001)."

National Studies

The FACES study of Head Start classrooms (1999) and the ECLS study of kindergarten students (Zill and West. 1999, 2000, 2001) around the nation provide large-sample data on children's preparation for schooling and correlates of school success. These provided the framework for the data gathering effort in the Hawai`i study in which this observational project arose. Findings directly relevant to the results of this chapter are noted in the Discussion.

Preschool and Beyond Study

This study developed for the Kamehameha Schools involves extensive collection of home and school data for 500 children in 42 preschool classes. The strongest predictors of gains in language scores were found within the classroom environment. High scores on post-tests in the spring were strongly correlated with: a) the teachers' highest level of education ($r = .735$); b) the number of college courses the teacher had taken in elementary education ($r = .511$); c) whether the teacher was certified in early childhood education ($r = .436$); d) the number of college courses the teacher had taken in other areas of education ($r = .419$). Classroom features that correlated with post-test gains were that higher performing classrooms had a higher percent of Hawaiian or part-Hawaiian children; a lower percent of children speaking pidgin-English in class; a lower number of non-English languages spoken by the children in the past; and teachers who rated their class' pre-reading skills as low, at the beginning of the year.

Home Literacy and Signs of School Success

Features of home environments associated with school success have tended to be those that enable sustained, attentive, responsive parent-child interactions (Laosa, 1982; Martini, 1995). It is hypothesized that in these sustained parent-child interactions children are exposed to and learn effective conceptual models that enable them to more effectively organize their understandings of their day-to-day worlds and to learn from their experiences. Only children, oldest and youngest children, who have been found to receive the most intense parent-child contact tend to perform best in school.

Although middle class parents tend to spend somewhat more time in school-like activities, what differentiates them most from lower-class parents are the ways in which they interact with their children (Beals & Dickinson, 2001; Yaden, Rowe, MacGillivray, 1999). Middle class parents, and mothers with some higher education, in particular, tend to have more egalitarian relationships and interactions with their children (Laosa 1982). They tend to use authoritative, rather than authoritarian or permissive parenting styles (Baumrind, 1989). Emotional warmth and responsiveness, egalitarian parent-child relations, lower control of children but higher expectations for performance—these combine to characterize the authoritative style.

In these egalitarian relations, children talk more, initiate more turns and topics, and speak as much as the parents. The topics and direction of the conversations are steered as much (or more) by the children as by the parents (Martini & Mistry,1993). In the current study we predict that these interactive characteristics will differentiate effective from less effective teachers as well.

The parents and children co-participate in these discussions and build up shared realities in the process. In these discussions, parents mention, model and demonstrate useful conceptual frameworks, which children listen to, assimilate and then use to mentally organize their perceptions and thoughts. Levine, Resnick and Higgins (1993), McGillicuddy-DeLisi (1985), and Sigel, Stinson and Kim (1993) review research associating particular parenting practices with children developing representational-symbolic competencies, and succeeding in school. School success is strongly associated with parents who place high demands on their children to think, reason, and understand with language. These parents engage children in discourse routines such as: reporting, defining, interpreting, demonstrating, sequencing, analyzing, evaluating, inferring cause and effect, generalizing, planning and resolving conflict (Sigel, et al., 1993).

Martini (2001a), in studies comparing high vs. low scoring Hawaiian children, and Beals & Dickinson (1994), and others in the Harvard Home-School Learning Project also find that parents of children who are successful in school spend significantly more time during mealtimes engaging their children in discussions of non-present and non-observable topics. School success is also strongly associated with egalitarian parent-child relationships that enable the child to remain in contact with parents long enough to develop shared mental realities and to perform operations (interpreting, evaluating, analyzing, etc.) on these realities.

Educational success is also linked to parents scaffolding their child's learning by structuring learning conditions to pose challenges to the child that are just at the top of the range of the child's current capacities. These practices enable the child to develop new skills based on his or her existing knowledge. Parents of successful students also introduce discrepancies or conflict in children's belief systems to spur them on to a more advanced cognitive synthesis (Sigel et al., 1993).

"Learning with Understanding"

The principles of "Learning with Understanding" were put forward by Bransford, Brown and Cocking (2000) to stimulate research, notably: a) to determine conditions under which children engage in optimal or in-depth learning, and then b) to reproduce these conditions in everyday classroom contexts.

In-depth understanding is said to occur when students attend extensively to what they are learning, and produce products that indicate high levels of understanding. Depth understanding is measured in terms of how well the student can apply learned materials to fashion projects, inquiries, reports and demonstrations that are more complex than the materials through which the student originally learned the skills. The students are able to do something with the new information or skills that is more complicated than the tasks they completed in order to learn the material. They are able to use knowledge to solve real life problems.

Hypotheses

The hypotheses of this study are that depth learning will be facilitated under at least eight conditions, namely when: 1) the child can relate the material to what s/he already knows; 2) the teacher understands and builds upon what the child already knows; 3) the teacher presents explicit models to the child for organizing perceptions; 4) the teacher provides focused activities related to the conceptual theme; 5) the teacher enables children to structure their own problem solving around problems of interest to them, without microstructuring their efforts; 6) the teacher provides many opportunities for the child to present her understandings and discoveries to others; 7) the teacher provides relatively long periods for focused individual work; and, 8) the teacher relates "interest center" work to the conceptual themes of the day, week or study unit. To fulfill these conditions, the teacher must provide both structure and extensive opportunities for students to work independently.

The difference between classrooms as environments for in-depth learning or for less integrated learning can be summarized in two models of preschool education:

> *Model 1*: Preschools following a thematic approach in which activities were planned to fit within a central conceptual framework, daily, weekly or by unit; and
>
> *Model 2*: Preschools stressing development of discrete skills (pre-reading, pre-writing, pre-science skills) but not within a unifying conceptual framework.

In the following example, the teacher of a Model 1 classroom integrates learning around the theme of how animals and plants grow and survive.

Example of a Large Group Activity from One of Our Study Classrooms: Observing Nature

Teacher: Remember going to the farm last week?
Children: Yes.
Teacher: What is this?
Children: A mango.
Teacher: What's happening to it?
Children: It's squishing out . . . it rotting . . . a ant get inside
Teacher: Yes, the mango is splitting; it's squishing out. Brenda said she saw an ant inside it.
Child: Put it in the microwave
Teacher: What would happen if I put it in the microwave?
Child: It would smell.
Teacher: What is this one (a dried flower)?
Children: A flower.
Teacher: What kind of flower? What's it shaped like?

Children: Like a bird.

Teacher: This one smells good; this one is all dried up...Can I get Brenda's help? Brenda, you're our weather observer—go outside and find out why this flower is all dried up and looks like this. Thank you.

(Brenda goes outside).

Teacher: Children, what do we need rain for? The rain makes the ground wet so all of the plants can what?

Children: Drink.

Teacher: That's right...

In contrast, the following is an example of a similar large group activity in a Model 2 classroom stressing development of discrete skills:

Example of a Large Group Activity from One of Our Study Classrooms: Filling in the Calendar

Teacher: Okay, children, help me spell the month of April.
   (Children help her spell: A-P-R-I-L)

Teacher: What day of the month is it?

Children: 25.

Teacher: What year?

Children: 2000.

Teacher: What do I need to put at the end of the sentence?

Children: A period.

Teacher: Yes. (She writes and says), "Today is Thursday." What was yesterday?

Children: Wednesday.

Teacher: Yes. What is tomorrow?

Children: Friday.

Teacher: Yes, tomorrow will be Friday. Eyes up here, please. How many boys are in school? (She writes this, too). Do we need a period here?"

Children: No, a question mark.

Teacher: That is right. I forgot. I was trying to trick you. Boys, stand up.
   (They do)

Teacher: Everybody—count the boys. Where are your counting fingers?
   (Some children raise their counting hands.)

Teacher: Good job, Brenda.
   (Children count to 8 boys).

Teacher: (writes 8) How many girls do we have? Girls, count yourselves.
   (Girls do this and get to 9).

Teacher: We have 9 girls. (Writes) We have 8 boys and 9 girls. Do we
     have more girls than boys?
Children: More girls.
Teacher: Yes, more girls.

The prediction was that more High Gain (HG) classrooms would re-
semble Model 1 in which children are provided regular conceptual frames
for understanding and given many opportunities to solve their own problems and make their own products, using those frames.

The hypothesis is, then, that HG classrooms will be characterized by
more features of "Learning with Understanding" in the above domains,
than will LG classrooms. Teachers of HG classrooms: 1) will provide a
clearer conceptual focus, each day, in the form of stated topics, themes
or problems; 2) that they will integrate the purposes of learning center
tasks around these themes; 4) will set up more open-ended, child-designed
problems and projects in these centers, related to the conceptual themes;
5) will be more responsive toward children, including questioning what
they already know; 6) will convey more information in the form of models
for understanding topics; and 7) will be less critical and controlling of
children.

Also, teachers of High Gain classrooms will: 1) conduct a wider range
of activities that call for high level reasoning and language; 2) be more
egalitarian in following children's leads (answering their questions, using
their input, listening to them, asking them to report on their views); 3) scaffold more complex group discussions; 4) enable more sharing of personal
knowledge and interests; and 5) scaffold richer one-on-one conversations
with children around the child's products, interests or activities.

RESEARCH DESIGN

Methods

The Sample
Forty-two classrooms, comprising 841, 4-year-old children, were sys-
tematically observed. Complete data sets were collected on 35 of these
classrooms. Children in 13 of these 35 classrooms exhibited significant
gains in average standard scores on the PPVT-III from the beginning to
end of the year. Children in these High Gain (HG) classrooms made an
average gain of 10.5 Standard Score points in the preschool year.

Children in another 12 classrooms lost, on average, .32 Standard Score
points across the year, even though they had started the year at exactly the

same level as children in the High Gain classrooms. (Children in both sets of classrooms averaged a score of 92 at the beginning of the year). (The Low Gain classrooms are abbreviated as LG classrooms).

The sample is described in detail in: The Pre-Kindergarten Year: Kamehameha Schools Preschool and Beyond Study: Year One Report, (SMS Research & Marketing Services, Inc., December 2002).

Pre- and post-tests were conducted on 433 students. Half the participating students were male, half, female. Most were 4 years old during the last year, but 36 percent were less than 48 months old at the time of the pretest. About 93 percent of the children were of Hawaiian ancestry. Nearly all (96%) of the children speak Standard English as their primary language. Nearly all (93%) of the children were described as very healthy or healthy by their parents. Most were in preschool 30 hours a week or more.

Teachers ranged in age from 25 to 55. All were women. Roughly one third were less than 35 years old; one third, 35–44; and one third older than 45. Thirty two percent were Hawaiian or Part-Hawaiian; 27%, Japanese; 27% Mixed or other; and 14% Caucasian. Roughly a third had a BA or less; a third had courses beyond the BA and a third had Master's degrees or more. Roughly a third had less than 5 years experience; 16% had 5–9 years experience; 29% had 10–14 years; and 37% had 15 or more years of experience teaching.

Most of the preschool programs in this study were yearlong, full-day programs serving four-year old children. Fifty-five percent of the classrooms had fewer than 20 students. Eighty percent of the classrooms had at least 50 percent Hawaiian students." (pp. 1–7).

The Key Test Used to Separate the HG and LG Classrooms

All children were individually tested during the first month of school and again during the last month of school, using the PPVT-III (Peabody Picture Vocabulary Test-III). The PPVT is widely used in the United States to determine young children's levels of talking and thinking with words. It is highly controversial in that it draws from Standard American English vocabulary. Attempts to write an indigenous Pidgin English form of the test have had little success in differentiating pidgin speakers from standard speakers in Hawai`i. Highly vocal children, whether they speak Standard American English or pidgin, tend to do better on this test than less talkative children. The test has very high reliability and construct validity. It relates strongly with tests of verbal reasoning.

PPVT average scores for classrooms were used to separate HG and LG groups independent of the observations that are the subject of this study.

Classroom Observations

Eight domains of the preschool environment were examined to determine features that significantly differentiate High Gain from Low Gain classrooms: 1) the physical setting, including presence of learning materials and structured opportunities for learning; 2) the temporal flow of the day, including measures of the proportion to time spent in large group, small-groups and individual activities; 3) the level of integration of the various learning opportunities in the classroom; 4) the complexity of the tasks children were asked to perform in learning centers; 5) the kinds of communications teachers sent when they talked with the children, (e.g., did they speak in mainly long sentences with large vocabularies?); 6) whether teachers scaffolded children's learning or not, and if so, how; 7) the skills that children practiced at the various learning centers; and 8) how children acted differently and spent their times differently in the two sets of classrooms.

Data Collection

Each of the 42 classrooms participating in the Preschool and Beyond Study was observed by fieldworkers from SMS Research, Inc. The six observers worked in pairs. Two workers observed for an average 211 minutes (3.5 hours) in each classroom at the same time. They observed during morning sessions, from the beginning of the school day. The observers sat along the edges of the room, writing as unobtrusively as possible. They moved around to position themselves closer to the area they were observing.

The observers were trained to understand the concepts involved in classroom observation, the procedures to follow in making observations, and how to record discrete behavior in checklist forms. Observers were not aware of the conceptual models tested or of the hypotheses. Two observers observed the same large group activities in the same classroom providing numerous checks on reliability. Data were entered randomly from either one or the other observation form for these activities.

Observation Instruments

Most of the observation instruments were "spot observations" or "time-sampling checklists" on which the observer quickly noted the presence of listed features. Observers also wrote verbatim transcripts of the main teacher's language in the following way. After completing observations of the large group setting and small group lesson, the observer moved close to the teacher and wrote a running account of the teacher's talk for a five minute period. Content and process analyses were later conducted on these typed transcripts of talk of 34 of the original 42 teachers.

The questions asked and instruments used to answer those questions are described below.

Activity Centers. For the first 10 minutes, each observer scanned the room and filled in an "Activity Centers Checklist" in which they checked the presence or absence of specific learning centers. Reliability was high for this straightforward method.

Teachers' Communication in Large Group Settings. Next, the observers did a 30-minute time-sampling of teacher actions during morning circle. They observed teacher-child interactions during this opening meeting of the day in which children and adults sat in a circle on a large rug in all classrooms. The observers observed the teacher for two minutes, and then spent a minute filling in a checklist for the presence of certain features during that segment. They repeated this for a total of 10 samples. At the end of 30 minutes the observers wrote notes about the content of the morning circle. They noted whether or not conceptual themes of the day had been introduced and learning centers explained in relation to those themes. Later, data entry staff randomly entered either the first or second of these entries. Activities that were double coded were used to calculate reliability for the time-sampling instrument.

Teachers' Communication in Small Group Settings. The same form and method were used by the two observers to observe the teacher in small group lessons.

Functions and Complexity of typical Teacher Talk. After observing 30 minutes of large group activity and 30 minutes of small group activity, the two observers wrote, verbatim, what the teacher said for the next 5 minutes. They wrote as quickly as possible to capture as much of the teacher's language as possible. Again, double entries enabled checks on reliability.

Skills Children Exercise at each Activity Center. The two observers then shifted to observing in the numerous learning centers or "interest corners" in the classroom. Each observer was designated half the centers (usually 5 or 6) to observe for 5 minutes each. S/he observed the first center and activities for 4 minutes and then spent a minute filling in the checklist of items and actions observed. Then s/he moved on to the second center on the list, and so on.

The Activity Center Description checklist has 9 sections. Section 1 is a list of observable features that indicate the degree to which the activity at the center is carefully structured, adequately explained, complex and related to a conceptual theme. Each of sections 2–9 consists of a list of skills, arranged from simplest to most complex, in 8 skill domains that children might exercise at the learning center. The observer sits close to the learning center and listens and watches for 3 minutes and then spends two minutes filling in the 9 checklists.

The domains coded were: 1) verbal reasoning skills (the simplest level was "child observes and labels"; the most complex level was "child explains cause and effect"); 2) book use skills (e.g., from "child looks at a book" to "child sounds out consonants"); 3) narrative skills (e.g., from "child tells a story" to "child speculates, imagines and describes improbable events"); 4) pre-writing skills (from "draws picture" to "pretends to write a letter, story"); 5) pre-math skills (from "uses containers to pour sand or water" to "writes some numbers" to "does quantity or proportion play"); 6) pre-science skills (from "takes 'notes' on an observation" to "uses science equipment, such as a microscope"); 7) Hawaiian Science/Nature skills (from "makes a project about nature in Hawai`i" to "learns about ancient Hawaiian methods (such as house building); 8) Hawaiian cultural skills or knowledge (from "does a Hawaiian craft" to "does chants, dances and songs with others").

Data-entry workers calculated the percent of items checked within each section, giving an approximation of the intensity and complexity with which children exercised that category of skills at that center during the observed period. In this way, a record was collected for each learning center in the classroom.

Children's Behavior at Activity Centers.   The observers then observed 10 children, each, in succession. They watched each child for 2 minutes and then filled in a checklist of activities. In this way, a record was collected for each child of typical behaviors.

Distribution of Activities in the Classroom across the Morning.   Observers filled in a balance of activities grid, using their observations of the amount of time the class spent in large group activities; small group activities; individual activities; free-play outdoors and maintenance (transitions, lunch).

Coding and Analysis of Verbatim Transcripts of Teacher Talk

Units of Analysis
Each teacher's language record was segmented into utterances. In research on language development an utterance is defined as the span of talk that is uttered within one breath and that has a single intonational contour.

Once delineated, teacher utterances were coded for: 1) their length in terms of the number of morphemes included in the utterance; 2) the communicative function the utterance served; 3) the number of grammatical markers the utterance contained; and 4) the level of complexity of reasoning elicited from children, if the utterance was a question or a demand.

Measuring the Complexity of Teacher Talk

The length of each utterance was measured in the teacher transcripts by counting the morphemes contained in the utterance. We then averaged these counts across utterances for each teacher to get the teacher's mean length of utterance (MLU). This coding system is used in numerous developmental studies of language learning (Ochs, 1972).

Coding for Complexity of Reasoning Demanded of Children

Next, we examined each question, request or command by a teacher and coded the level of reasoning required of the child to respond appropriately to this request.

This system stems from the work of Sigel (1990), who described 12 levels of cognitive demands on children in terms of the number and complexity of mental operations children need to perform in order to answer the questions or complete the assigned tasks. Each teacher utterance was coded in relation to this level system. We coded for four levels of complexity.

Very Low Level of Complexity of Demand. At levels 1 and 2 teachers ask children to attend to items the teacher displays; to follow simple commands; to repeat what the teacher says, to imitate what she does, to find or point to what the teacher says, to label things the teacher indicates, and to match similar items. These tasks develop children's abilities to attend to, recognize and label items.

Low Level of Complexity of Demand. At levels 3 and 4 teachers ask children to describe features of the items they indicate, to sort items in relation to their features, to seriate , sequence and count items; to recognize letters, numbers, syllables, or punctuation marks; to sound out some letters, to read simple words; to report on events which happened in the past; to specify the child's own wishes, wants, opinions and moods.

Medium Level of Complexity of Demand. At levels 5–7, teachers ask children to compare and contrast items or events in relations to specific features. Children need to use metaphors and analogies and to describe part-whole relationships. They need to describe differences and similarities. They use comparison terms such as "same as," "different than," "bigger than," and others. Teachers also ask children to sequence events in time and to specify temporal occurrences.

High Level of Complexity of Demand. At levels 8–12, children use complex symbolic reasoning to interpret events, to explain happenings, to attribute meanings, to demonstrate properties and processes, to analyze cause and effect, to determine means to an end, to analyze peoples' motives, and to answer "what if?" questions. They also solve problems, identify central themes; propose alternatives; invent new functions; give differing options; speculate about timeless, internal or future events; create fantasy scenarios; make up puppet plays; write stories and construct fantasy worlds.

FINDINGS

Similarities Among the Classrooms

The two sets of classrooms were similar in many ways, indicating culturally standard approaches to educating young children. Physically, most classrooms consisted of a central meeting area (such as a large rug on which children and teachers sat in a circle) for large group activities, a number of small-table learning centers arranged along the walls of the room for small group or individual learning, a cluster of tables for eating and doings crafts, cubbies, a kitchen area and access to an outdoor play area.

Morning sessions in most classes included: 1) an initial large group meeting ("circle time") at which daily routines, planning and presentation of the daily theme occurred; 2) individual choice time for children to play/learn in centers of their choice; 3) teacher-led small group activities (in some cases, related to the daily theme) (doing crafts, science, story reading, lessons on numbers, letters or verbal reasoning); 4) snack; 5) outdoor play; and 6) maintenance routines (getting ready for lunch, lining up, going to the restrooms, clean-up time, etc.). The HG and LG classrooms did not differ significantly in the balance of time spent in large group, small group and individual activities.

Teachers in the two sets of classrooms conducted the initial "circle time" meeting differently. Circle time in the effective, HG classrooms more consistently included a daily "conceptual" theme (such as how chickens hatch, how plants and animals differ, or a Hawaiian myth). HG teachers tended to present new information about that theme in the form of a demonstration or reading, and to give instructions on how to use materials in the learning centers to explore that theme. Circle time in the less effective, LG classrooms focused more on daily procedural routines in which the content remained the same from day to day. For example, many LG teachers led children in: singing the daily "morning song", choosing helpers, doing attendance, naming the days of the week, labeling the colors of children's clothing, etc.

Teachers' Use of Language

Across the 35 classrooms, teachers used language in specific ways that differed slightly across the large-group, small group and individual learning settings and from HG to LG classrooms.

In general, teachers *directed* children at least once during about 75% of the observed segments.[1] For example, they commanded and instructed children step by step through activities during 78% of the observed segments. They also *offered new information* at least once (e.g., by explaining or reading out loud) during 75% of the observation segments. They *asked didactic questions* to see whether children were assimilating this new information during 58% of the observed segments.

Teachers *encouraged* children during half the observed segments. For example, they *praised* children during 53% of the observed segments; *helped* them during about 50% of these segments; *answered* their questions in 43% of the observed segments; *asked for new information; followed children's initiations* at least once in about 28% of the observed segments and *joked* around with them in about 30% of the segments.

Teachers spent the least amount of time *correcting, scolding, ignoring* or *punishing* children. These occurred only in an average of 10–15% of the observed segments.

Differences in Teachers' Language Use

An unexpected finding was that High Gain teachers did not model significantly more complex language in this study. However, they did demand significantly higher levels of verbal reasoning from the children ($p. = .006$).

Teachers used more *directive* and *corrective* language during group activities in which they needed to keep large numbers of children on the same track at the same time. They used more *supportive* and *encouraging* language during Individual activities and one-to-one interactions with children, in which they could respond to the single child, answer her questions and support her goals.

HG teachers used: 1) *directive* language more frequently than did LG teachers: 2) *supportive* language more frequently (e.g., joking around with children and answering their questions) and 3) *corrective* language less frequently than LG teachers. In addition, they spoke in long sentences in a significantly greater percent of the observed segments.

Individualized Learning

In addition to providing more consistent conceptual frames at the beginning of the day, HG teachers also provided more opportunities for individualized learning and more focused yet complex activities at the learning centers.

---

[1] Italicized terms for communications are coding categories. More information about the coding scheme is available from the author.

Children in both sets of preschools were given the same amount of time on the observed mornings to play at individual learning centers. However, HG and LG classrooms differed in terms of: 1) the number and kinds of centers children could choose from; 2) the complexity of the activities set up at each center; 3) the clarity of instructions for what children could do at each center; and 4) the way in which teachers related these activities to the theme of the day or week. HG classrooms had more centers (p < .05), more centers involving complex verbal reasoning (p < .05) and more focused yet individualized projects at these centers.

Typical Learning Centers

Most of the 35 classrooms had the following learning centers, which (with the exception of computer corners) reflect traditional beliefs about appropriate activities for young children: 1) arts and crafts center (91%); 2) blocks and construction corner (83%); 3) reading center/book corner (71%); and, 4) computer center (71%).

About half the classrooms also had the following centers specializing in academic learning: 1) writing center (63%); 2) science center (63%); 3) dramatic play corner (area for playing house, etc.) (63%); 4) music center (49%); and 5) math center (48%).

Only a third or fewer of the classrooms had the following more specialized centers: 1) listening center (34%); 2) Hawaiian music center (28%); 3) play store or other fantasy setting (23%); and 4) Hawaiian nature and science center (14%).

Differences in Learning Centers Across HG and LG Classrooms. High Gain classrooms had significantly more learning centers (Mean = 15 for HG; 12 for LG; F = 7.4; p = .012), and, in particular, centers encouraging fantasy play, literacy projects (writing, drawing, making books) and science observation and recording.

Significantly more HG than LG classrooms had: a) Writing centers (including book-making) (13 HG vs. 8 LG classrooms; chi-square = 5.16; p = .023); b) Pretend stores or other fantasy settings (9 HG vs. 3 LG classrooms; chi-square = 4.89; p = .027); c) Hawaiian music and dance centers (12 HG vs. 5 LG classrooms; chi-square = 7.35; p = .007); and e) Listening centers (for hearing tape recorded books) (12 HG vs. 7 LG classrooms (chi-square = 3.95; p = .047).

More HG than LG classrooms had the following centers, but differences did not reach the .05 level of significance: 1) Math centers were in 11 HG vs. 9 LG classrooms; 2) Water or sand tables were in 11HG vs. 8 LG classrooms: 3) Puppet stages were in 8 HG vs. 6 LG classrooms; and 4) Hawaiian Nature centers were in 7 HG vs. 5 LG classrooms.

Skills Exercised at Individual Learning Centers

Children applied, practiced and exercised many different skills during morning sessions in these preschools. The skills they exercised most were: Verbal Reasoning skills (26% of the listed verbal reasoning skills were used in all 2 minute observation segments); Pre-Science skills (18%); Narrative skills (16%); Book-use skills (16%); Pre-Writing skills (15%) and Math skills (14%).

Children used different skills in different learning contexts. Academic skills were exercised in both the relevant academic learning centers (writing, reading, etc.) and in the more open-ended "play" centers.

Children used Verbal Reasoning skills most consistently in the math (45%) and science centers (34%). But they also used these frequently during unscripted puppet play (35%), while building structures in the block corner (34%) and while playing computer games (30%). (Verbal Reasoning skills include: labeling, matching, comparing, explaining categories, describing cause and effect, predicting events and verbal problem solving).

Children used Narrative skills most frequently during Puppet play (46%); Dramatic Play (36%); Writing (23%) and Hawaiian music (25%). Narrative skills include: telling a well structured story, reporting, providing adequate background information, developing scripted pretend play, acting out stories, and other such language skills.

Children practiced Book skills most consistently at the reading (52%), writing (45%) and computer centers (28%). (For example, at these centers they held books correctly, tried to read letters, sounded out consonants, pretended to read and write, and used formulaic expressions used in narratives, such as "Once upon a time".)

Children used Emerging Writing skills consistently at the Writing Centers (66%). However, they also used these consistently when doing arts projects at the Crafts center (51%) and at the Hawaiian Arts center (25%). (Emerging writing skills include drawing records and journal entries, writing some letters, writing notes, making books of drawings, and writing some words.)

Children used Pre-Math skills most consistently at the sand or water table (45%), next most, at the math center (22%) and also at the Pretend Store (10%). They used pre-science skills in the science center (34%), but also at the sand and water table (12%).

Differences Between HG and LG Children in Exercising Skills

Children in HG classrooms exercised academic skills equally in both academic and more open-ended, free-play contexts, while children in LG classrooms tended to use academic skills in their relevant centers only. For example, while playing with blocks, HG children exercised Verbal

Reasoning, Pre-Math and Pre-Science skills significantly more consistently than did LG children.

Children in HG classrooms tended to do more complex, project or experiment type activities in these learning centers, while children in LG classrooms more frequently engaged in rote or worksheet kinds of activities.

For example, in 64% of the HG writing centers, children made books, wrote and drew journals, notes, letters and science records related to other classroom activities. Children in only 33% of the LG writing centers did these kinds of activities. In 67% of the observed writing centers, children copied letters and numbers, wrote their names and did readiness worksheets.

Similarly, in 90% of the observed science centers in HG classrooms, children worked on multi-step projects discussed, earlier that day, in group activities. They observed and drew caterpillars and sea creatures, fed animals, organized their own collections, dissected dead insects and geckos, cared for plants, made butter, did experiments and recorded plant growth. Complex, hands-on activities occurred in only 33% of the observed science centers in LG classrooms. In 67% of the LG science centers, children played sorting and matching games, colored science worksheets and labeled animal and plant parts (chi-square = 7.226; p = .027).

HG classrooms also provided significantly more opportunities for fantasy play. In addition to the traditional "home corner," several of the HG classrooms had puppet stages and pretend stores.

Children's Activities

HG children tended to spend a larger percent of time writing, reading, doing Hawaiian activities, singing and dancing and helping others than did the LG children, but none of these differences reached the .05 level of significance. Similarly, HG children tended to spend less time wandering and fighting. However, there was no difference in the amount of time children were on task, and the LG children spent significantly more time trying new activities and problem solving.

DISCUSSION

The teachers in effective classrooms more consistently: 1) provided, daily, an explicit conceptual framework for the children, and 2) provided more activity opportunities in which children could try out the new conceptual learning to produce products of their own design or to solve self-chosen problems. We hypothesized that these two components—conceptual clarity, coupled with open-ended but focused opportunities for experimentation—characterized the Model 1 classroom and worked together to enhance children's learning.

The findings of this study corroborated and extend those of several previous studies of effective preschools. As in the Early Childhood Longitudinal Study and the Head Start FACES study, teacher's level of education, number of child development and early childhood courses, and number of other education courses all correlated strongly with positive child outcomes. As delineated in the FACES study as well, the most effective teachers in this study: were more responsive (in terms of answering children's questions, asking their views) and very rarely ignored children's questions. They offered information, conceptual models for understanding new material and methods for accomplishing tasks, more than did the less effective teachers. In addition to planning and providing quality conceptual coherence, they provided a larger number of individualized discovery activities in both structured and free play centers. They structured complex tasks. They spent more time during the day in teacher directed learning and less time in transition. They encouraged egalitarian relationships and scolded and punished less. Significant differences did not emerge in descriptions of how the children acted, moment to moment, however, HG children tended to do more complex literacy activities and science and math projects related to a central conceptual theme.

Our findings extend those in the literature in that the teachers in the Model 1, HG classrooms served, primarily, as conceptual guides who modeled coherent intellectual activity, monitored children's experimentation and scaffolded children into using complex interpretative models to understand reality. LG classrooms resembled Model 2 settings in which teachers functioned, mainly, as guides for children learning a wide range of discrete, relatively disconnected skills and information.

A larger number of features characteristic of "Learning with Understanding" emerged in the HG than in the LG classrooms. This confirmed our hypothesis that children learn concepts, information and skills more deeply and completely when they need them for their own purposes and when they are helped to learn a delimited range of aspects in depth rather than when children practice a wide range of basic skills without a clear, teacher-provided conceptual framework.

REFERENCES

Beals, E. E., and Dickinson, D. K. (1994). Not by print alone: Oral language supports for early literacy development. In: Lancy, D. F. (ed.) *Children's Emergent Literacy: From research to practice*, Praeger Publishers, West Port, CT, p. 29–40.

Bransford, J. D., Brown, A. L., and Cocking, R. R. (2000). *How people learn: Brain, mind, experience, and school.* National Academy Press, Washington, DC.

Cotton, K. & Conklin, N. F., Research in Early Childhood Education. In: *School Improvement Research Series.*

D'Amato, J. (1986). "We Cool, that's why" A study of personhood and place in a class of Hawaiian second graders. Unpublished PhD dissertation, University of Hawai`i at Manoa, Honolulu, HI.

Dickinson, D. K., and Tabors, P. O. (2001). *Beginning Literacy with Language.* New York: Brookes Publishing.

Early Childhood Longitudinal Study, Study Brief (2000). National Center for Education Statistics.

Family and Child Experiences Study (FACES) (1999). *Report on Findings: www.acf.hhs.gov/programs/core/pubs_reports/faces/meas_99_exec_summary.html.*

Farren, D., Mistry, J., Ai-Chang, M., and Hermann, H. (1993) "Kin and Calabash: the social networks of preschool part-Hawaiian children." In: Roberts, R. (ed.) *Coming home to preschool.* Ablex Publishers, Norwood, NJ.

Forester, M. A. (1995). *The Development of Young Children's Social-Cognitive Skills,* Psychology Press.

Greenfield, P. M. and Cocking, R. (1994). *Cross-cultural roots of minority child development.:* Lawrence Erlbaum Associates, Hillsdale, NJ.

Howard, A. (1974). *Ain't no big thing: Coping strategies in a Hawaiian-American Community.* University of Hawai`i Press, Honolulu, HI.

SMS Research, Inc., (2002). *Kamehameha Schools: Preschool and Beyond Study: Year One Report, The Pre-Kindergarten Year.* SMS Research, Honolulu, HI.

Laosa, L. M. (1982). Families as facilitators of children's intellectual development at 3 years of age: A causal analysis. In: Laosa and Sigel (eds.), *Families as learning environments for children,* Plenum, New York, pp. 1–46.

Levin, P., Tibbetts, K., McClelland, M., and R. Heath. "Hawaiian parents teaching styles." In: Roberts, R. (ed.) *Coming home to preschool,* Ablex Publishers, Norwood, NJ.

Lynn, Leon (1997). Language-Rich Home and School Environments are Key to Reading Success. *Harvard Education Letter,* July/August, 1997. pp. 1–3.

Lyon, R. (1997). Language and Literacy Development. *Early Childhood Update.*

Martini, M. (1995). Features of home environments associated with children' school success. *Early Child Development and Care* 3:49–68.

Martini, M. (1996). What's new? at the dinner table: Family dynamics during mealtimes in two cultural groups in Hawai`i. *Early Development and Parenting* pp. 23–34.

Martini, M., and Mistry, J. (1993). Talking at home and test-taking at school. In: Roberts, R. (ed.). *Coming home to preschool.* Ablex Publishers, Norwood, NJ.

Mikulecky, Larry (1996). Family Literacy: Parent and Child Interactions. In: EDS? *Family Literacy: Directions in Research and Implications for Practice,* January 1996, Department of Education Publications.

Mistry, J., and Martini, M. (1993). Preschool activities as occasions for literate discourse. In: Roberts, R. (ed.) *Coming home to preschool.* Ablex Publishers, Norwood, NJ.

Nord, C., Lennon, J., Liu, B., and Chandler, K. (1999). *Home Literacy Activities and Signs of Children's Emerging Literacy, 1993 and 1999.* In National Center for Education Statistics.

West, J. (1999). *Early Childhood Longitudinal Study: Project Summary: Kindergarten Class Report 1998–99.*

Wilson, V. (2000). Can Thinking Skills be Taught? *The Scottish Council for Research in Education Newsletter.*

Yaden, D. B., Rowe, D. W., and MacGillivray, L. (1999). *Emergent Literacy: A Polyphony of Perspectives.* A Center for the Improvement of Early Reading Achievement report #1–005.

Zill, N. and West, J. (2001). *Entering Kindergarten: A Portrait of American Children When they begin school: Findings from the National Condition of Education Study*, 2000. NCES 2001–035, Washington D.C.

AUTHOR NOTE

As a study of preschools with high proportions of Hawaiian children, the project was designed to locate the presence of particular cultural features in teachers' approaches and children's learning styles. However, with the exception of Hawaiian content in many of the schools (Hawaiian myths, history, traditional instruments, hula, singing, greetings, and nature study), culturally specific teaching and learning styles were not apparent. This may reflect the standardization of early childhood teacher training in Hawai`i and the United States in general OR the applicability of these approaches across cultures. Future studies in Hawai`i might profitably focus on schools whose main purpose is to specialize in culturally specific teaching and learning methods. For example, specifically Hawaiian teaching styles might be found in Hawaiian language immersion schools. However, a second possibility is that providing children with coherent conceptual models and structuring opportunities for them to use these for their own purposes might be effective practices across cultures.

Parts of this chapter were prepared as a report for the Kamehameha Schools, Policy Analysis and System Evaluation branch in connection with the Preschool and Beyond Study. Data collection and analysis were conducted by SMS Research & Marketing Services, Inc. under contract to Kamehameha Schools. The support and extensive efforts of Shawn Kana'iaupuni, Director, PASE, and James E. Dannemiller, SMS, are gladly acknowledged.

Chapter 7

Learning Connections
A Home-School Partnership to Enhance Emergent Literacy and Emergent Math Skills in At-Risk Preschoolers

Barbara D. DeBaryshe and Dana M. Gorecki

INTRODUCTION

The consequences of neglecting to provide all children with adequate early learning experiences are sobering. Social disadvantage based on ethnicity and class is associated with lower academic readiness at the time of school entry (Jordan, Huttenlocher & Levine, 1994; Whitehurst & Lonigan, 2001) and the achievement gaps between low- and high-SES groups widen as children progress through elementary school (Alexander & Entwisle, 1988). In the past several years there has been a renewed focus, particularly at the level of governmental policy, on prevention efforts for at-risk preschoolers (Shonkoff & Phillips, 2000). This is because high quality childcare, early intervention, and preschool programs can have marked impacts on cognitive, social, and behavioral outcomes (Barnett, 1995; Campbell & Ramey, 1994; Peisner-Feinberg et al., 2000); in some cases, positive effects can still be identified in early adulthood (Barnett, 1995; Garces, Thomas & Curie, 2000).

Unfortunately, for young children in the United States, experience in high quality early childhood education and care settings is more often the exception than the norm (Cost, Quality and Child Outcomes Study

175

Team, 1995; Galinsky, Howes, Knotots & Shinn, 1994). Even the Head Start program, which was specifically designed to redress the negative effects of social disadvantage on children's academic achievement, has identified school readiness as an area in need of improvement (Bryant, Burchinal, Lau & Spaulding, 1994; Dickinson & Sprague, 2001; Zill, Resnick & McKey, 1999). We do not mean to imply that preschool children need an intensive academic environment, which in some studies, had been linked to lower elementary school achievement and reduced motivation to learn (Stipek, Feiler, Byler, Ryan, Milburn & Salmon, 1998). Rather, young children need increased access to instructional experiences with literacy and math that are designed to be responsive to their interests and developmental needs.

The purpose of this chapter is to describe and present outcome data on the Learning Connections (LC) curriculum. LC is a research-based curriculum designed to enhance emergent literacy and math skills in three- and four-year-old children. LC was developed in response to a perceived need for a teacher-friendly, empirically-validated curriculum that provides purposeful, individualized instruction in developmentally appropriate early academic skills. In designing the LC curriculum, we drew from research on early literacy and mathematics development, early childhood pedagogy, staff development, parent involvement, and culturally compatible instruction. The end product was an add-on curriculum that can be used as an adjunct to more comprehensive and holistic curricula, in order to provide an enriched focus on literacy and mathematics.

PROMOTING THE DEVELOPMENT OF LITERACY AND MATHEMATICS SKILLS IN EARLY CHILDHOOD: THE RESEARCH BASE

Emergent Literacy

Preschool and kindergarten children with strong oral language and emergent literacy skills do better in terms of reading, writing, spelling, and overall academic performance throughout the school years (Barnhardt, 1991; Juell, 1988; Scarborough, 2001; Stanovich, 1986). Such evidence has led to a consensus among educators that developmentally sensitive emergent literacy instruction should be provided in all early childhood settings, and that this instruction should promote (a) oral language competence, (b) phonemic awareness, and (c) knowledge of the alphabet and print concepts (IRA and NAEYC, 1998; Snow, Burns & Griffin, 1998; Vellutino & Scanlon, 2001).

The quality of teacher-child conversation affects children's oral language growth, especially conversations that occur one-on-one or in small group settings (McCartney, 1984; Beals, DeTemple & Dickinson, 1994; Dickinson & Sprague, 2001). A technique that is well-suited to supporting rich verbal interaction is small-group, dialogic reading. In this technique, adults engage children in active discussion of books during read-aloud sessions. The adult scaffolds the conversation by asking leading questions and making responsive comments that extend the conversation and draw the children in to longer and more complex discussion sequences. Dialogic reading has been used effectively by teachers and parents. When treatment fidelity is high, dialogic reading programs lead to significant and lasting gains in expressive vocabulary and the grammatical and semantic complexity of children's speech (Hargrave & Sénechal, 2000; Whitehurst, Arnold, Epstein, Angell, Smith & Fischel, 1994; Whitehurst et al., 1988).

Phonemic awareness is the ability to hear and manipulate the individual sounds (phonemes) of which words are composed (Snow et al., 1988; Whitehurst & Lonigan, 2001). Phonemic awareness is one of the most robust predictors of concurrent and future literacy (Adams et al., 1998; Juel, 1988; Nation & Hulme, 1997; Stanovich, Cunningham & Feeman, 1984); children who enter school with high phonemic awareness usually learn to read and write well, regardless of the method of literacy instruction to which they are exposed (Byrne & Fielding-Barnsley, 1995; Griffith, Klesius & Kromrey, 1992). Controlled laboratory studies of phonemic awareness interventions have shown success with children from preschool through grade 1, and the more intensive interventions show positive effects on reading and writing skills one to three years later (Bradley & Bryant, 1983; Byrne & Fielding-Barnsley, 1991, 1995; Cunningham, 1990; Treiman & Baron, 1983). When phonemic awareness instruction is implemented by classroom teachers rather than research assistants, smaller but still significant child gains are found (Blachman et al., 1994; Byrne & Fielding-Barnsley, 1995; Lundberg, Frost & Petersen, 1988). In sum, there is a good research base of validated techniques for promoting preschoolers' language and phonemic awareness skills.

Other domains of early literacy instruction have received less scientific attention. Correlational evidence linking early knowledge of print concepts (e.g., book handling, print tracking) and early alphabet knowledge (e.g., letter recognition, letter naming, letter-sound correspondence) with later reading is plentiful (Scarborough, 2001; Snow et al., 1998; Vellutino & Scanlon, 2001). However, we were able to locate only a handful of studies that validated the causal role of print concept or alphabet knowledge using experimental methods. Short-term research designs indicate that children who are taught to identify a set of letters by name show rudimentary ability to apply this knowledge to phonetic decoding (Roberts, 2003; Treiman & Rodriguez, 1999). For example, if a child is taught the names for the letters

B and T, the child shows some success in reading the printed word "bt" as "beet."

Somewhat surprisingly, emergent writing has received little attention in the research-based reviews of recommended instructional practices (e.g., Snow et al., 1998). Basic developmental studies indicate that children's writing attempts follow a reliable developmental progression (Sulzby, Barnhart & Hieshima, 1989) and emergent writing skills correlate both concurrently and predictively with conventional measures of spelling and reading processing (Barnhardt, 1991; McBride-Chang, 1998). Daily journal writing is a classroom technique that is included in some curricula, yet journaling has not been subject to experimental validation. Qualitative evidence suggests that journaling increases children's understanding of the functions of print, motivates children to put their thoughts on paper, and helps them progress to more advanced levels of emergent writing (Baskt & Essa, 1990; Fang & Cox, 1999; IRA and NAEYC, 1998; Pontecorvo & Zucchermaglio, 1989). Based on this evidence, we included emergent writing as a focus of the LC curriculum, resulting in four main content areas for literacy instruction—oral language, phonemic awareness, alphabet knowledge/print concepts, and emergent writing.

Emergent Mathematics

The emergent perspective in mathematics is based on the premise that mathematical universals are present in all cultures, and that children develop an impressive level of intuitive i.e., non-abstract, understanding of mathematics in the course of everyday activities (Baroody & Wilkins, 1999; Klein & Starkey, 1988; NAEYC & NCTM, 2002; Saxe, Guberman & Gearhart, 1987). Recent standards for early childhood mathematics instruction (NAEYC & NCTM, 2002; NCTM, 2000) make it clear that preschool mathematics involves considerably more than rote counting and the identification of basic shapes. These standards emphasize the breadth of early mathematical knowledge, including the domains of numbers and operations, geometry, measurement, data analysis, probability, algebra, problem-solving, reasoning/proof, communication, connections, and representation. There is increasing agreement among researchers in the area of early mathematics that preschool children should be exposed to purposeful and challenging math experiences, with the caveat these experiences are based in concrete, meaningful, and enjoyable activities (Baroody & Wilkins, 1999; Clements, 1999; Nelson, 1999; Sophian, 1999; NAEYC & NCTM 2002). However, teacher preparation programs and public policy initiatives relating to preschool quality (e.g., Early Reading First), devote much more attention to issues of early literacy instruction than to improving early math instruction. Many early childhood educators receive minimal preparation in developmentally appropriate mathematics instruction (Balfanz, 1999; Nelson, 1999). Teachers may hesitate to even introduce children to math, mistakenly believing that mathematical activity necessarily involves abstract symbols and formulae.

A small, but growing number of controlled evaluations indicate that early childhood math interventions have positive effects. Griffin and Case (1996) developed an enumeration program for disadvantaged first-grade children; their program strengthened children's numerical skills, and this outcome showed transference to enhanced performance on other mathematical tasks. Arnold, Fisher, Doctoroff, and Dobbs (2002) implemented a 6-week intervention in Head Start classrooms. Teachers were provided a resource book of short math activities and were asked to select 1–2 activities per day. Children showed gains on the Test of Early Mathematical Abilities (effect size = 1.21) while teachers reported improvements in both children's interest in math, and in their own attitudes about math instruction. Klein and colleagues developed a preschool math curriculum focusing on enumeration, number operations and spatial knowledge (Klein, Starkey & Ramirez, 2002). Middle-class preschoolers who received the curriculum showed stronger math skills than did a comparison group (Klein, Starkey & Wakely, 1994), and a home-based variation of the curriculum also showed positive effects on the number and spatial skills of Head Start children (Starkey & Klein, 2000).

Content areas for the LC curriculum were drawn from this conceptual and empirical literature. Three main learning domains were selected—numbers and operations, geometry, and spatial sense. As a secondary emphasis, LC math activities were designed to also incorporate mathematical communication, reasoning, and graphing.

Teacher Professional Development

The success of any curriculum is highly dependent on the teachers who implement the program. In-service training is most effective when the training provided is (a) specifically designed for the curriculum to be implemented, (b) teachers are given ample opportunity for hands-on practice, (c) on-site observation and feedback are provided by a supportive mentor over an extended period of time and (d) teachers are encouraged to reflect on and evaluate their new practices (Bowman, Donovan & Burns, 2001; Malone, Straka & Logan, 2000; Odell, 1990). It is also important to match the content of training and supervision activities to each teacher's developmental level (Glickman, 1981; Spodek, 1996).

When properly implemented, staff development and mentoring efforts lead to demonstrable improvements in teachers' knowledge, attitudes and classroom practices (Fantuzzo et al., 1996; Kontos, Howes & Galinsky, 1996; Nurss, Abbott-Shim & McCarty, 1998). For this reason, a substantial education and mentoring component was included as part of the LC curriculum package.

Parent Involvement

Parental involvement enhances children's academic outcomes (Blevins-Knabe & Musun-Miller, 1996; Reynolds, 1992; Weissberg & Greenberg, 1998) and provides an extra boost beyond the gains affected by high-quality classroom environments (Bryant et al., 1994). Parents' self-efficacy, beliefs about children's acquisition of academic skills, and their personal comfort level and interest in learning-related skills all predict the kind of learning environment that parents provide at home (DeBaryshe, 1995; DeBaryshe, Binder & Buell, 2000; Stipek et al., 1992). Low-SES children are less likely than middle class children to receive consistent, frequent home interactions and activities of the type that promote academic skills. Differences are found in the frequency, content, and complexity of adult-child speech, adult-child picture book reading, and other joint activities involving writing and number concepts (Burns & Casbergue, 1992; Feitelson & Goldstein, 1986; Hart & Risley, 1995; Payne, Whitehurst & Arnold, 1994; Phillips & McNaughton, 1990; Saxe et al., 1987). At first glance, the magnitude of these differences does not seem large—for example, reading to one's child every other day as opposed to two or three times per day (DeBaryshe, 1993; DeBaryshe 1995). But seemingly small differences in home practices can have a large cumulative impact over time.

Major barriers to parent involvement include school, home, and cultural obstacles (Lopez & Scribner, 1999). School barriers occur when the school is unwelcoming and/or resistant to parental involvement. Home barriers include time and resource constraints and mismatches between staff and parents' expectations about what the appropriate home and school roles should be. Cultural barriers occur when families and school do not share deeply-rooted beliefs, values, and expectations about social interaction and/or learning processes (Rogoff, Mistry, Goncu & Mosier, 1993; Tharpe, 1989).

When home-school barriers are reduced, children benefit in terms of enhanced self-perceptions, motivation and academic achievement (Arunkumar, Midgley & Urdan, 1999; Tharp, 1989). One way to increase parental involvement is to invite families to serve as partners in developing learning activities that are personally and culturally meaningful and compatible with the goals parents hold for their children (Delgado-Geitan, 1991; Holloway et al., 1995; Tharp, 1989). The LC curriculum enlists the family as active partners in their children's learning by providing consistent home activities that were designed with parental input to be both engaging and culturally relevant. Parents also receive ongoing education and mentoring regarding family involvement.

DEVELOPMENT AND CONTENT OF THE LEARNING CONNECTIONS CURRICULUM

Educational Needs of Hawai`i's Multicultural Preschoolers

Hawai`i has a unique multicultural population, which, in many ways, provides a model for the increasingly diverse face of the continental U.S. The ethnic composition of the state is 24% Caucasian, 20% Native Hawaiian/part Hawaiian, 18% multi-ethnic, 16% Japanese, 14% Filipino, 5% other Asian/Pacific Islander and 2% African American (DBEDT, 2002). Hawai`i's predominantly Asian and Pacific Islander (API) children do not fit the stereotype of the API "model minority." In the most recent state assessment of school readiness, 80% of entering kindergarten children scored below age level for vocabulary, and 59% showed moderate to severe language deficiencies (Office of Children and Youth, 1993). There is also ongoing controversy regarding the effectiveness of the States' public school system. For example, in 1998 National Assessment of Educational Progress, 55% of Hawai`i fourth grade students scored below the basic level in reading and 47% scored below the basic level on math (compared with 39% and 38% of their peers nation-wide).

Despite these academic risks, the State's API population exhibits many strengths. Family is central to local culture and the importance placed on family solidarity is exhibited by indicators such as high rates of intergenerational living, shared family meals and leisure time, children's contact with grandparents, and family observation of cultural practices (Center on the Family, 1999). Although API families vary widely in terms of national origin, religion and immigration history, members of this composite ethnic group tend to share key culturally-relevant values. Distinctive API values include collectivism (emphasizing the needs of the group more than the needs of the individual), respect for parents and elders, cherishing of children, and high expectations for family obligation (Blaisdell & Mokuau, 1991; Sue & Sue, 1990; Uba, 1994). This suggests that API families may be especially receptive to efforts that promote family involvement in preschool education.

Curriculum Goals and Methods

Learning Connections is a culturally sensitive literacy and math curriculum for use in preschools serving low-income Asian and Pacific Islander children. Curriculum development was supported by a Head Start-University Research Partnership grant. For the first two years, project team members included Dr. Catherine Sophian, Melodie Vega, and the authors of this chapter. Sophian had primary responsibility for developing the learning goals, instructional materials and assessment protocols for the math portion of the curriculum; author DeBaryshe played the same role regarding the literacy portion of the curriculum. After one year of development activities, each portion of the curriculum was piloted in the 2001–2002 school year. Results indicated that language pilot classrooms tended to show the largest gains in literacy skills (DeBaryshe, 2003) and math pilot classrooms tended to show the largest gains in math performance (Sophian, 2004). Based on a combination of the pilot test results and extensive teacher feedback on each lesson, a revised, combined math and literacy curriculum was developed. The revised curriclm included roughly 75% of the pilot year literacy activities and 50% of the pilot year math activities; additional lessons were developed to replace the earlier materials that were not retained. The complete revised curriculum was tested in the 2002–2003 shool year. The results of this evaluation form the core of the present chapter.

Distinctive aspects of the revised curriculum package include:

An Eclectic Theoretical Orientation to How Children Learn

The theoretical basis for the curriculum was multi-faceted. The goal of developing the learner's knowledge base, strategic repertoire, problem-solving skills and metacognitive awareness comes from information processing theory. The careful sequencing of activities to promote successful learning is based on both social learning theory and Montessori teaching methods. A strong focus on mediated learning and scaffolding of interactions within the child's zone of proximal development was rooted in social learning and sociocultural theories.

User Collaboration on Curriculum Development

During the development year, a committee of Head Start teachers, parents and administrators worked with the LC staff to develop learning goals and curriculum activities. Volunteer teachers and parents implemented the activities on a limited basis and provided feedback on developmental appropriateness, cultural relevance, ease of use and appeal to children and adults.

Table 1. Curriculum Domains and Specific Learning Goals

Oral language
  Expands vocabulary
  Engages in conversations of increased length and complexity
Phonemic awareness
  Segments and blends syllables
  Recognizes and generates rhymes
  Recognizes and generates words with the same initial, medial and final sounds
  Segments and blends phonemes within words
Alphabet knowledge and print awareness
  Identifies upper and lower-case letters and knows letter-sound correspondence
  Tracks print
  Aware of environmental print
  Aware of the usefulness of print
  Spells and reads consonant-vowel-consonant words
Emergent writing
  Attempts to convey meaning via writing
  Strengthens fine motor muscles
  To use tools in preparation for writing and drawing
  Shows increasingly higher levels of emergent writing
  Begins to spell simple words
  Follows a left-to-right orientation when writing
Numbers and mathematical operations
  Counts forwards and backwards using one-to-one correspondence
  Understands both quantities and numerals from 0–10
  Understands alternative counting units
  Understands that adding/taking away objects increases/decreases number
  Uses manipulatives to indirectly perform addition and subtraction operations
  Uses manipulatives to indirectly perform multiplication and division operations
Measurement
  Distinguishes alternate dimensions of measurement, e.g., height, width
  Uses nonstandard units of measurement
  Understands concepts of weight, volume, and area
  Conserves volume and area
Geometry
  Defines math vocabulary terms
  Identifies basic shapes
  Aware that news shapes may be made from two or more instances of a given shape
  Identifies a given shape within a larger array
  Counts occurrences of a specific shape
  Compares and categorizes shapes by attribute

Learning Goals Derived from the Research Literature

The curriculum was based on 33 discrete learning goals (DeBaryshe, 2003; Sophian, 2004), organized into seven more general knowledge domains (see Table 1). The learning goals and general domains were articulated with both the Head Start Performance Standards and the State of Hawai`i Preschool Standards. A series of 85 developmentally sequenced activities were developed for use in the preschool classroom. Each activity addressed one or more of the 33 discrete learning goals. A set of 24 family activities were also developed. These activities addressed one or more curriculum learning goals and extended the lessons that children received at school to the home setting. Finally, the LC curriculum was designed with a prospective intent (Sophian, 2004). The intent was to promote both current learning and also to address the conceptual foundation of skills that children would address in elementary school, e.g., phonics, graphing, multiplication, subtraction.

Small Group, Individualized Instruction

Teachers were provided with daily lesson plans for an introductory circle time and three or four literacy and math activities to be done during learning center rotations. Each activity was conducted with small groups of one to four children, with group size changing as a function of children's skills and needs for support. Teachers were encouraged to keep the composition of learning groups consistent. They were also encouraged to make the LC materials available to children as free-choice activities.

A teacher's manual included detailed instructions for each LC activity, along with suggestions for individualizing the lesson to match participating children's levels of skill. A compact documentation form was developed in order to allow teachers to collect ongoing assessment information and review each child's progress at a glance.

Cultural Sensitivity

To be more meaningful for Hawai`i's multicultural population, curriculum content (e.g., concepts, vocabulary, materials) uses many examples of "local" culture. For example, both widely available rhyming books, and pidgin (aka Hawai`i Creole English) versions of classic nursery rhymes were used to introduce the concept of rhyming. Pictures, bingo cards, and other vocabulary stimuli were made to represent a variety of familiar foods, plants, sea creatures, and articles of clothing that are common in Hawai`i but not often represented in commercially available materials. Many of the family activities had a cultural focus, for example, compiling a simple counting book that uses objects that are unique to the family's culture, and parents were encouraged to conduct the home activities in their heritage language.

Ongoing Teacher Mentoring

Following principles of effective professional development practices, teacher mentoring and ongoing technical assistance were integral to the curriculum package An experienced master's level teacher spent two full mornings per month in each LC classroom. She used this time for technical assistance and individualized coaching. Every three to four weeks, the classroom mentor and lead researcher visited each site to provide ongoing curriculum training. The small group nature of the ongoing training allowed for considerable interaction, practice and reflective conversation.

Family Involvement and Support

The parental involvement component was designed to increase the frequency and quality of parent-child learning interactions. The family curriculum consisted of 24 weekly home activities that paralleled the lessons children received at school. Parents were given a simple written description of the activity and any needed materials. Most activities yielded a product (e.g., a home-made book, a collection of objects obtained on a scavenger hunt) that parents placed in their child's classroom portfolio. Parents were also encouraged to borrow books on a weekly basis, and to complete ratings and comments on each week's activity. The mentor visited each classroom on a biweekly basis, bringing a display board with examples of the next two home activities (Sophian, 2004). The mentor met informally with parents, either individually, or in small groups, as they dropped off their children. She used this time to explain the purpose of the new activities, answer parents' questions and discuss their experiences with prior activities, and provide suggestions for making learning interactions more effective.

AN EXPERIMENTAL EVALUATION OF THE LEARNING CONNECTIONS CURRICULUM

A quasi-experimental evaluation of the revised LC curriculum was conducted in the 2002–2003 school year. It was hypothesized that:

- Children in the LC curriculum would show larger gains on vocabulary, emergent reading and writing, phonemic awareness, letter-sound correspondence, enumeration, mathematical operations, measurement, and geometry skills than children in a comparison curriculum. The only area for which no group differences were expected was letter naming, which is not emphasized in the LC curriculum.
- A dose-dependent relationship would be found in which more frequent exposure to high-fidelity implementation of LC activities both at school and at home will predict greater gains among children within LC classrooms.

Methods

Sampling and Participants

Classroom Selection.   Nine Head Start centers on the island of O'ahu participated in the study. These centers had a total of 11 classrooms and ran on an extended-day schedule. Experimental and control sites were matched for observed teaching quality, child demographic characteristics, and urban vs. rural location. All teachers in the study used the Creative Curriculum (Dodge, 2002) as their base curriculum, as required by their Head Start program. The control sites used the Creative Curriculum as the basis for all instructional activities. LC sites implemented LC as their language, literacy and math curriculum, and followed the Creative Curriculum for the remaining instructional areas, e.g., motor development, creativity, science.

Participants.   Participants were 169 preschool children, their parents, and their Head Start teachers. This number represents 89% of the original sample of children who remained enrolled in the classroom throughout the 24 week study period and for whom both pre- and posttest data were collected. The children's mean age was 47.6 months (range = 31 to 59), 53% were male, 23% were identified by their teachers as English language learners, and 5% had an identified disability. The ethnic background of the children was 29% Native Hawaiian/part Hawaiian, 20% East Asian, 12% Pacific Islander, 12% Filipino, 7% African American, 7% Hispanic, 6% Caucasian, 4% Southeast Asian and 3% not reported. The mean parental age was 31.9 years (range = 18 to 60). Twelve percent of parents had less than a high school education, 46% had a high school diploma, 35% had some college or a two-year associate's degree and 7% had a four-year college degree. Demographic data were reported for 29 of the 35 teachers. The mean teacher age was 38.2 years (range = 22 to 63) and their mean preschool teaching experience was 12.3 years (range = 1 to 32). Teacher educational attainment was as follows: 7% high school diploma or GED, 38% child development associate certificate, 28% associate's degree, 28% bachelor's degree. All but one teacher was female.

Measures

Child Assessment Battery

Children were assessed on an individually-administered battery of standardized tests and structured performance measures. Oral language was assessed using the Expressive One-Word Picture Vocabulary Test (Brownell, 2000); this instrument shows high internal consistency ($\alpha = .96$) and test-retest reliability ($r = .85$) for preschool children, as well as convergent validity with other measures of vocabulary. The Test of Early Reading Abilities-3 Form B (Reid, Hresko & Hammill, 2001) was used to assess emergent reading. This instrument covers the domains of alphabet knowledge, print conventions, and communication of meaning. The TERA also shows high internal consistency ($\alpha = .91$) and test-retest reliability ($r = .98$) with 3- to 6-year-old children; convergent validity with other measures of reading skill has been demonstrated ($r = .52 - .67$) when administered in the early elementary grades. Phonemic awareness was assessed on a 30-item task developed by the authors that included syllable recognition and the recognition and generation of rhyming and alliterative words. The rhyme and alliteration recognition items were adapted from a pre-publication version of the Preschool Comprehensive Test of Phonological Processing (Lonigan, n.d.). Emergent writing was also assessed using a procedure developed by the authors. Children were asked to write their name and then, a list of "all the words or letters that you know." Both samples were scored for level of emergent writing based on Sulzby, Barnhardt & Hieshima, 1989, and the list was scored for the number of unique letters and unique recognizable words. A total score was created by summing the four sub-scores. Both the phonemic awareness battery and the emergent writing sample show acceptable internal consistency ($\alpha = .71$ and .74), converge with the EOW and TERA scores, and have been shown to be sensitive to intervention effects (DeBaryshe, 2003). Children's emergent math skills were assessed on two instruments. The mathematics and logical operations scale of the Developing Skills Checklist (CTB/McGraw-Hill, 1990) covers counting, numeral and shape identification, patterning, seriation, number conservation and part-whole relations. It has good internal consistency for preschoolers (KR-20 = .89) and convergent validity with the ESA math achievement scale ($r = .59 - .73$). A math performance battery adapted from Sophian (2004) included 11 items that were more closely aligned with concepts covered by the LC curriculum including measurement, area, volume, and spatial sense. The math performance battery converges with the DSC ($r = .56$).

Parent Surveys

Parents were administered surveys developed for this project. Content included demographic information and self-reported frequency of home teaching interactions. Six items addressed literacy stimulation (e.g., "How often do you read aloud to your child?") and six items addressed math stimulation (e.g., "How often do you play games that use shapes, like puzzles or origami?"). Each item was rated on a 7-point Likert scale, with response options ranging from "never or rarely" to "daily." Two composite variables were formed, home literacy stimulation ($\alpha = .88$) and home math stimulation ($\alpha = .87$), by taking the mean response across component items. These composites were computed at both pre- and posttest. Parents in the experimental group were also asked six items addressing consumer satisfaction with the LC currciculum.

Teacher Survey

Teachers were administered a posttest survey that was developed for this project. Content included demographic information, teaching history, and, for LC teachers only, six items addressing consumer satisfaction with the LC curriculum.

Classroom Data

To measure treatment dosage, attendance records were collected from the Head Start administration. In LC classrooms, the mentor kept logs of the number of home activities returned by each family. In addition, LC families reported on a weekly basis the number of books borrowed from the classroom, and rated the quality of that week's home activity (using a 4-point Likert scale ranging from "poor" to "excellent").

Procedure

Pretest child assessments and parent surveys were administered at the start of the school year. Learning Connections was implemented in the experimental classrooms over a 24-week time span, including an additional 2-week review period during the winter holidays. Child posttest assessments and parent and teacher surveys were administered immediately after the implementation period ended.

Results

Pretest Equivalence

The LC and control groups were compared for pretest equivalence on all child, parent, and teacher measures. Significant pretest differences were found for only two variables. Children in the LC group had higher EOW vocabulary scores, $M = 82.77$ vs. 76.63, $t_{156} = 2.46$, $p < .02$, and the proportion of English language learners (ELL) was higher in the control group (35% vs. 16%), $\chi^2_1 = 8.16$, $p < .004$.

Treatment Fidelity

The classroom mentor worked with teachers individually to help insure that LC lessons were implemented with the prescribed frequency and in an appropriate manner. Overall, implementation fidelity for the parent component was moderate to good; on the average, families completed and returned 60% of the home activities. On both pre- and posttests, parent reports of home literacy and math stimulation were close to ceiling level. Although it was expected that home math and literacy stimulation would increase for the LC families, this was not the case. Parents in both groups reported a significance increase in literacy stimulation over time, $F_{1,124} = 8.82$, $p < .004$ and no change in home math stimulation.

Group Differences on Child Literacy and Math Skills
One-way analysis of covariance procedures were used to test the hypothesis that gains on children's literacy and mathematics performance would be higher for the LC group. Separate analyses were conducted for each dependent measure. Group (LC vs. control) served as the between-subjects factor, and child pretest age and the relevant pretest score were the two covariates. Both statistical significance and partial η^2 were computed for the group and covariate effects. In this situation, η^2 represents the proportion of variance in the dependent measure explained by the target effect, adjusting for all other effects. A standard deviation-based effect size was also computed for the group effects, using covariate-adjusted means (see Table 2).

Significant treatment effects were found for three of the six literacy outcomes and one of the two math outcomes. Controlling for age and pretest performance, LC children scored significantly higher than control children on the TERA emergent reading, $F_{1,149} = 4.95$, $p < .03$, $ES = .26$; phonemic awareness, $F_{1,154} = 38.52$, $p < .001$, $ES = .81$; letter-sound correspondence, $F_{1,154} = 8.72$, $p < .004$, $ES = .41$; and DSC math measures, $F_{1,156} = 5.23$, $p < .02$, $ES = .24$. There were no significant group differences on the EOW vocabulary standard scores, letter naming, the emergent writing composite, or math concepts measures. (There were significant differences favoring the LC group on EOW raw scores and the name-writing sub-score of the writing composite.)

Individual Differences in Developmental Gains
Because interventions or curricula are never uniformly effective for all participants, it is important to understand what factors are associated with individual differences in participant change. We were particularly interested in identifying possible dosage effects and child characteristics that correspond with developmental progress. Partial correlations, controlling for pretest performance, were used to identify correlates of child literacy and math gains over time.

To reduce the number of variables involved, children's test data were transformed into composite scores by standardizing and summing each child's results on the relevant pre or post-test instruments. Two home

Table 2. Analysis of Covariance Results on Child Assessment Data

Dependent Variable/ Effect	F	df	p	η^2	ES	Experimental		Control	
						Mean	SD	Mean	SD
EOW									
Age	0.02	1,154	.65	.001					
Pretest	342.36	1,154	.001	.69					
Condition	2.48	1,154	.12	.02	.14	87.70	0.84	83.63	1.00
TERA									
Age	43.95	1,149	.001	.23					
Pretest	146.52	1,149	.001	.50					
Condition	4.95	1,149	.03	.03	.26	89.86	0.95	86.55	1.15
Phonemic Awareness									
Age	9.29	1,154	.003	.06					
Pretest	43.72	1,154	.001	.22					
Condition	38.53	1,154	.001	.20	.81	16.84	0.62	10.89	0.73
Letter Sounds									
Age	11.26	1,154	.001	.07					
Pretest	27.85	1,154	.001	.15					
Condition	8.72	1,154	.004	.05	.41	2.28	0.15	1.58	0.18
Letter Names									
Age	1.19	1,154	.53	.003					
Pretest	69.47	1,154	.001	.31					
Condition	0.60	1,154	.44	.004	−.10	2.31	0.18	2.52	0.21
Emergent Writing									
Age	4.66	1,153	.03	.03					
Pretest	45.05	1,153	.001	.23					
Condition	0.07	1,153	.78	.001	.03	18.20	0.80	17.87	0.93
DSC									
Age	7.35	1,156	.007	.04					
Pretest	94.01	1,156	.001	.38					
Condition	5.23	1,156	.02	.03	.24	17.53	0.50	15.78	0.57
Math Concepts									
Age	3.66	1,155	.06	.02					
Pretest	26.24	1,155	.001	.14					
Condition	0.80	1,155	.37	.005	.12	9.67	0.26	9.32	0.29

Note. Tabled means and standard deviations are covariate-adjusted

stimulation change measures were also computed, one measuring change in home literacy stimulation, and one measuring change in home math stimulation. These scores were computed by taking the residual of posttest literacy or math stimulation regressed on pretest literacy or math stimulation.

Literacy gains in the LC group were highest for: English language learners (partial $r = .26$, $p < .01$), children with high attendance rates (partial $r = .24$, $p < .05$), and children whose families increased their level of home stimulation above what would have been predicted based on family practices at pretest (partial $r = .37$, $p < .01$). There were no associations with age or home activity return rate. In the control group, literacy gains were higher for younger children(partial $r = -.35$, $p < .01$), and again, for children who attended school most frequently (partial $r = .29$, $p < .05$). There were no significant correlates of math gains for children in either group.

Classroom Stability and Developmental Gains

Analyses of classroom stability were conducted for LC classrooms only. Classroom stability was defined in two ways. In terms of *learning group stability*, LC classrooms were encouraged to use consistent small groups (i.e., the same teacher and 3–4 children working together across the school year) when doing LC activities. Four of the six LC classrooms attempted to implement stable learning groups. *Teacher stability* was a factor not under staff control. The lead teachers in three LC classrooms were frequently away from their sites serving on a program-wide staff development team. Two classrooms also lost assistant teachers and had difficulty finding replacement staff. When progress within the LC group was examined, results suggested that classroom stability was associated with children's learning gains. Classrooms A and B (high on both teacher and grouping stability) scored above the aggregate mean for child gains, especially for literacy outcomes. Classrooms C and D (both were low on teacher stability, and C did not use stable learning groups) showed the smallest gains.

Finally, a natural experiment occurred within Classroom D. This classroom organized four learning groups, but was affected by the loss of an assistant teacher (whose position remained open for several months) and the frequent absence of the lead teacher. When staff members were absent, other teachers would attempt to cover for the missing teacher(s). Within Classroom D, literacy gains were significantly higher for children in the two learning groups that kept the same teacher throughout the school year.

Consumer Satisfaction

Consumer satisfaction with LC was high, especially for parents. The percentage of teachers who reported being "satisfied" or "very satisfied" with different aspects of the LC curriculum was as follows: mentoring and implementation support, 100%; quality of LC materials, 94%; children's learning, 94%; teacher's own mastery of LC, 94%; teacher teamwork within the classroom, 88%; parent involvement, 71%. Parents rated each LC home activity on a four-point scale, ranging from "poor" to "excellent"; the mean activity rating was 3.38 ($SD = 0.42$). Between 98% and 100% of parents "agreed" or "strongly agreed" that the classroom and home curricula contributed to their child's learning, that the home activities were clearly written and fun to do, and that they would recommend LC to other parents. Two percent of parents rated the curriculum package as "poor," 28% described it as "good," and 70% rated LC as "excellent."

DISCUSSION

Overall, LC was an effective and well-received curriculum. Controlling for age and pretest performance, LC was found to benefit children's development in math, emergent reading, letter-sound correspondence, and phonemic awareness. Gains in all these areas were both statistically and educationally significant, with changes in phonemic awareness being particularly strong. The home component of the curriculum was largely successful in engaging parents in their children's learning and parent consumer satisfaction was especially high.

The comparison curriculum used in the evaluation project was the Creative Curriculum (Dodge, 2002), which is widely implemented in Head Start programs nation-wide. The current findings suggest that LC may be a more effective approach for literacy and math instruction. Why might this be the case? Both curricula have literacy and math learning goals that align with the Head Start Performance Standards. LC goals, however, are more numerous and specific, especially in the math domain. Other differences between the curricula are more striking. First, LC provides teachers with detailed, specific instructional activities and lesson plans that, if followed, ensure that purposeful instruction in literacy and math occurs on a daily basis. In the Creative Curriculum, teachers have latitude to design, select, and schedule activities. This provides more professional freedom, but also introduces variation in instructional content and time. Second, LC was implemented in the context of ongoing classroom mentoring and technical assistance. This is a valuable professional development resource that may be beyond the means of many early childhood programs. Third, LC includes a substantial parent curriculum, including weekly home activities and parent support. This degree of intensity in expected parental involvement is unusual for center-based programs. Because LC was implemented as a package, we cannot determine the degree to which different curriculum components contributed to the evaluation outcomes.

LC is a relatively intensive program to implement, and it is legitimate to question whether the observed magnitude of child outcome gains are worth the effort it takes to implement the curriculum. Teachers had to make several changes in their classroom practices. These changes included (a) altering schedules, (b) using more small-group instruction,

(c) incorporating literacy and math content on a more frequent basis, (d) using all staff members (not just lead teachers) to implement instructional activities, and (e) conducting ongoing assessments on a weekly basis. Although these changes were not necessarily easy to do, results of this evaluation suggest that teachers and parents felt their efforts were rewarded.

LC was developed in part to meet the needs of Hawai`i's multicultural API population. Culturally responsive practices help build cultural awareness, cultural competence, and self-esteem (Tharp, Estrada, Dalton & Yamauchi, 2000). It has been suggested that ethnic minority children are best served when culturally responsive teaching and educational excellence are mutually supporting tenets of classroom practice (Delpit, 1995; Ladson-Billings, 1995). By focusing simultaneously on developmentally appropriate academic content, culturally-responsive instruction, teacher professional development, and parental involvement, we hoped to maximize the benefits provided to our Head Start children. Because effective early childhood education can reduce academic risk (Barnett, 1995; Campbell & Ramey, 1994; Peisner-Feinberg et al., 2000), a curriculum like LC may be useful in improving the longer-term educational prospects of at-risk preschool children. LC improves preschoolers' academic readiness skills, which should positively affect their success in elementary school. In addition to strengthening children's cognitive skills, LC strengthened aspects of the parent-child system. By working with their children on a regular basis, parental self-efficacy increased and parents became more aware of their children's capabilities. By changing parents' behaviors, the positive benefits of LC may be better maintained in the future. If their families continue to hold high expectations and remain actively engaged in their children's learning, children should show lasting advantages in terms of academic performance and motivation. We are currently planning a kindergarten follow-up study of LC graduates, to determine whether the academic gains are maintained once children enter the formal school system and whether LC has long-term effects on parents' educational involvement.

REFERENCES

Abbott-Shim, M. (2001). *Validity and reliability of the Creative Curriculum for Early Childhood and the Developmental Continuum for Ages 3–5.* Available from Teaching Strategies, Inc., Box 42243, Washington, DC 20015.

Adams, M. J., Treiman, R., and Pressley, M. (1998). Reading, writing, and literacy. In: I. E. Sigel and K. A. Renninger (eds.). *Handbook of child psychology,* 5th ed. Volume. 4: *Child psychology in practice,* Wiley, New York, pp. 275–356.

Alexander, K. L., and Entwisle, D. R. (1988). Achievement in the first 2 years of school: Patterns and processes. *Monographs of the Society for Research in Child Development*. 53(No. 2, Serial 218).

Arnold, D. H., Fisher, P. A., Doctoroff, G. L., and Dobbs, J. (2002). Accelerating math development in Head Start classrooms. *Journal of Educational Psychology* 94:762–770.

Arunkumar, R., Midgley, C., and Urdan, T. (1999). Perceiving high or low home-school dissonance: Longitudinal effects on adolescent emotional and academic well-being. *Journal of Research on Adolescence* 9:441–466.

Balfanz, R. (1999). Why do we teach young children so little mathematics? Some historical considerations. In: J. Copley (ed.), *Mathematics in the early years*. National Council of Teachers of Mathematics, Reston, VA, pp. 3–10.

Barnhardt, J. E. (1991). Criterion-related validity of interpretations of children's performance on emergent literacy tasks. *Journal of Reading Behavior* 23(4):425–44.

Barnett, W. S. (1995). Long-term effects of early childhood programs on cognitive and school outcomes. *The Future of Children* 5(3):25–50.

Baroody, A. J., and Wilkins, J. L. M. (1999). The development of informal counting, number and arithmetic skills and concepts. In: J. Copley (ed.), *Mathematics in the early years*. National Council of Teachers of Mathematics, Reston, VA, pp. 48–65.

Baskt, K., and Essa, E. L. (1990). Emergent writers and editors. *Childhood Education* 66:145–150.

Blachman, B. A., Ball, E. W., Black, R. S., and Tangel, D. M. (1994). Kindergarten teachers develop phoneme awareness in low-income, inner-city classrooms. *Reading and Writing: An Interdisciplinary Journal* 6:1–18.

Blaisdell, K., and Mokuau, N. Kanaka maoli: Indigenous Hawaiians. In: Mokuau, N. (ed.). *Handbook of social services for Asian and Pacific Islanders*. Greenwood, New York, pp. 131–154.

Blevins-Knabe, B., and Musun-Miller, L. (1996). Number use at home by children and their parents and its relationship to early mathematical performance. *Early Development and Parenting* 5:35–45.

Bowman, B. T., Donovan, M. S., and Burns, M. S. (2001). *Eager to learn: Educating our preschoolers*. National Academy Press, Washington, D.C.

Bradley, L. and Bryant, P. (1983). Categorizing sounds and learning to read—a causal connection. *Nature* 301:419–421.

Byrant, D. M., Burchinal, M. B., Lau, L. B., and Sparling, J. (1994). Family and classroom correlates of Head Start children's developmental outcomes. *Early Childhood Research Quarterly* 9:289–309.

Byrne, B., and Fielding-Barnsley, R. (1995). Evaluation of a program to teach phonemic awareness to young children: A 2- and 3-year follow-up and a new preschool trial. *Journal of Educational Psychology* 87:488–503.

Byrne, B., and Fielding-Barnsley, R. (1991). Evaluation of a program to teach phonemic awareness to young children. *Journal of Educational Psychology*, 83:451–455.

Burns, M. S. and Casbergue, R. (1992). Parent-child interaction in a letter-writing context. *Journal of Reading Behavior* 24:289–311.

Campbell, F. A., and Ramey, C. T. (1994). Effects of early intervention on intellectual and academic achievement: A follow-up study of children from low-income families. *Child Development* 65:684–698.

Center on the Family (1999). Hawai`i family touchstones. Author, Honolulu, HI. Available from the University of Hawai`i Center on the Family, 2515 Campus Road, Honolulu, HI 96822.

Clements, D. H. (1999). Geometric and spatial thinking in young children. In: Copley, J. (ed.), *Mathematics in the early years*. National Council of Teachers of Mathematics Reston, VA, pp. 66–79.

Cost, Quality and Child Outcomes Study Team (1995). Cost, quality and child outcomes in child care centers, public report, 2nd ed. University of Denver, Denver. Available from the Department of Economics, University of Denver, Denver, Co.

CTB/McGraw-Hill (1990). Developing Skills Checklist norms book and technical manual. Author, Monterey, CA.

Department of Business, Economic Development and Tourism (DBEDT), 2002, The State of Hawai`i data book 2002; http://www.hawaii.gov/dbedt.

DeBaryshe, B. D. (1993). Joint picture-book reading correlates of early oral language skill. *Journal of Child Language* 20:455–461.

DeBaryshe, B. D. (1995). Maternal belief systems: Linchpin in the home reading process. *Journal of Applied Developmental Psychology* 16:1–20.

DeBaryshe, B. D., Binder, J.C., and Buell, M. J. (2000). Mothers' implicit theories of literacy instruction: Implications for children's reading and writing. *Early Child Development and Care*. 160:119–131.

Delgado-Geitan, C. (1991). Involving parents in the schools: A process of empowerment. *American Journal of Education* 100:20–46.

Delpit, L. (1995). *Other people's children: Cultural conflict in the classroom*. Plenum, New York.

Dickinson, D. K., and Sprague, K. E. (2001). The nature and impact of early childhood care environments on the language and early literacy of children from low-income families. In: S. B. Neuman and D. K. Dickinson (eds.), *Handbook of early childhood literacy research*. Guilford, New York, pp. 263–280.

Dodge, D.T. (2002). *The creative curriculum for preschool*, 4th Ed. Teaching Strategies, Inc., Washington, D.C. (Available from Teaching Strategies, Inc., Box 42243, Washington, DC 20015).

Fang, Z., and Cox, B. E. (1999). Emergent metacognition: A study of preschoolers' literate behavior. *Journal of Research in Childhood Education* 13:175–187.

Fantuzzo, J., Childs, S., Stevenson, H., Coolahan, K. C., et. al. The Head Start teaching center: An evaluation of an experiential, collaborative training model for Head Start teachers and parent volunteers. *Early Childhood research Quarterly* 11:79–99.

Feitelson, D., and Goldstein, Z. (1986). Patterns of ownership and reading to young children in Israeli school-oriented and nonschool-oriented families. *The Reading Teacher*. pp. 924–930.

Galinsky, E., Howes, C., Kontos, S., and Shinn, M. (1994). The study of children in family child care and relative care. Families and Work Institute, New York. Available from the Families and Work Institute, 330 7th Ave., New York, NY 10001.

Garces, E., Thomas, D., and Currie J. (2000). Longer term effects of Head Start. Labor and Population Program working paper series 00–20. Available from the Rand Corporation.

Glickman, C. (1981). *Developmental supervision: Alternative practices for helping teachers improve instruction*. Association for Supervision and Curriculum, Alexandria, VA.

Griffin, S., and Case, R. (1996). Evaluating the breadth and depth of training effects when central conceptual structures are taught. In: Case, R. and Okamoto, Y., *The role of central conceptual structures in the development of children's thought. Monographs of the Society for Research in Child Development* 61(1–2):v–265.

Griffith, P. L., Klesius, J. P., and Kromrey, J. D. (1992). The effect of phonemic awareness on the literacy development of first grade children in a traditional or a whole language classroom. *Journal of Reserach in Childhood Education* 6:87–92.

Hargrave, A. C. and Sénéchal, M. (2000). Book reading interventions with language-delayed preschool children: The benefits of regular reading and dialogic reading. *Early Childhood Research Quarterly* 15:75–90.

Hart, B. and Risley, T. R. (1995). *Meaningful differences in the everyday experiences of young American children*. Brookes, Baltimore, MD.

Holloway, S. D., Rambaud, M. F., Fuller, B., and Eggers-Pierola, C. (1995). What is "appropriate practice" at home and in child care?: Low-income mothers' views on preparing their children for school. *Early Childhood Research Quarterly* 10:451–473.

International Reading Association and the National Association for the Education of Young Children (1998). Learning to read and write: Developmentally appropriate practices for young children. *Young Children* 53:3–46.

Jordan, N. C., Huttenlocher, J., and Levine, S. C. (1994). Assessing early arithmetic abilities: Effects of verbal and nonverbal response types on the calculation performance of middle- and low-income children. *Learning and Individual Differences* 6:413–432.

Juell, C. (1988). Learning to read and write: A longitudinal study of 54 children from first through fourth grades. *Journal of Educational Psychology* 80:437–447.

Kana'iaupuni, S. M., and Ishibashi, K. (2003, June). Left behind? The status of Hawaiian students in Hawai`i public schools. (PASE report No. 02.03.13). Kamehameha Schools, Honolulu, HI; http://www.ksbe.edu/services/pase/pdf/Reports/k-12/-2_-3_13/pdf.

Klein, A., P. Starkey and A. B. Ramirez. (2002). *Pre-K mathematics curriculum-Early childhood*. Scott Foresman.

Klein, A., and Starkey, P. (1988). Universals in the development of early arithmetic cognition. *New Directions for Child Development* 41:5–26.

Klein, A., Starkey, P. and Wakely, A. (1999, April). Enhancing pre-kindergarten children's readiness for school mathematics. Paper presented at the Annual Meeting of the American Educational Research Association, Montreal. (ERIC document ED431556).

Kontos, S., Howes, C. and Galinsky, E. (1996). Does training make a difference to quality in family childcare? *Early Childhood Research Quarterly* 11:427–445.

Ladson-Bilings, G. (1995). But that's just good teaching! The case for culturally relevant pedagogy. *Theory into Practice* 34:159–165.

Lopez, G. L., and Scribner, J. D. (1999, April). Discourses of involvement: A critical review of parent involvement research. Paper presented at the annual meeting of the American Educational Research Association, Montreal, Canada.

Lundberg, I., Frost, J., and Petersen, O. (1988). Effects of an extensive program for stimulating phonological awareness in preschool children. *Reading Research Quarterly* 23:263–284.

Malone, D. M., Straka, E., and Logan, K. (2000). Professional development in early intervention: Creating effective inservice training opportunities. *Infants and young children* 12:53–63.

McBride-Chang, C. (1998). The development of invented spelling. *Early education and development* 9:147–160.

McCartney, K. (1984). Effect of day care environment on children's language development. *Developmental Psychology* 20:244–260.

Nation, K., and Hulme, C. (1997). Phonemic segmentation, not onset-rime segmentation, predicts early reading and spelling skills. *Reading Research Quarterly* 32:154–167.

National Association for the Education of Young Children and the National Council of Teachers of Mathematics, Early childhood mathematics: Promoting good beginnings, 2002, April.; http://www.naeyc.org/resources/position_statements/psmath.htm.

National Council of Teachers of Mathematics (2000). *Principles and standards for school mathematics*. Author, Reston, VA.

National Center for Education Statistics (1999). *The condition of education* [Online].; http://nces.ed.gov/nationsreportcard/TABLES//SDTTOOL.HTM). [Accessed 04/14/00.)

Nelson, G. D. (1999). Within easy reach: Using a shelf-based curriculum to increase the range of mathematical concepts accessible to young children. In: Copley, J. (ed.), *Mathematics in the early years.* National Council of Teachers of Mathematics, Reston, VA, pp. 135–145.

Nurss, J., Abott-Shim, M., and McCarty, F. (1998). Writing in the transition classroom: Results of an effective staff development plan. ERIC documents #ED436004.

Odell, S. (1990). *Mentor teacher programs.* National Education Association, Washington, D.C.

Office of Children and Youth (1993). The bottom line: A complication of data on children and youth. State of Hawai`i, Honolulu, Hawai`i. (Available from the Office of the Governor, Office of Children and Youth, P.O. Box 3044, Honolulu, HI 96802).

Payne, A. C., Whitehurst, G. J., Angell, A. L. (1994). The role of the home literacy environment in the development of language ability in preschool children from low-income families. *Early Childhood Research Quarterly* 9:427–440.

Peisner-Feinberg, E. S., Burchinal, M. R., Clifford, R. M., Culkin, M. L., Howes, C., Kagan, S. L., Yazejian, N., Byler, P., Rustici, J., and Zelazo, J. (2000). *The children of the Cost, Quality, and Outcomes Study go to school: Technical report.* University of North Carolina at Chapel Hill, Frank Porter Graham Child Development Center, Chapel Hill.

Phillips, G., and McNaughton, S. (1990). The practice of storybook reading to preschool children in mainstream New Zealand families. *Reading Research Quarterly* 25:196–212.

Pontecorvo, C., and Zucc101hermaglio, C. (1989). From oral to written language: Preschool children dictating stories. *Journal of Reading Behavior* 21:109–126.

Reid, D. K., Hresko, W. P., and Hammill, D. D. (2001). *The Test of Early Reading Ability,* 3rd. ed. Pro-Ed, Austin.

Reynolds, A. J. (1992). Comparing measures of parental involvement and their effects on academic achievement. *Early Childhood Research Quarterly* 7:441–462.

Roberts, T. A. (2003). Effects of alphabet-letter instruction on young children's word recognition. *Journal of Educational Psychology* 95:41–51.

Rowell, E. H. (1998). A letter a week, a story a day, and some missed opportunities along the way: A study of literacy in pre-kindergarten classes. *Child Study Journal* 28:201–222.

Saxe, G. B., Guberman, S. R., and Gearhart, M. (1987). Social processes in early number development. *Monographs of the Society for Research in Child Development.* 52:(2 Serial No. 216).

Scarborough, H. S. (2001). Connecting early language and literacy to later reading (dis)abilities: Evidence, theory, and practice. In: Neuman, S. B. and Dickinson, D. K. (eds.). *Handbook of early childhood literacy research.* Guilford, New York, pp. 97–110.

Shonkoff, J. R., and Phillips, D. A. (2000). *From neurons to neighborhoods: The science of early childhood development.* National Academy Press, Washington, D.C.

Snow, C. E., Burns, M. S., and Griffin, P. (eds.). (1998). Preventing reading difficulties in young children. National Academy Press, Washington, D.C.

Sophian, C. (2004). Mathematics for the future: Developing a Head Start curriculum to support mathematics learning. *Early Childhood Research Quarterly,* 19, 59–81.

Sophian, C. (1999). Children's ways of knowing: Lessons from cognitive development research. In: Copley, J. (ed.), *Mathematics in the early years,* (pp. 11–20). National Council of Teachers of Mathematics, Reston, VA, pp. 11–20.

Spodek, B. (1996). Selecting professional development activities for early childhood teachers. *Early Childhood Development and Care* 117:113–121.

Stanovich, K., E. (1986). Matthew effects in reading: Some consequences of individual differences in the acquisition of reading. *Reading Research Quarterly* 21:360–407.

Stanovich, K. E., Cunningham, A. E., and Feeman, D. J. (1984). Intelligence, cognitive skills, and early reading progress. *Reading Research Quarterly* 19:278–303.

Starkey, P., and Klein, A. (2000). Fostering parental support for children's mathematical development: An intervention with Head Start families. *Early Education and Development* 11:659–680.

Stipek, D., Feiler, R., Byler, P., Ryan, R., Milburn, S., and Salmon, J. M. (1998). Good beginnings: What difference does a program make in preparing young children for school? *Journal of Applied Developmental Psychology* 19:41–66.

Sue D. W. and Sue, D. (1990). *Counseling the culturally different: Theory and practice*, 2nd ed. Wiley, New York.

Sulzby, E., Barnhart, J., and Hieshima, J. A. (1989). Forms of writing and rereading from writing: A preliminary report. In: Mason, J. M. (ed.). *Reading and writing connections*. Allyn and Bacon, Boston, pp. 31–61.

Tharp, R. G. (1989). Psychocultural variables and constants: Effects on teaching and learning in schools. *American Psychologist* 44:349–359.

Tharp, R. G., Estrada, P., Dalton, S. S., and Yamauchi, L. A. (2000). *Teaching transformed: Achieving excellence, fairness, inclusion, and harmony*. Westview, Boulder, CO.

Treiman, R., and Baron, J. (1983). Phonemic-analysis training helps children benefit from spelling-sound rules. *Memory and Cognition* 11:382–389.

Treiman, R., and Rodriguez, K. (1999). Young children use letter names in learning to read words. *Psychological Science* 10:334–338.

Uba, L. (1994). *Asian Americans: Personality patterns, identity and mental health*. Guilford, New York.

University of Hawai`i Instructional Research Office (2002). Enrollment of Hawaiian students, University of Hawai`i Manoa Fall 2001. Author, Honolulu, HI.

Vellutino, F. R., and Scanlon, D. M. (2001). Emergent literacy skills, early instruction, and individual differences as determinants of difficulties in learning to read: The case for early intervention. In: Neuman, S. B. and Dickinson, D. K. (eds.), *Handbook of early childhood literacy research*. Guilford, New York, pp. 295–321.

Weissberg, R. P. and Greenberg, M. T. (1998). School and community competence-enhancement and prevention programs. In: I. E. Sigel and K. A. Renninger (eds.), *Handbook of child psychology*, 5th ed., Volume 4. *Child psychology in practice*. Wiley, New York, pp. 877–356.

Whitehurst, G. J., Arnold, D. S., Epstein, J. N., Angell, A. L., Smith, M, and Fischel, J. E. (1994). A picture book reading intervention in day care and home for children from low-income families. *Developmental Psychology* 30:679–689.

Whitehurst, G. J., Falco, F. L., Lonigan, C. J., Fischel, J. E., DeBaryshe, B. D., Valdez-Menchaca, M. C., and Caulfield, M. B. (1988). Accelerating language development through picture book reading. *Developmental Psychology* 24:552–559.

Whitehurst, G. J. and C. J. Lonigan (2001). Emergent literacy: Development from prereaders to readers. In: Neuman, S.B. and Dickinson, D.K. (eds.), *Handbook of Early Literacy Research*. New York and London: Guilford, New York and London, pp. 11–29.

Zill, N., Resnick, G., and McKey, R. H. (1999, April). What children know and can do at the end of Head Start and what it tells us about the program's performance. Paper presented at the Biennial Meeting of the Society for Research on Child Development, Albuquerque, NM.

Section III

Approaches to Supporting Learning in Middle- and High-School Settings

The three chapters in this section report research programs that involve learning in adolescence. The researchers examine social and cognitive development in the institutional settings of middle- and high-schools. The headline of Laurie Schick's chapter, "You cannot cheat the footwork," is a quote from a dance teacher who instructs adolescents in complicated dance moves at the same time that he provides them with moral training. Schick's in-depth linguistic analyses of the teacher's use of "cheating," "lying," and "blame" make the link between the context of the dance class and the greater context of participating as moral agents in society. Schick's groundbreaking work makes the link between the literatures of moral development and language socialization. The chapter is an elegant demonstration of fieldwork methodology in a context where learning about morality could be easily taken for granted. The "learning with understanding" that happens in the dance classes is deepened by the use of moral metaphors in the embodied context of dancing. The notion that a simple metaphor is worth a thousand words applies here: one could imagine a much more lengthy discussion of morality in an ethics class that might not have the same effect on the adolescents' learning.

Lois Yamauchi, Tasha Wyatt, and Jacquelin Carroll summarize research on enacting five critical standards of effective pedagogy in a high-school program that was designed to be culturally-relevant. Based on sociocultural theory, the five standards of effective pedagogy are focused on the contextualized collaboration between students and teachers in a productive activity, where student learning is supported through small group discourse, extensive speaking and writing, and thoughtful feedback from the teacher. It is clear from the ethnographic field notes that are used in the chapter to describe the learning experiences of high school students that the five standards provide a way to make education more culturally relevant and effective at the same time. Several levels of the learning context are considered, with links between the high school students, their teacher, and the university consultant who both guides and studies the process. The authors conclude the chapter by noting that the five standards can be adopted by new teachers and in classrooms for all students, not just those from diverse backgrounds.

Nina Buchanan reports research that makes sociocultural theory come to life. Buchanan describes the West Hawai`i Explorations Academy (WHEA), a context of learning that integrates research from motivation, learning, and intelligence into a curriculum that meets the educational needs of students, many of whom might otherwise reject school. Students in the WHEA program learn English composition, math, and science in the service of projects which they design themselves. Students also learn about self-motivation and responsibility, as they are held accountable to deadlines and to showing progress in each area of education. The learning at WHEA described by Buchanan appears to be seamlessly connected to everyday life and problem-solving. From the reader's perspective, it seems that WHEA students learn a great deal about core subjects as well as personal development without getting bogged down in the usual achievement tests and milestones found in most schools; further, the students seem to learn without even realizing they are, a key component of culture as a process of learning.

Chapter 8

"You Cannot Cheat the Footwork"
Moral Training in Adolescent Dance Classes

Laurie Schick

INTRODUCTION

In this chapter I examine how language socialization and embodied practice, performed together in middle dance school classes, can train students
how to behave morally as well as how to dance competently. More specifically, I examine how one teacher uses dance as a vehicle for teaching his
students not only how to understand but also how to practice the moral
concepts and values that are entailed in this classroom's use of the English
words 'cheat,' 'lie,' and 'blame.'

Part of the title for this chapter, "You cannot cheat the footwork," is
taken from an admonition uttered by a middle school dance teacher while
instructing a class of 7th and 8th graders on how to do the waltz. At the
time of the utterance, the teacher, Mr. B, was in the introductory stages of
teaching his class how to do the basic waltz 3-step. When he saw that many
of the students were doing two steps instead of three, he stopped the class
and gave them an admonition as well as detailed instructions in the form
of demonstrations (Trans. 1a; see Appendix for Transcription Key):

Transcript 1a: You cannot cheat the footwork (Waltz lesson)

1.	Mr. B	**you CANNOT CHEAT the FOOTwork.**
2.		*((Mr. B demonstrates wrong footwork))*
3.		('at's) cheating the footwork =
4.		= I'm taking two steps =

5.   = it has to be
          ((starts demonstrating the right footwork on "be"))
6.   o:ne . two . three
7.   o: ne . two . three
8.   °('t) has to be three steps°
          ((stops demonstrating))
9.   can we now do four *((meaning 4 sets of the 3-step))*

If we examine this short sequence of interaction in isolation, i.e., if we take it out of the larger context of this classroom's ongoing interaction, it is possible to think that Mr. B is using the term 'cheat' primarily as a kind of rhetorical device in order to emphasize for his students the importance of taking the requisite number of steps. For by identifying the taking of two steps instead of three as a matter of cheating rather than merely as a mathematical miscalculation, Mr. B is also conveying a negative moral judgment toward any student who may be taking those two steps instead of three. For as any current or former student in any U.S. middle school can tell you, there is practically nothing worse for a student in a class than to be accused of cheating on a test and nothing worse for a kid on the playground than to be accused of cheating in a game. Given this, as a non-participating observer I might well ask whether Mr. B is over dramatizing the importance of learning how to do the waltz while at the same time needlessly shaming the two-stepping students by using the term 'cheat' to describe what, in the "greater scheme of things," might appear to be a very minor offence. What I hope to show by the end of this chapter is that instead of capitalizing on the power of the term 'cheat' to teach his students the waltz, Mr. B is in fact using dance instruction as a means to teach his students the skills they need in order to both understand and practice a number of culturally shared moral values, with not cheating being only one of them.

FIELDWORK AND METHODOLOGY

The research presented in this chapter is part of a larger study of the language socialization of morality among older children and adolescents at a public middle school in the Los Angeles area. The data from the larger study include approximately 100 hours of videotape collected in three middle school dance classes, one middle school drama class, one middle school social studies class, and one high school dance club (which met on the middle school campus). In addition to the videotaping, data collection includes notes from informal conversations and interviews with students, teachers and administrators and the collection of artifacts such as copies of assignments and student journals.

All of the videotaped sequences discussed here come from one Beginning and one Advanced dance class, with both being taught by the same teacher, Mr. B. Mr. B is an experienced professional performer as well as dance teacher with a resume that includes three decades of teaching public schools students in grades 1–8 as well as teaching in an after school program for students in grades 9–12. The Beginning class discussed in this chapter had 34 students; virtually all of them were 6th graders aged 11–12. The Advanced class had 29 students who were all 7th and 8th graders aged 12 to 14. Both of these classes roughly reflected the ethnic and economic profile of the school itself. Official records for the first year of data collection for the school report: 0.3% American Indian; 5.1% Asian; 18.4% Black; 1.8% Filipino; 33.2% Hispanic; 0.5% Pacific Islander; 40.8% White (this includes a number of recent Armenian and Russian immigrants). Approximately 50% of the students were from middle and upper-middle class backgrounds and 50% from lower and lower-middle class backgrounds, with 40% of all students at the school participating in school lunch programs.

Data analysis is qualitative and focuses on the transcription and micro-analysis of the ways in which language and embodied practice are being used to socialize both the cognitive understanding as well as the performative instantiation by individuals of this community's shared definitions of 'lying,' 'cheating,' and 'blame.' Transcription techniques follow overall those used in conversation analysis, with slight variations that include the addition of frames taken from the videotapes (see Appendix for a transcription key). Macro-analytical techniques such as ethnographic analysis are used to help (a) identify culturally shared values and practices and (b) analyze how language is being used to foster individual behavior that adheres to these shared values and practices. As examples of this process, I analyze four sequences of interaction: one in which the teacher operationally defines the term 'cheating,' two in which the he defines 'lying,' and one in which he describes the kinds of actions for which students deserve 'blame.' In addition to examining how the teacher operationally defines these terms, I also analyze how he uses embodied demonstrations and student practice in order to help his student learn (a) skills which will help them NOT to lie or cheat and (b) what they need to do in order to take responsibility to prevent and/or remedy the consequences of lying and cheating.

THEORETICAL FRAMEWORK: LANGUAGE
SOCIALIZATION AND EMBODIED PRACTICE

An Interdisciplinary Perspective

In his social intuition theory of moral development, Jonathan Haidt (2001) compares the findings of researchers from a number of different disciplines. In giving his rationale for doing so, Haidt cites Edward O. Wilson's (1998) "resurrection" of the term 'consilience' (p. 839). In Haidt's summary of the concept, 'consilience' refers "to the degree to which facts and theories link up across disciplines to create a common groundwork of explanation" (p. 839). Accordingly, Haidt suggests that we as researchers will be able to get a fuller understanding of how individuals develop the moral intuitions upon which moral judgments are made only by integrating the findings of researchers who have examined the subject from a variety of different perspectives. This approach calls to mind the old East Indian parable of the six blind men; the blind man who felt the tail thought the elephant was like a rope, the man who felt the ear said it was like a fan, and so on. In the words of the American poet John Godfrey Saxe, who transmitted this parable to a Western audience in poetic form, "Though each was partly in the right, all were in the wrong" (1852/2003). In an effort to get it more right than wrong, Haidt formulated his social intuitionist theory by taking into account the findings of a number of different kinds of research perspectives. This is his summary of his social intuitionist theory:

> Moral development is primarily a matter of the maturation and cultural shaping of endogenous intuitions. People can acquire explicit propositional knowledge [e.g., knowledge expressed through language] about right and wrong in adulthood, but it is primarily through participation in custom complexes (Shweder et al., 1998) involving sensory, motor, and other forms of implicit knowledge (Fiske, 1999; Lieberman, 2000; Shore, 1996) shared with one's peers during the sensitive period of late childhood and adolescence (Harris, 1995; Huttenlocher, 1994; Minoura, 1992) that one comes to feel, physiologically and emotionally (Damasio, 1994; Lakoff & Johnson, 1999), the self-evident truth of moral propositions (p. 828).

While the data and analyses presented in this chapter support overall most of the above propositions, they particularly support Haidt's (2001) claim as a social psychologist, Shweder's (1991, 1998) claim as a cultural psychologist, and Damasio's (1994) and Lieberman's (2000) claim as a cognitive neuroscientist, that physical movement, practice, and repetition are key to the way children, adolescents, and even adults develop the social, cognitive, affective and language skills they need to become morally competent members of the communities in which they live and interact on a daily basis.

Agreeing with Haidt (2001) and Wilson (1998) that it is important to integrate a number of different research methods and findings, I have adopted here an approach to language socialization that allows me, as researcher, to study the reciprocal role of language socialization and embodied practice in the socialization of morality among early adolescents in middle school. In the analysis presented here, I am primarily integrating two approaches to understanding how language socializes ideas, feelings, beliefs and values within the context of everyday interaction. These two approaches are: (a) Hilary Putnam's (1975) "socio-linguistic" theory of 'meaning' in language and (b) Elinor Ochs and Bambi Schieffelin's (Ochs, 1996, 2001; Ochs & Schieffelin, 1979, 1984; Schieffelin & Ochs, 1986, 1996) theory of language socialization.

Hilary Putnam's Socio-linguistic Theory of Meaning

In his socio-linguistic theory of "The Meaning of 'Meaning'" (1975) in language, Putnam argues that all words in any language need to be "operationally definable" in order for them to have real meaning for speakers in any given linguistic community (p. 251). This includes even deceptively simple words such as 'pencil'; nouns like 'pencil' are deceptively simple because they refer to common objects in the environment and thus are generally thought to need little or no contextualization to be understood. Putnam, however, claims that even these kinds of words need to be "operationally" defined within the socio-cultural context in which they are used. In addition, and perhaps even more importantly for the discussion at had, the operational definitions that these word acquire will also depend on the experience, social role, and, just as importantly, the social obligations that come to be associated by the speaker with any given word at any given time in any given linguistic community. Putnam (1975) explains his idea this way:

> The nature of the required minimum level of competence depends heavily upon both the culture and the topic. . . . In our culture speakers are required to know what tigers look like (if they acquire the word 'tiger,' and this is virtually obligatory); they are not required to know the fine details (such as leaf shape) of what an elm tree looks like. English speakers are *required by their linguistic community* to be able to tell tigers from leopards; they are not required to be able to tell elm trees from beech trees (p. 249, his emphasis).

In addition, as Putnam also points out, there are also different levels of linguistic competence within language communities as well. For example, what the word 'gold' means to me, especially from an operational point of view, is very different from what the word 'gold' means to a chemist or an assayer whose job it is to determine scientifically whether and to what degree a chunk of shiny, gold-looking metal is in fact a valuable piece of gold on the open jewelry market or perhaps the type of gold that can be used in manufacturing or in dentistry.

What I am proposing here is that both the need for operational definitions and the existence of different levels of expertise is even more true of words that tend to have socio-cultural and moral meanings (as opposed to word like 'pencil' and 'tiger' because their meanings are referentially tied to objects). With regard to the data examined here I am therefore also arguing that English-language speakers need to achieve more than linguistic and cognitive competence with regard to their use and understanding of words such as 'lying,' 'cheating,' and 'blame'—speakers are also generally required to reach a minimum level of operational or behavioral competence as well. But how do members gain such competence? One way to help answer this question is to use the methodologies associated with disciplines such as language socialization, linguistic anthropology, and conversation analysis to examine the processes by which individuals become competent, functioning members of their respective communities.

Ochs' Language Socialization and Related Pedagogical Theories

Elinor Ochs, one of the founders of language socialization theory and research methodology, defines the discipline this way:

> Language socialization research examines how language practices organize the life span process of becoming an active, competent participant in one or more communities.... Unlike language acquisition research, the analytic focus rests neither on less experienced persons as acquirers nor on more experienced persons as input but rather on socially and culturally organized interactions that conjoin less and more experienced persons in the structuring of knowledge, emotion, and social action (2001, p. 227).

This idea of "conjoining less and more experienced persons in the structuring of knowledge, emotion, and social action" is also echoed in Lev Vygotsky's (1978) zone of proximal development (ZPD), Wood, Bruner, and Ross' (1976) scaffolding, Barbara Rogoff's (1990) guided participation, and Shirley Brice Heath's (1998) research on collaborative adult-youth work projects. Heath's discussion of how older children learn by "Working through Language" (1998) as they collaborate with adults on joint arts and athletic projects is perhaps especially appropriate here in that it argues that not only very young children but also older children and adolescents are able to learn a number of skills that prepare them for adulthood by "working through language" as they work on projects with more experienced adults. In the dance class interactions described below, I am proposing that the adolescents who are enrolled in these classes are also "working through language" as they are learning a number of skills that will help prepare them to act according to the moral-ethical principles that are considered important not only in their immediate classroom but also in the larger communities in which they live and interact. In addition, I am also proposing that far from being extraneous, the kind of adult guidance that I found in these dance classes, particularly during practice and rehearsal, can constitute an important contribution to the older child's and adolescent's development of the knowledge and skills he or she needs not only to *reason about* but also to *practice* that which is operationally entailed in the linguistically expressed moral concepts of 'lying,' 'cheating,' and the giving and taking of 'blame.'

LANGUAGE SOCIALIZATION IN DANCE CLASS

I begin with a brief overview of the pedagogical and embodied practice routines typical of Mr. B's dance classes. Most of the dances taught in these classes are performed for recreational purposes both in a wide variety of foreign countries and in many different communities throughout the United States. American examples include the square dance, polka, swing and waltz. The international dances come from a number of different countries including Algeria, Bulgaria, China, Ghana, Ireland, Mexico, and Samoa, to name a few. Not surprisingly, one of the stated goals of Mr. B's classes is to teach students respect and understanding for diverse cultures through teaching those cultures' dances.

As already mentioned above, the vast majority of the students in Mr. B's Beginning classes are 6th graders (mostly aged 11, some start when they are 10 and some finish when they are 12). About half of the students have had little or no dance experience prior to enrolling in Mr. B's Beginning classes, and a few have had considerable dance experience given their age. Almost none of the students, however, have had experience learning and performing dances from so many diverse cultures. Nearly all the students in Mr. B's Advanced classes are 7th and 8th graders (aged 12–14) who have had one semester (about 17 weeks) of dance experience in one of Mr. B's Beginning classes.

Classroom and Instruction Routines

The routine of activities for a typical class period is similar for both Beginning and Advanced classes. As each period begins students change into their dance clothes, get their journal notebooks out of their designated cupboard, sit on the dance floor, and begin answering the daily journal question, which is already written on the chalkboard. Mr. B takes roll while students are writing their answers to the question. After roll Mr. B conducts a brief discussion on the journal question. Then students put away their journals and spread out on the dance floor for warm-ups. At the beginning of the semester in Beginning classes Mr. B will lead warm-ups, but after a week or two, a different student will volunteer each day to lead warm-ups. Often for the Advanced classes Mr. B will have the students do their warm-ups without a leader; the logic here is that every student is now experienced enough to take responsibility for doing a proper warm-up by herself.

After warm-ups the lesson(s) of the day will begin. The activities for the daily lessons will vary somewhat depending on whether Mr. B is introducing a brand new dance or whether the class is at various stages of practicing, refining, or rehearsing an already-introduced dance that they will perform either for fun or for a theatrical production. In all cases these lessons are taught in a recurring cycle of (a) teacher-fronted instruction, which includes embodied demonstrations, of a particular step or choreography; (b) embodied practice or performance by students of the dance task at hand, with this practice being led, depending on the level of competence being displayed by the dancing students, by a demonstrating Mr. B; and then (c) an evaluation of the practice or performance (which can come from students as well as the teacher). These cycles are similar to those that have been identified as typical classroom Initiation-Response-Evaluation (IRE) patterns (Cazden, 2001; Mehan, 1979). One way in which they are similar is that each cycle is generally short and is usually followed by yet another cycle or more of instruction and practice, with each cycle usually being based on the immediately prior evaluation. The first three sequences of classroom interaction under examination here take place during the early stages of introducing a new dance step; the last sequence occurs during a classroom performance for fun of a dance that the class has already ostensibly learned well and performed correctly many times before.

Sequence 1: Cheating the Footwork

The first sequence to be examined here is the same one I introduced at the start of this chapter as, "You cannot cheat the footwork" (repeated in Trans. 1b, which is the same as Trans. 1a except with an added frame grab). When I first introduced the sequence I gave very little information as to how it fit within the larger context of this class' ongoing interaction; now I will be giving more.

"You cannot cheat the footwork" takes place about halfway through the semester of an Advanced class. This means (a) the students have already had a fair amount of experience learning how to dance different kinds of traditional and recreational dances and (b) they are familiar with this classroom's routines and expectations for performance. However, and as already stated above, for this lesson the students are receiving their first instruction on how to do the particular step at hand, which is the basic waltz 3-step. In addition, and making the learning task more complicated, the students are also learning how to do the step (a) with a partner, (b) so that they and their partner will be able both to rotate around each other, and (c) so that they and their partner will be able to revolve together (while rotating) as they dance around the floor in a large circle.

To facilitate today's demonstration-and-practice session Mr. B has asked the students to place themselves in one large circle around the dance floor facing inward so that they can see him in the center as he demonstrates and leads practice (see Trans. 1b for a photograph of the formation). In order for the students to be able to do the step so that they can both rotate and revolve around the circle with a partner, they must make sure that they are actually taking three rotating steps instead of just taking two big ones as they travel to their next spot around the circle. However, after several cycles of practice, there are still some students who are not taking three steps. This is when Mr. B stops the practice and reframes the lesson by characterizing the taking of two steps instead of three as "cheating" (Trans. 1b).

Transcript 1b: You cannot cheat the footwork (Waltz lesson)

| 10. | Mr. B | **you CANNOT CHEAT the** FOOT**work.** |
| 11. | | *((Mr. B demonstrates wrong footwork))* |

12.   ('at's) cheating the footwork =
13.   = I'm taking two steps =
14.   = it has to be
             ((starts demonstrating the right foogwork on "be"))
15.   o:ne .   two . three
16.   o: ne .   two . three
17.   °('t) has to be three steps°
             ((stops demonstrating))
18.   can we now do four *((meaning 4 sets of the 3-step))*

Without looking at the embodied demonstration, i.e., by just looking at the language, it might be easy to conclude that Mr. B is simply defining cheating as a question of mathematical calculation, i.e., as a matter of taking two steps instead of three. However, by examining his demonstration we can see that the definition is much more complex. First, Mr. B demonstrates the incorrect move by taking two very wide steps such that he is able to cover as much or more ground as he would have covered had he taken the proper three. Moreover, he does not rotate in the required manner but merely steps sideways; in addition, with his arms out and palms inward he is, through his body positioning, further emphasizing the sideways trajectory of the incorrect movement. With this embodied demonstration, Mr. B operationalizes or entails his definition of cheating as not simply the taking of two instead of three steps, but also as the taking of two exaggeratedly big steps such that he is able at least to cover the required distance, thereby compensating for, if not also "covering up," the fact that he is actually doing the step incorrectly.

Although many of the students are still taking two steps instead of three, it is nevertheless the case that they are still in the early stages of learning. In other words, they may not yet have the skills to cover the ground they need to cover without cheating. As if to give them the benefit of the doubt, Mr. B does the following: (a) he provides them with an opportunity to practice the step again (Trans. 1, Line 9), thereby also giving them an opportunity to attain the skills they need to become competent enough not to cheat; and (b) he does not directly accuse anyone of cheating but frames his proposition as a general definition, i.e., as more of an "academic" lesson than as an allegation. He accomplishes this in part by the way he frames their current action of cheating as something that is being done to the footwork rather than something that is being done to a person with whom one has a social relationship. In other words, by telling the students not to "cheat the footwork" and the footwork only, Mr. B is essentially defining cheating here as a concrete operation or embodied action, and not necessarily as a social or interpersonal action. In the next sequence, however, Mr. B does include the social or interpersonal dimension in his operational definition not of what it means to "cheat the footwork" per se, but of what it means to actually "lie" to someone by not doing the footwork the way one should.

Sequence 2: Lying to Me

In the next sequence, "Lying to me" (Trans. 2a-b), Mr. B and one of his Beginning classes are in what I would identify as the second stage of learning an Irish 3-step. Despite the fact that these are Beginning students in the early stages of learning this particular step, they have nevertheless already had a few months of experience learning other kinds of dances in Mr. B's class, including other 3-steps. In addition, and contrary to the waltz lesson, here Mr. B is only asking the student to perform the step in a practice line; i.e., he is not yet asking them to move according to any kind of choreography such as rotating with partners while revolving in a circle on the dance floor. What is more, even though the students are still in the early stages of learning this step, they have already seen Mr. B demonstrate it several times and they have had several opportunities to practice the step as Mr. B continues to demonstrate along with their practice. This kind of "guided practice" routine could also be identified as a variation of what Rogoff (1990) defines as "guided participation" and what Haidt (2001) and Shweder (1998) identify as an immersion in the repeated practice of culturally established routines.

In order to show more clearly how this particular guided practice routine works, I have divided the "This is lying to me" sequence into two parts, which are represented in Transcripts 2-a and 2-b respectively. I begin with the first part (Trans. 2-a), which contains two of the several mini-practice sessions that occur immediately prior to Mr. B's operational definition of lying. The sequence below begins at the end of one of Mr. B's routine cues to begin practice (these cues usually start with "ready?" and end with "and").

Transcript 2a: This is lying to me (Irish 1-2-3 practice)

1.	Mr. B	A:ND	((Cues students for practice))
2.		ONE TWO THREE,	
3.		we need three hundred of them.	
4.		one two three?	((Kids practice steps while Mr. B calls steps and demonstrates))

5.	one two three?	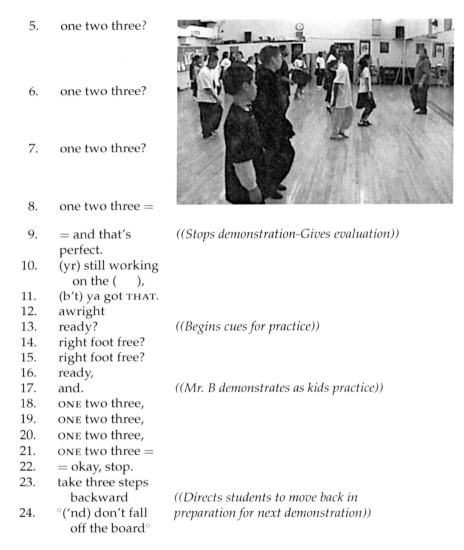
6.	one two three?	
7.	one two three?	
8.	one two three =	
9.	= and that's perfect.	*((Stops demonstration-Gives evaluation))*
10.	(yr) still working on the ( ),	
11.	(b't) ya got THAT.	
12.	awright	
13.	ready?	*((Begins cues for practice))*
14.	right foot free?	
15.	right foot free?	
16.	ready,	
17.	and.	*((Mr. B demonstrates as kids practice))*
18.	ONE two three,	
19.	ONE two three,	
20.	ONE two three,	
21.	ONE two three =	
22.	= okay, stop.	
23.	take three steps backward	*((Directs students to move back in*
24.	°('nd) don't fall off the board°	*preparation for next demonstration))*

After Mr. B stops the practices, he asks the students to move back from the mirror as preparation for the next part of the lesson (Trans. 2-a, Lines 23–24). As soon as he sees they have moved back, Mr. B essentially announces that the next topic in the lesson will be to give an operational definition of 'lying' by saying emphatically, "THIS IS LYING TO ME" (Trans. 2-b, Line 25). Instead of immediately explaining what "this" is in words, Mr. B first adds the directive, "don't lie to me" as he turns to face the mirror, thereby framing what is to follow as morally significant directive (Line 26). Then, once he has turned, he restarts his statement about what lying is, except that this time he verbally says only, "THIS IS" and then replaces the words "lying to me" with a demonstration of the incorrect way to do the step (Line 27), thereby defining lying to him as doing the step incorrectly.

Transcript 2b: This is lying to me (Irish 1-2-3 practice)

25. Mr. B   THIS IS LYING
             TO ME.
26.   don't LIE to
             me.
             *((turns to face
             mirror as he
             speaks))*
27.   THIS IS,   *((Mr. B demonstrates 'lying to me'))*

28.   *((demonstrates
             a step while
             facing the
             mirror))*

29.   am I
             stepping
             on all three
             steps?
             *((turning to
             class as he
             speaks))*
30. Girl   no:::

On the surface, it could appear as though Mr. B is defining 'lying' as he did 'cheating' (Trans. 1), i.e., simply as a concrete, embodied operation having everything to do with doing the footwork correctly but little or nothing to do with interpersonal or social interaction. This, however, is not the case because here Mr. B did not say simply, "This is lying" but, rather, "This is lying to me" (Line 25). By adding the phrase "to me," Mr. B is using language to define 'lying' here as not only (a) an embodied, sensorimotor kind of operation, but also as (b) a social, interpersonal and interactional kind of operation. The addition of this interpersonal dimension is also accomplished by the way in which "to me" indexes, and thus makes relevant, the social roles that students and teachers are expected to fulfill when interacting within the classroom environment.

There are additional entailments with respect to the opertaionalization of 'lying' within the context of classroom interaction as a 'situated activity' (Goodwin, 1990). For example, it is the job and thus also the obligation of the teacher to give instruction on the academic subject of the class; but it is also the job and obligation of the students to respond to that instruction with their best effort to learn thereby. More specifically and with respect to the notion of 'lying,' if my teacher asks me to do something and I respond by saying "no" or by clearly refusing in some other way, I may be labeled as being "uncooperative" but probably not as "lying" per se. However, if I am asked to perform a task for which I have been given considerable instruction and practice and which I simply perform, without asking for help, the easy rather than the proper way, then I could easily be labeled as "lying" as well as "uncooperative."

There is also one additional operational entailment associated with the situated activity in which this definition of lying is embedded. Although Mr. B does not directly accuse anyone of lying, he does so implicitly because of the placement of the definition within this class' typical IRE pattern. Specifically, both the definition and admonition about lying occur in a typical evaluation position, i.e., after the students have performed the step in question. What is more, this evaluation occurs after the students have performed the step not once but several times. Therefore this definition and admonition about lying can be construed not only as (a) an evaluation of student performance but also as (b) an implicit accusation by the speaker that some students are not only lying, but also that they are lying to him personally.

In the above sequence, then, 'lying' is being defined both as an embodied and as a social or interpersonal act. Moreover, 'lying' is not being defined as necessarily something a student *says*, but more as something that a student actually *does*. Thus from both an embodied and a social-interpersonal point of view, 'lying' becomes operationally entailed as (a) something that is *done* rather than something that is merely said and (b) as something that is done to another person or other people with whom one has at least an immediate if not also an ongoing social relationship.

Sequence 3: "There are children lying"

In the next sequence, "There are children lying" (Trans. 3), Mr. B takes the operational definition of 'lying' a step further. Once again, this sequence also takes place in one of Mr. B's Beginning classes, except that this time the lesson is salsa and the primary teacher is not Mr. B but a guest teacher, whom I call Mr. L. Mr. L is a very experienced salsa dancer (having competed in professional competitions) and also an experienced middle school teacher, except that he usually teaches a subject other than dance. As a dance teacher per se, then, he is much less experienced than Mr. B.

Another difference between the "Lying to me" sequence (Trans. 2a-b) and this one is that instead of merely defining 'lying' and/or implicitly suggesting some students may be lying to him, Mr. B is now explicitly saying that at least some of the students are actually lying right then and there during the class. In addition, this time he is not just *warning* them about lying to *him*—now he is explicitly *accusing* them of lying to a third party, i.e., their guest teacher, Mr. L. Following is a discussion of Mr. B's warrant for doing so.

Prior to the start of "There are children lying" (Trans. 3), Mr. L has already begun his lesson by demonstrating and guiding the students as they practice, in lines and without choreography, the basic salsa step. At this point in the lesson Mr. L. has already demonstrated the step in front of the class, led the students through practice first without music, and is now leading them through practice with the music. As in "This is lying to me" (Trans. 2), Mr. L, as teacher, has not yet asked students to do the step either with partners or with any kind of choreography. Nevertheless, many of the students are still having trouble just doing the basic salsa.

As the sequence begins, the music is still playing as Mr. L brings this mini-practice to a close by asking the students whether they are doing the step (Trans. 3, Line 2); more specifically, he is asking them to let him know whether they think they've got the basics or not. But none of the students answers. Mr. L's "awright" (Line 3) in response to the students' silence is evidence that he has apparently taken their lack of response as an affirmative answer, i.e., that they are able to do the basic step okay. Mr. B, however, is not content to let this affirmative-answer-by-default stand, as can be seen in the way he stops the music and interrupts Mr. L before he can progress on to the next stage of the lesson (Lines 4–6).

Transcript 3: There are children lying (Salsa lesson)

1.   ((*music playing; kids talking*))
2.   Mr. L.   yeah? you guys (doin') it?
3.   awright

4.		*((Mr. B stops musci; kids still talking))*
5.	Mr. B.	Mr. L., I'd like to report that
6.		**there are children LYing to you**
7.	Mr. L.	what
8.	Mr. B.	LY:ing, Mr. L. looks like this
9.		one two three four *((softer voice))* *((demonstrates the step as he talks))*
10.	Mr. L.	*((Mr. L walks toward Mr. B, looking at Mr. B's feet))*

Mr. B.

11.	Mr. B.	one two three four
12.		one two three four *((stops demonstration))*
13.		why is that a lie?
14.		**we talked about this before**
15.	kid	(because . . .)
16.	Mr. B.	why is that a lie?
17.	kid	(because)
18.	Mr. B.	because (I have the step wrong)
19.		isn't that awful,
20.		**children are lying**
21.	Mr. L.	you guys
22.	Mr. B.	(steppin'---foot)
23.	Mr. L.	awri:ght
24.		I'm glad somebody's watchin' out for me *((smiling, as he walks to front of class))*
25.	listen	*((faces mirror to begin another demonstration of the basic step))*

There are both similarities and differences between this sequence and the previous ones (Trans. 1b and Trans. 2a-b). The main similarity is that in all three sequences Mr. B is defining both 'cheating' and 'lying' as not necessarily something someone says but as something that someone does. Sequences 2 and 3 are similar in the way that Mr. B includes an interpersonal dimension by defining 'lying' as "lying to me" in Sequence 2 (Trans. 2-b, Line 25) and by accusing the students of lying to Mr. L in Sequence 3 (Lines 5–6).

One difference between Sequences 2 and 3 is that in Sequence 2 Mr. B directly addresses the students by saying "this is lying to me. don't lie to me" (Trans. 2, Lines 25–26), but in Sequence 3 he is addressing his comments directly to Mr. L. by telling him, "there are children LYing to you" (Trans. 3, Line 6). By addressing his accusation of students lying directly to Mr. L instead of to the students, Mr. B is not only taking the students to task but Mr. L as well. For by addressing his accusation directly to Mr. L, Mr. B is also accusing Mr. L of not fulfilling his responsibility for teaching the students just as surely as he is accusing the students of not taking responsibility for their part in the learning process as well. The implied accusation against Mr. L is based on the fact that he let the children lie to him about having gotten the step, thereby indicating also that they needed no more special practice at this time. That Mr. L accepts Mr. B's criticism is apparent by his comment, "I'm glad somebody's watchin' out for me" (Line 24). In addition to displaying Mr. B's position as expert teacher, the interaction in Sequence 3 also demonstrates clearly that participants can display multiple levels of expertise not only with regard to their ability to dance, but also with regard to (a) their abilities to do dance training and, perhaps even more importantly here, (b) their abilities to recognize and address the consequences of lying within this particular social context.

Another example from Sequence 3 that illustrates the instantiation of different levels of expertise can be found in the way that Mr. B characterizes the lying students as "children" (Lines 6 and 20). This is a common practice for Mr. B, especially in his beginning classes. When the students are lying or cheating or being lazy or mean to other students, Mr. B tells them they are either acting like children or, possibly worse yet, like elementary school students. When they are being honest, hard working, respectful and kind, he characterizes them as acting more like middle school students. In this salsa lesson, the students were acting like children because they were lying, and they therefore needed adult intervention. But Mr. L did not intervene, thereby giving Mr. B warrant to address his initial accusations of children lying to Mr. L, who, according to Mr. B's point of view as senior instructor, should have been the one to intervene first. And intervene is precisely what Mr. B does once again in the following sequence, but this time his intervention is not only even more drastic than it was in the salsa interaction—it is also addressed directly to a whole group of students themselves.

Seqence 4: Blame

In this final sequence, Mr. B once again intervenes while students are performing a dance, except that this time he is doing so not in order to clarify the operational meaning of such morally questionable actions as 'lying' or 'cheating'; this time he is clarifying the operational meaning and consequences of not taking responsibility, which in this case he operationally defines as the taking and remediation of 'blame.' More specifically, by his intervention Mr. B not only defines for students what it means to deserve the 'blame' for irresponsible behavior; he also gives them a practice session in order to teach them how to take responsibility for addressing and/or remedying their own irresponsible actions.

As this sequence opens, the class is in the middle of doing a dance for fun that they have already been taught and should already know well. The dance is a set dance because the dancers are moving together in a series of predefined or already "set" formations. For the portion of the dance being done in Sequence 4, the formation requires the following: (a) dancers are to be dancing as couples and (b) all the couples in the set have to place themselves in two lines with partners facing each other. In the traditional version of the dance all the ladies would be in one line facing their gentlemen partners who are in turn facing them in a parallel line. The choreography for this part of the dance requires the head couple (i.e., the couple who are facing each other at the head of the each line) to move crisscross down the lines as they take turns hooking elbows and circling first each other, then the next couple, then each other, then the next couple, and so on until they reach the bottom of the lines (see photograph in Transcript 4).

On this day, all of the students in the class have divided themselves into two sets. Although both "sets" of students seem to be having a great time dancing, right in the middle of the dance and just before the start of the Sequence 4, Mr. B abruptly turns off the music and then, as the sequence starts, says, "ugh-uh not acceptable" (Trans. 4, Line 1), after which he then proceeds to make the entire set of dancers do the dance again, this time without music.

Transcript 4: Blame (Set dance)

1 Mr. B.   ugh-ah <u>not</u> acceptable
2   <u>GET</u> BACK UP here

 3   2 Girls   *((starting back to the head of the lines))*
 4   Mr. B   <u>not</u> acceptable
 5   it's a <u>DA</u>:nce
 6   2 Girls   (0.3) *((girls still walking up to head of lines))*
 7   Mr. B   <u>right</u> elbow <u>three</u> half turns
 8   <u>GO:</u>
 9   2 Girls   *((start the turns at top of lines))*
10   Mr. B   one, two, three
11   (left to the si:de)
12   **I blame these two,**
13   **and <u>every</u> <u>single</u> <u>couple</u> in the set**
14   **cuz <u>every</u> <u>single</u> <u>couple</u>**
15   **did the wrong elbow with Heather**
16   2 Girls   *((start turns going down the lines with other students))*
17   Mr. B   and Dale?
18   (chu- fr-) <u>you</u> know this <u>da:nce</u>
19   2 Girls   (10 sec.) *((Heather-Dale as couple continue turns down the lines))*

Heather   Dale

20   Mr. B   three halves at the bottom
21   2 Girls   *((reach the bottom and start their turns))*
22   Mr. B   one two (three)
23   (holding hands)
24   2 Girls   *((get into their places at bottom of the lines))*
25   Mr. B   fine
26   *((starts music))*

What happens in "Blame" (Trans. 4) is similar to "Children are lying" (Trans. 3) in that in both sequences Mr. B clearly does more than just define 'lying' and 'blame' operationally from an embodied and social interactional point of view. He does more than define these terms as abstract or general moral concepts. He defines them as concrete actions that are pragmatically instantiated within the context of the culture (i.e., the shared values and routine practices) of this particular classroom. What is more, Mr. B is also providing guided practice in order to help students to acquire the skills they need in order to perform the tasks in question in the correct way. This is the case even in "Children are lying," for by taking Mr. L as well as the students to task, Mr. B is also effectively directing Mr. L to begin another cycle of demonstration and practice of the basic salsa step. Moreover, by requiring every dancer in the set to do the problematic choreography over again, Mr. B is in effect also giving every single dancer an opportunity both to remedy their transgression and to learn to do better by doing the same step again, but this time correctly. What is more, by requiring this remediation in the "Blame" sequence, Mr. B is not simply applying some sort of general principle that everyone in the group is responsible for the actions of every one of its members. Rather, Mr. B is making it crystal clear that he is having every single dancer in the set do it over because, in actual fact, "every single couple did the wrong elbow with Heather" (Trans. 4, Lines 14–15).

Along with blaming every single couple for doing the wrong step (Trans. 4, Lines 14–15), Mr. B is also implying that he blames them not simply for cheating the footwork but also for lying about cheating as well. This implication of lying can be construed from the fact that virtually every single student in this class has had ample opportunity to learn, practice and perform this dance, and has even demonstrated that they can perform this dance correctly on many previous occasions. Therefore, from an operational point of view, they could easily be seen as 'lying' in a similar way to the students in the "Children are lying" sequence; i.e., they were being seen, in effect, as lying about their level of knowledge and skill because they did the turn the wrong way despite the fact that they had in the past demonstrated they knew better. That knowing better is an important criterion for assigning blame is in turn demonstrated in the way that Mr. B singled out Heather's partner, Dale, for special culpability. Based on this criterion of "knowing better," Mr. B's warrant for singling Dale out is twofold: (a) Dale ended up doing the wrong elbow with Heather not once like the other dancers but as many as six different times because of the fact that she was Heather's partner in this set; and (b) Dale had been publicly acknowledged to be one of the best dancers in the class and had in the past been given and taken responsibility for helping other students learn new dance steps. In sum, then, by making it clear that he blames every single couple in the set because they in fact did the wrong thing, Mr. B is also making it clear that both blame and responsibility are to be applied not simply on the basis of an abstract principle (e.g., the group is responsible for the actions of its members), but on the basis of actions that people take when they are interacting with each other moment-to-moment within the context of spontaneously unfolding social circumstances. By having the students perform the remedial action of doing the elbow turns once again, Mr. B is also socializing his students in becoming increasingly expert at both understanding and practicing (a) what it means to lie and cheat during the course of performing an activity such as dance, (b) what it means to take the blame for lying or cheating, and also (c) what it means to take responsibility for both acquiring and practicing the skills they need not only to become competent dancers but also to become morally competent members of their communities as well.

CLOSING THOUGHTS ON LANGUAGE SOCIALIZATION AND EMBODIED PRACTICE

The dance class data presented above, as analyzed from a language socialization and embodied practice perspective, supports a number of claims that have already been made about the socialization and development of moral judgment and conduct by researchers using other investigative methodologies. For example, this language socialization study supports, generally speaking, Shweder's (1991, 1998) basic claim that moral values are learned through participation in discourse that is carried out within the context of culturally-based custom complexes. In addition, this study also supports, again generally speaking, Lakoff and Johnson's (1980; 1999) idea that we as human beings construct abstract concepts similarly to the way we construct metaphors, that is, by grounding these concepts in how we experience physical structures and embodied practices. This idea applies not only to how we conceptualize abstract ideas in general but also to how we conceptualize moral principles and values in particular (Lakoff and Johnson, 1999, pp. 290ff.).

In connection with this idea that abstract concepts are often (if not always) formulated by a kind of metaphorical or analogical connection with embodied experience, my study also supports Haidt's (2001) claim as a social psychologist, Shweder's (1991, 1998) claim as a cultural psychologist, and Damasio's (1994) and Lieberman's (2000) claims as cognitive neuroscientists, that physical movement, practice, and repetition are key to the way we as human beings develop the kinds of social, cognitive, affective and language skills we need to become morally competent members of our communities. However, perhaps the importance of practice, repetition, and/or rehearsal in the socialization of responsible and moral behavior is nowhere more clearly summarized than in the following excerpt from a speech Mr. B gave one of his dance classes after they failed to behave responsibly during a fire drill (Trans. 5).

Transcript 5: Rehearsal for a Fire Drill

1.	Mr. B	I take [fire drills]. <u>very</u> <u>ser</u>iously
2.		you are not to talk
3.		one of the facts of performers is that
4.		you re<u>hears:e</u> . in the <u>stu</u>dio,
5.		to try ta get to a hundred percent.
6.		to try to get things <u>per</u>fectly.
7.		your technique and everything.
8.		when you perform on STAGE
9.		you end <u>u:p</u> with your technique about seventy-five percent.
10.		because other things take over.
11.		the audience, performing,
12.		being aware of the sta(ge)-
13.		you known it REALLY DOES af<u>fect</u>,
14.		so:. the point is
15.		if you can <u>GET</u> to a hundred percent in the <u>stu</u>dio,
16.		that seventy-five percent('s) <u>aw</u>fully good
17.		(0.25)
18.		and it looks perfect.
19.		>because all the other things add to it < too
20.		(0.5)
21.		but- the lo:ss of technique is made up =
22.		= by your <u>sta:ge</u> presence and all o' <u>that</u> stuff
23.		IT'S THE SAME THING with FIRE drill
24.		(0.25)
25.		if you can re<u>hearse</u> it at a hundred perCE::nt
26.		when it really-
27.		if you go ou:t and start smellin' the <u>smoke</u> 'r seeing <u>fla:</u>mes
28.		and you've re<u>hearsed</u> it.
29.		a hundred per<u>ce:nt</u>.
30.		then the SEVENTY-FI:VE. sixty percent that we're LEFT with =
31.		= when people start. a:ll that adrenaline comes in =
32.		= because you <u>actually</u> <u>see</u> something going <u>wro:ng</u>
33.		(it) still leaves us o-<u>KA:Y</u>

Lakoff and Johnson (1980) say that the activities and terminology associated with physical activities such as dance can provide excellent embodied metaphors for understanding and talking about social and moral values and behavior. What I am proposing here, and I have no doubt that Mr. B would concur, is that dance not only provides a metaphor for talking and thinking about abstract concepts such as moral values. Dance also provides the kind of embodied practice that can help any novice to become more expert at behaving "okay," even when the "adrenaline comes" as "you actually see something going wrong." This kind of embodied practice is thus not only the way a dancer can learn what is entailed in not "cheating the footwork"—she can also learn the skills she needs in order not to cheat in life as well.

Anecdotally, I can say that I witnessed noticeable changes in the way that many of the students in the Mr. B's classes started to take practice and rehearsals seriously; more specifically, I saw students begin to take responsibility not only for their own performance but also for the performances of others as well as themselves, especially within the context of performing set dances for fun and ensemble dances for theatrical performance. This responsibility took the form of requesting more practice based on self-evaluation, gently helping classmates who were having trouble getting the steps, and even asking uncooperative dancers to shape up. This increasing competence in the students' moral as well as dance performance was due, I believe, not so much to any rules that Mr. B imposed, but rather to the way in which students were able to gain, in part through the process of guided practice, the skills they needed not only to know *what* to do, but also *how* to do it.

Appendix: Transcription Key

underline	LOUDER VOICE
SMALL CAPS	Slightly higher pitch
FULL CAPS	SIGNIFICANTLY HIGHER PITCH
small caps with underline	SLIGHTLY HIGHER PITCH WITH LOUDER VOICE
FULL CAPS WITH UNDERLINE	HIGHER PITCH WITH LOUDER VOICE
BOLD FONT	HIGHLIGHTS UTTERANCES THAT ARE KEY TO THE ANALYSIS
: (colon)	Lo:ng vowel or, with more colons, a lo::nger vowel
- (dash)	Cut off word (incomplete or abruptly stopped)

= (equal sign)	Latching; next speech is begun with no pause
(words in single parentheses)	Unclear or inaudible speech
((words or description in double parentheses))	Notes concerning context, environment, nonverbal expressions, etc. (e.g., laughing, background noise)
((double parentheses with italics))	Descriptions of embodied actions, gestures, etc.
. (period)	Full stop with lowering intonation
, (comma)	Slightly rising and/or lowering then slightly rising tone at the end of a word
○ ○	Quieter talk (compared to immediately prior speech)
> <	Faster talk (compared to immediately prior speech
? (question mark)	Rising tone (sounds like the tone at the end of a yes/no question on English)
! (exclamation point)	Emphatic
Kid	Student, unidentifiable, including by gender
Girl/s	Female student/s, identity unknown

REFERENCES

Cazden, C. B. (2001). *Classroom discourse: The language of teaching and learning* (Second ed.). Heinemann, Portsmouth, NH.

Damasio, A. R. (1994). *Descartes' error: Emotion, reason and the human brain*. Grosset/Putnam, New York.

Fiske, A. P. (1999). *Learning culture the way informants do: Observing, imitating, and participating.* Unpublished manuscript. University of California, Los Angeles.

Goodwin, M. H. (1990). *He-said-she-said: Talk as social organization among black children.* Indiana University Press, Bloomington.

Haidt, J. (2001). The emotional dog and its rational tail: A social intuitionist model of moral judgment. *Psychological Review* 108 (4):814–834.

Harris, J. R. (1995). Where is the child's environment? A group socialization theory of development. *Psychological Review* 102:458–489.

Heath, S. B. (1998). Working through language. In: Hoyle, S. M., and Adger, C. T. (eds.), *Kids talk: Strategic language use in later childhood*, Oxford University Press, New York, pp. 217–240.

Huttenlocher, P. R. (2002). *Neural plasticity: The effects of environment on the development of the cerebral cortex*, Harvard University Press, Cambridge, MA.

Lakoff, G., and Johnson, M. (1980). *Metaphors we live by.* University of Chicago Press, Chicago.

Lakoff, G., and Johnson, M. (1999). *Philosophy in the flesh: The embodied mind and its challenge to western thought.* Basic Books, New York.

Lieberman, M. D. (2000). Intuition: A social cognitive neuroscience approach. *Psychological Bulletin* 126(1):109–137.

Mehan, H. (1979). *Learning lessons: Social Organization in the Classroom,* Harvard University Press, Cambridge, MA.

Minoura, Y. (1992). A sensitive period for the incorporation of a cultural meaning system: A study of Japanese children growing up in the United States. *Ethos* 20(3):304–339.

Ochs, E. (1996). Linguistic resources for socializing humanity. In: Gumperz, J. J., and Levinson, S. C. (eds.), *Rethinking linguistic relativity,* Cambridge University Press, Cambridge, England, pp. 407–437.

Ochs, E. (2001). Socialization. In: Duranti, A. (ed.), *Key terms in language and culture.* Blackwell Publishers, Oxford, England, pp. pp. 227–229

Ochs, E., and Schieffelin, B. B. (1979). *Developmental pragmatics,* Academic Press, New York.

Ochs, E., and Schieffelin, B. B. (1984). Language acquisition and socialization: Three developmental stories and their implications. In: Shweder, R. and LeVine, R. (eds.), *Culture theory: Essays on mind, self and emotion,* Cambridge University Press, New York, pp. 276–320.

Putnam, H. (1975). The meaning of 'meaning', *Mind, language and reality: Philosophical Papers* Volume 2, Cambridge University Press, Cambridge, pp. 215–271.

Rogoff, B. (1990). *Apprenticeship in thinking: Cognitive development in social context,* Oxford University Press, Oxford, England.

Saxe, J. G. (1852/2003). *The blind men and the elephant.* Retrieved, from the World Wide Web: http://www.mastermason.com/BrotherGene/wisdom/blind_men_and_the_elephant.htm

Schieffelin, B. B., and Ochs, E. (1986). *Language socialization across cultures.* Cambridge University Press, Cambridge, England.

Schieffelin, B. B., and Ochs, E. (1996). The microgenesis of competence: Methodology in language socialization. In: Slobin, D. I., Gerhardt, J., Kyratzis, A., and Guo, J. (eds.), *Social interaction, social context, and language: Essays in honor of Susan Ervin-Tripp,* Lawrence Erlbaum Associates, Mahwah, NJ, pp. 251–263.

Shore, B. (1996). *Culture in mind: Cognition, culture, and the problem of meaning.* Oxford University Press, New York.

Shweder, R. A., Goodnow, J., Hatano, G., LeVine, R. A., Markus, H., and Miller, P. (1998). The cultural psychology of development: One mind, many mentalities. In: Damon, W. (ed.), *Handbook of child psychology,* 5th edition, Volume 1, Wiley, New York, pp. 869–937.

Shweder, R. A., (with Much, N. C). (1991). Determinations of meaning: Discourse and moral socialization. In: Shweder, R. A. (ed.), *Thinking through cultures: Expeditions in cultural psychology,* Harvard University Press, Cambridge, MA, pp. 186–233.

Vygotsky, L. (1978). *Mind in society: The development of higher psychological processes.* Harvard University Press, Cambridge, MA.

Wilson, E. O. (1998). *Consilience: The unity of knowledge.* Alfred A. Knopf, New York.

Wood, D., Bruner, J. S., and Ross, G. (1976). The role of tutoring in problem solving. *Journal of Child Psychology and Psychiatry* 17:89–100.

AUTHOR NOTE

Laurie Schick, Department of Applied Linguistics, University of California, Los Angeles.

The research for this paper was conducted as part of a larger study on the language socialization of morality among middle school students in performing arts classes.

This research was made possible in part through a Dissertation Improvement Grant in Linguistics from the National Science Foundation. I would also like to thank Marjorie Harness Goodwin for her guidance as my Dissertation Chair and Debra Friedman for her critique of an earlier draft of this paper. An earlier version of this paper was presented as part of a panel on "The Embodied Mind and Consciousness: Developmental Perspectives" at the Piaget Conference (2002).

Correspondence may be addressed to Laurie Schick, Dept. of Applied Linguistics & TESL, University of California, Los Angeles, Los Angeles, CA 90095–1531. Email is: schick@humnet.ucla.edu.

Chapter 9

Enacting the Five Standards for Effective Pedagogy in a Culturally Relevant High School Program

Lois A. Yamauchi, Tasha R. Wyatt, and Jacquelin H. Carroll

THE FIVE STANDARDS FOR EFFECTIVE PEDAGOGY

The Five Standards for Effective Pedagogy are principles of instruction for teaching students from culturally and linguistically diverse backgrounds. The Five Standards are (a) teachers and students working together in productive activity; (b) supporting students' language development across the curriculum through extensive speaking and writing; (c) contexualizing new information with what students already know, (d) supporting complex thinking by focusing on higher level thought and providing feedback; and (e) enacting instructional conversations—teaching through small group discourse (Tharp, Estrada, Dalton, & Yamauchi, 2000). Each of the Standards is discussed in more detail later in this chapter.

The Five Standards derive from Vygotsky's (1978) sociocultural theory. Vygotsky believed that social interaction was the basis of all higher psychological processes such as one's beliefs, values, strategies, and ways of viewing the world. According to this perspective, children interact through language and other symbols with adults and more capable peers and eventually appropriate those symbols. The Five Standards are helpful to educators because they translate sociocultural theory into pedagogical practice (Tharp et al., 2000). For example, they emphasize that teachers need to organize activities so that they have opportunities to discuss concepts with students and provide assistance for students as they engage in problem solving, analysis, and other higher level thinking.

The Five Standards can be considered aspects of good instruction for all students. However, they are particularly important for those who have typically had more negative experiences, as those individuals are the ones who have the most to benefit from reorganizing education in ways that maximize learning. The Standards emphasize an active role of teachers in the classroom. Although the cooperative learning movement focused attention on the importance of peer assistance, teachers often became less present in those settings, and students lost opportunities to learn from them.

The Five Standards also highlight the importance of the cultural context of learning. For Vygotsky (1978), all learning is situated in a particular sociocultural context that determines what, how, and from whom one learns. All students come to school with a unique history of knowledge, expectations, and goals that are shaped by interactions within their cultural communities. Those who have difficulty in school may have different goals and expectations than that of school personnel (Tharp, 1989; Tharp et al., 2000). For example, students who come from a more collective home culture, where the goals of the group are emphasized over that of the individual, may have difficulty adjusting to a more competitive and individualistic school environment.

In addition, some groups of students may have little experience with the concepts being taught in school. The third Standard, *Contextualization*, emphasizes that learning is promoted when new information is connected to students already know and expect from home, school, and community (CREDE, 2003; Tharp, et al., 2000). This includes teaching in ways that are familiar to students and using curriculum that connects academic concepts to students' prior knowledge. In this chapter, we discuss the Hawaiian Studies Program (HSP) at Wai'anae High School, a high school program that is exemplary for its contextualization of students' cultural experiences with more traditional academic learning. The purpose of the chapter is to describe program and to discuss the application of the Five Standards.

THE HAWAIIAN STUDIES PROGRAM (HSP)

The HSP is a community-based, culturally contextualized program for students in grades 10–12. The program is located at Wai'anae High School, a public high school on the rural, western tip on the island of O'ahu, Hawai'i. The primary goal of the HSP is "to empower students to become self-sufficient, productive, contributing members of their own community and of the global community, caring for the land and natural resources that make life possible" (Hawaiian Studies Program, 1997, p.2). The program was conceptualized as a science-based academic program that would help students make connections between academic concepts and the Hawaiian culture.

In 1995, three teachers, along with members of two community-based organizations, approached the principal of Wai'anae High School about starting a Hawaiian studies program. Their vision of the program included improving academic outcomes and making school more engaging and relevant for students. At a school where over half of the student population is Hawaiian or part-Hawaiian, it made sense to develop a program that was centered around Hawaiian cultural issues in order to nurture students' self of sense and to connect what students learn in school to what they already know.

The HSP founders saw firsthand the evidence of students' disconnectedness to and lack of success in school. The drop-out rate at Wai'anae High School is one of the highest in the State (Hawai`i State Department of Education, 2002a). Even when students stay in school, many fail to earn enough credits to advance to the next grade (Hawai`i State Department of Education, 2002b; 2003). In addition, standardized test scores at Wai'anae also tend to be low. The HSP founders were also motivated by evidence that Hawaiian students, in general, do not perform as well as other groups of students on standardized test scores, have higher drop out and grade retention rates, are under-represented in higher education, and over-represented in special education (Kanaiaupuni & Ishibashi, 2003; Office of Hawaiian Affairs, 1994; Takenaka, 1995; University of Hawai`i Institutional Research Office, 2002).

What resulted was the Hawaiian Studies Program at Wai'anae High School (HSP), a program that integrates the learning of Hawaiian values, knowledge, and practices with more traditional secondary curriculum in science, social studies, and English. Although the majority of students in the HSP is Native Hawaiian, the program is open to all students at the high school in Grades 10–12. Students who enroll in the program come from a wide range of academic backgrounds, including honors students, those in special education, and some who are at-risk for dropping out.

The program is built around weekly field work in the Wai'anae community that is conducted in cooperation with community members. For example, students participate in archaeological surveys and excavations of cultural sites in the Wai'anae Valley that are led by professional archaeologists. With consultation from the governmental agency that regulates water use, other students and teachers conduct chemical and visual tests of the Wai'anae and Makaha Valley stream environments to study the effects of diverting water for household consumption. Another group of students conducts field work at the Wai'anae Coast Comprehensive Health Center, shadowing health care professionals, planning and implementing community health care initiatives, and assisting in patient care.

There are a number of indicators that the HSP is succeeding in its goals to promote student learning and academic engagement. HSP students have good attendance, are less likely to drop out of school, and are more likely to enroll in post-secondary institutions of higher education or training than students in the high school at large (Carroll, 1999). Enrollment in the program is also associated with an increase in students' grades. In the only school year in which these data were analyzed (1998–99), 86% of first year Hawaiian Studies students and 64% of second year Hawaiian Studies students increased their GPAs from the previous year. An external evaluation of the program found that compared to peers at Wai'anae High School who were not enrolled in the program, HSP students felt more connected to their school and local communities, were more likely to agree that they were valued members of those communities by peers and adults, reported being more knowledgeable of and interested in Hawaiian history and culture, and also to be more likely to have thought about careers and post-secondary education (RMC, 2003).

Success of the program is also evident in HSP student awards and honors. Prior to HSP students entering the State Science Fair in 2000, students at Wai'anae High School had not entered the competition in 16 years. The first year that HSP students entered, they became the State first place winners in two categories. In 2001 and 2002, teams of HSP students also won another statewide science competition to create a model of a watershed. In 2001, students were invited to present their work at four national and regional water quality conferences, and a HSP student won the district science fair competition in Behavioral Sciences.

Enrolling about 2,000 students, Wai'anae High School is a large public high school. Such a large school enrollment itself presents challenges for youth adjustment. A national study of health-related behaviors showed that as school size increased, adolescents' feelings of connectedness to school and academic achievement decreased (Morrison, 2002). Students in larger schools also are more likely to drop out and are less likely to have parents who are involved in their education (Raywid, 1999). The HSP uses teaming and looping to create a smaller learning environment within a large high school. Teaming refers to a small group of teachers working with a sub-section of the student population (Trimble & Miller, 1998). Looping involves teachers moving with their students to the next grade level (Black, 2000; Little & Dacus, 1999).

In the HSP, three to four teachers teach 60–100 students, who remain with them for two years. Although the numbers of sophomores who elect to enroll in the HSP is increasing, most HSP students enter as juniors and remain for their senior year. Thus, for at least two consecutive years, students have the same teachers and peers for the majority of their course work. Students identify with their peers and the program and develop a connection to the HSP teachers and community partners. When asked what they liked most about the program, students most often mentioned the sense of *'ohana* or family in the program (Ceppi, 2000).

ENACTMENT OF THE FIVE STANDARDS IN THE HAWAIIAN STUDIES PROGRAM

The Center for Research on Education, Diversity, & Excellence (CREDE) is a federally-funded research and development center at the University of California. CREDE sponsored 31 research projects nationwide that focused on how to best educate students from culturally and linguistically diverse backgrounds. In 2001, CREDE adopted the HSP as a demonstration school because it exemplified enactment of a number of the Five Standards (Yamauchi, 2002). As part of the demonstration site activities, HSP teachers receive professional development to learn about the Five Standards and plan for ways to enact the Standards in their classroom and field instruction. The teachers also evaluate enactment of the Standards by watching videotaped excerpts of each other's instruction and rating the lessons using the Standards Performance Continuum (SPC), an instrument developed by CREDE researchers to measure enactment of the Standards (CREDE, n. d. a.).

The SPC provides criteria for evaluating the enactment of each Standard along a continuum of "not observed" to "integrating." The highest level of intergrating is achieved when three or more of the Standards are rated at the enacting level. Thus, for each of the Standards, evaluators must decide whether a particular lesson meets the criteria for "not observed," "emerging," "developing," or "enacting." In the following sections we describe the Five Standards and discuss some of the ways they have been enacted in the HSP. We refer to criteria from the SPC that is used to determine the extent to which each Standard is observed in a particular lesson. (See Table 1).

Joint Productive Activity

Joint Productive Activity (JPA) is the process in which teachers and students engage in activities that result in tangible or intangible products

Table 1. Criteria for the Developing and Enacting Levels of the CREDE
Standards Performance Continuum (SPC)

Standard	Developing	Enacting
Joint Productive Activity	The teacher and students collaborate on a joint product in a whole-class setting, OR students collaborate on a joint product in pairs or small groups.	The teacher and a small group of students collaborate on a joint product.
Language and Literacy Development	The teacher provides structured opportunities for academic language development in sustained reading, writing or speaking activities.	The teacher designs and enacts instructional activities that *generate* language expression and development of content vocabulary, AND *assists student language expression and development* through questioning, rephrasing, or modeling.
Contextualization	The teacher makes incidental connections between students' prior experience/knowledge from home, school, or community and the new activity/information.	The teacher integrates the new activity/information with what students already know from home, school, or community.
Challenging Activities	The teacher designs and enacts activities that connect instructional activities to academic content OR advance student understanding to more complex levels.	The teacher designs and enacts challenging activities with clear standards and performance feedback AND assists the development of complex thinking.
Instructional Conversation	The teacher converses with a small group of students on an academic topic AND *elicits student talk* with questioning, listening, rephrasing, or modeling.	The teacher: designs and enacts an instructional conversation (IC) with a clear academic goal; listens carefully to assess and assist student understanding; AND questions students on their views, judgments, or rationales. All students are included in the IC, AND student talk occurs at higher rates than teacher talk.

Note. From "Standards Performance Continuum," by the Center for Research on Education, Diversity, & Excellence (CREDE), n.d.a, Santa Cruz, CA: Author

(Tharp et al., 2000). Tangible products include artifacts such as reports, concept maps, math problems, debates, games, and plays. Intangible products are more conceptual, such as elaborated understandings, procedures, or other ideas. JPA goes beyond cooperative learning in that it requires that teachers become actively involved in group work, not just designing and observing student activity. Cohen and her colleagues (e.g., Cohen & Lotan, 1997) caution against teachers dominating participation in classroom conversations and other activity settings. While this can be a problem, teachers' presence in classroom activity is also necessary to push students to think in more complex ways (Tharp et al., 2000). For example, teachers and other adults can use their expertise to ask the right questions, provide feedback, model and use other forms of assistance that scaffold students' thinking.

Enacting JPA requires *collaboration* between teachers and students. CREDE (n. d.b) defines collaboration as "joint activity that results in shared ownership, authorship, use, or responsibility for a product." Group member contributions must add to the final product. For example, in order for a discussion to be a JPA, student and teacher comments should build toward the group's common understanding, what Vygotsky (1978) called intersubjectivity.

Implementing JPA at the enacting level also requires that the joint activity occur between teachers and a *small* group of students (typically defined as 5–7 individuals). A small group is necessary because it provides more assurance that all members will contribute in meaningful ways. Large group activities allow some students to be more passive or silent, and this can go unnoticed by the teacher. Thus, a teacher's collaboration in a whole class setting, or students collaborating in pairs or small groups without the teacher, is only considered to be JPA at the "developing" level.

An early assessment of the enactment of the Five Standards in the HSP, suggested that JPA has always been a strength of the program (Ceppi, 2000). This may be because the program was designed to incorporate small groups of students, teachers, and community members collaborating during weekly field work. The nature of the field projects lend themselves well to enacting this Standard in that students are divided into small groups and the projects are often organized around the development of tangible products (e.g., an archaeological map, a stream assessment, or a video to promote healthy behaviors). The projects often develop from community needs and focus on real problems for which the teachers may not have necessarily had a particular answer in mind. In addition, HSP teachers often do not have all the knowledge and skills necessary to solve problems generated by the field work and look to community partners to provide assistance in these less familiar areas. Thus, in the field, the teachers become learners with their students, adopting a role that fits well with the notion of JPA.

JPA in the HSP is also prominent in the development of student port-folios. Throughout the year, students are required to collect evidence that indicates how they are meeting the program objectives. The students are required to reflect on these work samples and to compile this documenta-tion in a portfolio. Students work on the portfolios in their English classes, but are also encouraged to discuss what to include in the portfolio with other teachers and community members who are involved in their field work. Teachers meet with small groups of students to discuss the meaning of the program objectives, what students might include in the portfolio, and why students believe selected artifacts reflect the objectives.

At the end of the year, students participate in a mock job interview that involves presenting their portfolios to "sympathetic strangers," con-sisting of community members from the university, government and local businesses. Teachers, community members, and peers provide students with suggestions on how to add more clarity to their portfolio reflections and how to best present themselves in the mock interview. Teachers and students role play and engage in practice interviews that are sometimes videotaped. After watching the videotapes, students provide self- and peer-critiques of the interviewee's performance.

Language and Literacy Development

The second Standard focuses on the goal of developing language and literacy in all classrooms, not just those designated as language arts (CREDE, n. d.c; Tharp et al., 2000). When teachers plan and enact activi-ties that are designed for students extended reading, writing or speaking, their lessons are considered at least at the "developing" level of this Stan-dard. In order to be scored at the "enacting" level, the lesson must actually generate students' oral or written language (CREDE, n. d.a). In addition, there should be evidence that the teacher assisted students' language de-velopment by questioning, rephrasing, or modeling language production. Thus, these criteria reflect both a teacher's focus on language develop-ment and students' willingness to produce the language initiated by these activities.

Language generation is viewed as important for two reasons (Hilberg, Doherty, Tharp, & Estrada, n. d.). When students are engaged in extended speaking and writing, they are often using higher level cognitive pro-cesses that require more elaboration of meaning, compared to when they are just listening or responding to brief, repetitive exercises. Second, sus-tained speaking and writing provides opportunities for students to use the vocabulary of the content area they are studying and to receive feedback on their use of language in these contexts.

In an example of the Language and Literacy Development Standard enacted in the HSP, Michael Kurose, the social studies teacher, conducted a lesson on the politics of funding public education in Hawai`i. To start the discussion, Mr. Kurose asked the students to generate a list of deteriorating facilities at their school. The teacher and the students came up with a list of items that included peeling paint, large amounts of trash on the ground, graffiti, and lack of toilet tissue in the bathrooms. Mr. Kurose and the students then took turns reading an article about which schools had received funding that year for various improvements. Mr. Kurose explained that funding for Hawai`i public schools derives largely from state taxes and determined by State legislators. The legislators are supposed to allocate money to health and safety repairs before extending funds to other development. However, only 10 of the 60 projects that were funded were those that dealt with health and safety. These included an all-weather track around the University of Hawai`i's athletic field, electrical upgrading and air conditioning of two schools, and extending another school's parking lot. Most of the schools on the list were not funded.

Mr. Kurose used the article as a springboard for a class discussion of the differences in political treatment of schools based on the income level of the communities they serve. He asked students to consider why politicians will advocate for new development at some schools, while overlooking repairs needed at others. The discussion was emotional and lively. The majority of the 15 students participated in the discussion, responding to peer and teacher comments. The lesson concluded with the students writing letters to their legislators about the conditions at Wai`anae High School and calling for more consistency and clarity in the way that money is spent on public education in the State.

Applying the SPC criteria to this lesson, the Language and Literacy Development Standard would be evaluated at the enacting level because Mr. Kurose designed and implemented activities that generated sustained student speaking and writing. He also assisted student language expression by questioning students about the topic. At one point, Mr. Kurose asked the students, "Which communities are growing fastest? What happens to the Kalihis and Wai'anaes (two communities on the island that have large low income populations)? Who do you think speaks out more, those with money or those who have no more money?"

Mr. Kurose also assisted students' language development by rephrasing students' statements. For example, as a student read the article aloud, she came across the word "fiscal" and had difficulty with the pronunciation. Mr. Kurose, took the opportunity to pronounce the word correctly and then expanded on its meaning to ensure that the students understood its meaning. He explained that, "Fiscal just means financial. It just means financial terms. Every year they allow a certain amount of the money to be spent. So, when they say a fiscal year, it means a year in which they have to calculate how much money was spent during that time period."

Contextualization

Teachers contextualize instruction when they tie new information with what students already know from prior experiences in their schools, homes and communities (CREDE, n.d.d; Tharp et al., 2000). If new information is contextualized, it is better remembered and understood. When students see the relevance to what they are learning to their lives outside of the classroom, they may also be more motivated to participate. The criterion for teachers enacting this Standard at the developing level of the SPC involves their make incidental connections between students' prior knowledge and the new knowledge of the lesson (CREDE, n.d.a). Incidental connections are unplanned comments or questions to students made "on the fly" as the lesson unfolds.

An example of incidental integration of students' prior knowledge comes from Dan Forman's English class. Mr. Forman was reading a novel aloud to his class when they came across a phrase that many students did not understand. Mr. Forman tried to clarify the meaning, "What does wreaked havoc mean? Yeah, havoc is your clue. Caused turmoil. Caused confusion. Messed up. Turmoil is like when you catch a wave and you eat it and you are swimming around." This is an example of an *incidental* connection between students' prior knowledge and the academic content because Mr. Forman decided to connect the meaning of the word *havoc* to the situation of "wiping out" in surfing. As Wai'anae High School is located on a beach and surfing is a common past time of many residents in the community, many students probably could relate to this comment. It is considered incidental because Mr. Forman probably did not plan this in advance. It was something he added at the moment to help his students better understand a new concept. The connection is also *incidental* because it deals with only a relatively minor aspect of the lesson, rather than being more integral.

In order for a lesson to be rated at the enacting level of Contextualization, the teacher needs to *integrate* new information with students' prior knowledge or experiences. This might be accomplished by designing an activity that requires students to apply academic concepts to a context from their homes or communities. This is exactly what the HSP founders had in mind when they conceptualized the field component of the program. The field projects were designed to apply academic concepts to a context that was familiar to students. For example, in their science classes, students learn about the scientific method and about concepts such as *ecosystem* and *sustainability*. In the environmental field rotation, those concepts and principles are applied as students' collect and analyze data on the ecosystem of the stream environment and discuss the sustainability of native plants and animals. Likewise, HSP teachers can use knowledge of students' field experience to contextualize their classroom instruction. For example, the HSP science teacher, Erich Smith, planned a lesson that involved groups of students constructing working models of a watershed that demonstrated knowledge about the sources and paths of water. This required students to use their knowledge of the Wai'anae Valley, developed both through field work and from living in the community.

Integration of prior information into a lesson can also refer to planning activities that build upon concepts that were learned previously in the same or other classes. The teaming of HSP teachers provides opportunities for teachers to be more informed about what their colleagues are emphasizing in their curriculum. This information can then be incorporated into their own lessons, so that students recognize how concepts from the different disciplines are related. For example, in their English classes, HSP students read accounts of political and environmental activism in Hawai`i. Discussions of these readings allow their teacher, Mr. Forman, to weave in references to concepts student have learned from their social studies, science, and field instruction.

Challenging Activities

The Challenging Activities Standard refers to teachers promoting students' engagement in complex thinking (CREDE, n.d.e; Tharp et al., 2000). There are four ways that this can be accomplished. First, teachers can ask students to consider the "why" and not merely the "what" or "how to" (CREDE, n.d.a). Second, teachers can implement activities that require students' use of complex thinking processes such as generating information, elaborating, analyzing, classifying, experimenting, synthesizing or interpreting. Third, teachers can make connections between the activity or content of the lesson and a more abstract idea or concept. For example, when Mr. Forman supervises students in their native plant field work, he explains that their effort to restore of native plants to a community area involves the Hawaiian value of *mālama i ka 'aina* (caring for the land) and the scientific concept of sustainability. These connections advance students thinking to more complex levels. Finally, teachers can assist students in improving their critical thinking, problem solving, or metacognitive skills. If teachers instruct students on how to develop an outline or a concept web of their ideas in order to organize their writing, they are also assisting students in their complex thinking.

If any of the above criteria is met, a lesson would be considered at least at the developing level of the Challenging Activities standard (CREDE, n.d.e). In order for it to be considered at the enacting level, the following additional criteria also need to be present: (a) students should be aware of the standards upon which their performances will be judged, (b) students should receive feedback on their performances, and (c) the teacher should assist students in the development of complex thinking.

An example of the Challenging Activity standard implemented at the enacting level of the SPC comes from a social studies lesson in which the students were learning about the effects of imperialism in the Hawaiian Islands by examining the political, economic, and cultural changes that resulted when American businessmen overthrew the Hawaiian monarchy. Students examined arguments between imperialists and the anti-imperialists presented in different texts. Their teacher, Mr. Kurose, divided the class into three groups, and each group focused on a particular text for 20 minute before rotating to another. In one case, a group discussed the meanings inherent in two poems, one from each side of the imperialist debate. The lesson was designed to engage complex thinking in that the students were required to analyze the texts in order to interpret the messages they conveyed. Mr. Kurose also asked the students to consider the author's voice, tone, and political intentions. Complex thinking was also engaged by connecting the activities to the more abstract concept of imperialism.

There was also evidence that the lesson incorporated the other criteria needed to consider it at the enacting level of Challenging Activities (CREDE, n.d.e). The students knew the standards upon which they would be judged because Mr. Kurose gave them guidelines for what he would use to judge their interpretations (clear reasoning, reference to the text, connections to imperialism). Mr. Kurose also *assisted* students' complex thinking through questioning and by demonstrating his own interpretation of a quote from one of the poems. Finally, he provided feedback to students about their interpretations and reasoning. The following excerpt exemplifies how Mr. Kurose helps one student interpret Kippling's poem *White Man's Burden*:

Mr. Kurose: Who is the half devil, half child?
Cyrus: The White Man.
Mr. Kurose: Is it? Is he referring to the White Man? Who is he talking about?
Cyrus: No, he is referring to everybody else.

Mr. Kurose: He's referring to everybody else, right?

Cyrus: Everybody but the White people.

Mr. Kurose: So, instead of using the word, half devil, half child, what is he saying about them?

Cyrus: They are savages.

Mr. Kurose: They are savages. They are uncivilized right? So, what is he saying that we should do?

Cyrus: It is saying that they got to take care of them and teach them, yeah?

Mr. Kurose: Yes, that's right! So, when he says, "Take up the White Man's Burden," what is the White Man's burden?

Cyrus: Civilize all of the savages.

Instructional Conversation

The fifth CREDE Standard, Instructional Conversation (IC), applies Vygotsky's (1978) emphasis on learning through discourse (CREDE, n.d.f; Tharp et al., 2000). IC is like other conversations in that (a) all individuals are expected to participate in the discussion, (b) what one conversational partner says influences how others respond, and (c) all contributions may steer the discussion onto different paths (CREDE, n. d.f; Tharp et al., 2003). An IC is unlike other conversations in that there is a focus on a particular learning goal. In ICs, teachers ask questions to assess what students know, and use this information to guide them toward new and more sophisticated understandings. This kind of talk contrasts with that of a more recitative classroom, where teachers dominate the discourse, asking questions for which the answers are already known, and students try to guess what their teacher is thinking (Mehan, 1979).

For a classroom discussion to be rated at the developing level of Instructional Conversation on the SPC, teachers need to converse with a small group of students and to elicit student talk through questioning, listening, rephrasing, and modeling (CREDE, n.d.a). Like the requirement of a small group necessary for Joint Productive Activity, it is necessary to have a small group of students to implement an IC because a more intimate group maximizes the possibility that all students will participate and that the teacher can be responsive to students' interests and comments.

In order for a lesson to be considered to be at the enacting level of IC, (a) the teacher must also question students on their views, judgments, and rationales; (b) all students must participate in the IC; and (c) student talk should occur at a rate higher than that of the teacher (CREDE, n.d.a). In our work with the HSP, we have found that this Standard is the hardest one for teachers to enact consistently. Part of the reason for this may be that the criteria for IC at the highest level requires teachers to organize their lessons in ways that would allow them to have extended discussions with students about academic topics. In secondary classrooms, this may be a challenge because of large class sizes.

Tharp and colleagues (Tharp et al., 2000) suggest creating space and time for small group discussions by organizing the classroom into multiple centers where students work independently on academic tasks. This frees the teacher to have extended conversations with smaller groups. Whereas such a model of classroom organization may be familiar to elementary teachers, particular those working in early childhood education, many high school teachers may not be exposed to such an organizational structure and need assistance in conceptualizing how it works. Our teachers commented that planning for multiple centers can be labor intensive and requires students to be more self-regulated than when a teacher is standing by to keep them on track. HSP teachers also suggested that IC was the most difficult standard to meet because the criteria for the enacting level includes students speaking at higher rates than the teacher does. In order for this to be realized, students must be comfortable being active participants in discussions with teachers and peers, and teachers must adopt a very different discourse pattern than may be typical for them.

One place in the HSP that ICs do occur frequently and easily is in the teachers' field instruction. Part of the reason for this may be that the field instruction has been designed as a small group activity involving students and teachers. In the field, the teacher is also not necessarily the expert and the problems to be solved are "real" issues of significance to the community that engender authentic conversations about them. Perhaps being outside of the classroom helps this situation as well, as teachers and students may find that they do not as easily fall into the discourse patterns they have developed over the years for instructional interactions that involve teachers doing most of the talking and students listening.

For example, Mr. Smith and the students he supervises for the environmental science field rotation must hike for approximately 40 minutes to reach the three sites where they routinely collect data for their stream analyses. During those hikes, Mr. Smith interacts with a smaller group of students than is typical of high school instruction. The small group is made possible by dividing students into small field groups that are supervised by teachers, community members, or a combination of the two. The long hikes provide excellent opportunities for Mr. Smith to engage students in ICs about the purpose of their field work and the scientific concepts that apply.

On one of their hikes into the valley, Mr. Smith conducted an IC about the relationships between dissolved oxygen, the amount of canopy cover, and the presence of invertebrates in the stream. He questioned students about these relationships and the factors that might influence them. For example, as part of their routine data collection, one student was trying to determine the amount of algae on the underside of a rock. Mr. Smith asked him how the algae might affect the general health of the stream,"Why would it be a worse rating if you had a lot of grass? What would that tell you about stream health?" Mr. Smith connected this point to their broader discussion on dissolved oxygen, the canopy, and invertebrates. Different students contributed their ideas until the group collectively decided that different amounts of sunlight filters through to the stream, depending on the density of the canopy. The sunlight influences plant growth in the water, which in turn supports varying numbers of invertebrates.

This example can be considered an application of IC at the enacting level because the teacher designed and enacted a discussion with a clear academic goal—Mr. Smith wanted students to analyze the relationships between three variables of the stream environment (CREDE, n.d.a). He listened to what students had to say, in order to assess and assist students' understanding by building on what they already knew. In addition, Mr. Smith questioned students on their views, all students were included in the conversation, and students spoke at rates higher than their teacher.

The Cultural Nature of Teaching and Learning

The Five Standards were designed to provide teachers with guidance in designing instruction that would promote achievement of students from culturally and linguistically diverse backgrounds. Each of the Standards reflects the cultural nature of teaching and learning. Joint Productive Activity and Instructional Conversation (Standards 1 and 5) are structures that develop intersubjectivity or common understanding among teachers and students. When teachers and students come from different cultural communities, they may start the school year with little in common. IC and other forms of JPA help to or build common experiences that become the basis of assisted performance and concept development.

Emphasizing language and literacy across the curriculum and complex thinking (Standards 2 and 4) are vehicles for students' acculturation into particular disciplinary communities. In order for students to learn science, they need to use the language of science, to engage in scientific thinking, and to receive assistance for these performances. This perspective views disciplines such as science and mathematics as cultural entities themselves, that include specific language, values, and ways of thinking.

Finally, Standard 3, *Contextualization*, highlights the importance of culturally relevant instruction by emphasizing the importance of connections between what is being learned and what students already know. Teachers can contextualize instruction by linking new information with students' prior knowledge both incidentally and through more "integrated" and planned actions. Contextualization can also be achieved by teaching in ways that are consistent with the interaction patterns found in students' homes and communities.

CONCLUSION

In this chapter, we described the Five Standards for Effective Pedagogy, principles for effective instruction that developed from sociocultural theory and research on how to best educate students from diverse cultural and linguistic backgrounds. We also presented how the Five Standards have been applied in the HSP, a culturally relevant program designed to improve education for students from a predominantly Native Hawaiian community. The Five Standards provide a framework for our work in assisting HSP teachers' instruction. They fit well with the teachers' and our beliefs that learning is situated and that positive outcomes can be fostered by presenting academic concepts within a context of what is familiar and comfortable to students. The Five Standards also provide a structure by which teachers can capitalize on what students do know and are familiar with to promote extensions to new ideas and more complex ways of thinking.

The design of the HSP—the use of weekly community based field work, teaming, and the integration of cultural values and knowledge—lends itself well to the Standards of Joint Productive Activity and Contextualization (Yamauchi, 2003). The other Standards, Language and Literacy Development, Challenging Activities, and Instructional Conversation, are also compatible with the program, but appear to require more deliberate planning and reflection in order for them to be consistently enacted. Over the last three years, we have implemented professional development activities for the teachers focused on the Five Standards. In these sessions, teachers meet regularly with a university facilitator to discuss the planning and implementation of the Standards. The first year of professional development focused on teachers learning about the Five Standards and conducting a baseline of teachers' enactment of the principles in classroom and field instruction. Later sessions focused on how to enhance implementation of the Standards.

In these more recent professional development sessions, teachers watch excerpts of each other's videotaped instruction both in the classroom and in the field and rate these lessons using the Standards Performance

Continuum. The group also reads articles about the Five Standards and related approaches (e.g., applying constructivism to one's classroom), seeking to further their understanding about how to implement these principles and why they are important. The approach to professional development also attempts to model enactment the Five Standards. Collaborative activities are planned for the teachers and facilitators to work together in coming to an understanding of the level at which the Standards were enacted (Joint Productive Activity). The facilitator plans activities to generate and assist the teachers' language expression and development (Language and Literacy Development). The activity integrates what teachers know about the Five Standards and their past teaching experiences (Contextualization). Teachers are required to analyze how the Standards are enacted in their lessons and also receive feedback about their performance from the group (Challenging Activities). Finally, the main activity of the sessions is a small group discussion about the Five Standards, where participants' views and rationales are questioned, there is a high level of participation, and "student" talk often occurs at higher rates than that of the facilitator's (Instructional Conversation).

The HSP teachers have suggested that the Five Standards substitute for Effective Pedagogy is a useful framework for their continued efforts to improve their instruction. After two years of professional development framed from this point of view, the teachers still felt that continuing to focus on the Five Standards would enhance their pedagogy because the Standards are complex and can be implemented in many different ways. We also note that the Five Standards can be useful to more novice educators in that they highlight important aspects of teaching that make a difference in student learning. This can be helpful because novice teachers are often overwhelmed by the details of teaching and are often unable to discern the most important things to focus on (Berliner, 1992). In the same way that the Five Standards are appropriate for all students' learning, not just those from diverse backgrounds, they provide a framework for all teachers to reflect on and improve their instructional practice.

REFERENCES

Berliner, D. C. (1992). The nature of expertise in teaching. In F. K. Oser, A. Dick, & J. L. Patry (Eds.), *Effective and responsible teaching: The new synthesis* (pp. 227–248). San Francisco, CA: Jossey-Bass.

Black, S. (2000). Together again: The practice of looping keeps students with the same teachers. *American School Board Journal, 18*(6):40–43.

Carroll, J. (1999). Final Report of the Field Initiated Studies Grant. Wai'anae High School Hawaiian Studies Center: Culturally Relevant Contextualized Education. Author, Honolulu, HI.

Ceppi, A. K. (2000). *Examining a culturally relevant, community based, secondary education program: The Wai'anae High School Hawaiian Studies Program.* University of Hawai`i, Honolulu, HI (Unpublished Dissertation).

Cohen, E. G. and Lotan, R. A. (1997). *Working for equity in heterogeneous classrooms: Sociological theory in practice.* New York: Teachers College Press.

CREDE (n.d.a). Standards performance continuum: A rubric for observing classroom enactments of CREDE's Standards for Effective Pedagogy. (Available from the Center for Research on Education, Diversity, and Excellence, 1156 High Street, Santa Cruz, CA 95064).

CREDE (n.d.b). Joint Productive Activity, University of California, Center for Research on Education, Diversity, and Excellence, (November 15, 2003); http://www.crede.ucsc.edu/standards/1jpa.shtml

CREDE (n.d.c). Developing language across the curriculum University of California, Center for Research on Education, Diversity, and Excellence, (November 15, 2003); http://www.crede.ucsc.edu/standards/2ld.shtml

CREDE (n.d.d). Contextualization, University of California, Center for Research on Education, Diversity, and Excellence, (November 15, 2003); http://www.crede.ucsc.edu/standards/3cont.shtml

CREDE (n.d.e). Teaching complex thinking: Challenge students toward cognitive complexity, University of California, Center for Research on Education, Diversity, and Excellence, (November 15, 2003); http://www.crede.ucsc.edu/standards/4chal_act.shtml

CREDE (n.d.f). Teaching through conversation: Engage students through dialogue, especially the Instructional Conversation, University of California, Center for Research on Education, Diversity, and Excellence (November 15, 2003); http://www.crede.ucsc.edu/standards/5inst_con.shtml

Hawai`i State Department of Education, 2002a, Wai'anae High School School Status and Improvement Report, Fall 2002, Hawai`i State Department of Education (July 31, 2003); arch.k12.hi.us/school/ssir/2002/leeward.html

Hawai`i State Department of Education, 2002b, Enrollment 2002–2003, Hawai`i State Department of Education (July 31, 2003); arch.k12.hi.us/school/ssir/2002/leeward.html

Hawai`i State Department of Education, 2003, 2002–03 Official Enrollment—School-by-School/Grade-by-Grade, Hawai`i State Department of Education (July 31, 2003); arch.k12.hi.us/school/ssir/2002/leeward.html

Hawaiian Studies Program (1997). Mission statement. Author, Honolulu, HI.

Hilberg, R. S., Doherty, R. W., Tharp, R. G., and Estrada, P. (n. d.). Standards Performance continuum manual for classroom observation. (Available from the Center for Research on Education, Diversity, and Excellence, 1156 High Street, Santa Cruz, CA 95064).

Kana`iaupuni, S. M., and Ishibashi, K. (2003). Left behind? The status of Hawaiian students in Hawai`i public schools. (PASE Report No. 02.03.13). Kamehameha Schools, Honolulu, HI, (June 2003).

Little, T. S., and Dacus. N. B. (1999). Looping: Moving up with the class. *Educational Leadership* 57(1):42–45.

Mehan, H. (1979). "What time is it, Denise?": Asking known information questions in classroom discourse. *Theory into Practice.* 18:285–294.

Morrison, D., 2002, Classroom management linked to lesser teen alienation from school, University of Minnesota, Center for Adolescent Health and Development (July 31, 2003); http://www.eurekalert.org/pub_releases/2002-04

Office of Hawaiian Affairs (1994). The Native Hawaiian Data Book. Author, Honolulu, HI.

Raywid, M. A. (1999). Current literature on small schools. ERIC Digest. Charleston, WV: ERIC Clearinghouse of Rural Education and Small Schools (ERIC Document Reproduction Service No. ED 425 049).

RMC (2002). CREDE evaluation report: Waianae High School. Author, Denver, CO.

Takenaka, C. (1995). *A perspective on Hawaiians*. A report to the Hawai`i Community Foundation. Hawai`i Community Foundation, Honolulu, HI.

Tharp, R. G. (1989). Psychocultural variables and constraints: Effects on teaching and learning in schools. *American Psychologist* 44:349–359.

Tharp, R. G., 1999, Effective teaching: How the Standards come to be. University of California, Center for Research on Education, Diversity, and Excellence (November 15, 2003); http://www.crede.ucsc.edu/standards/development.shtml

Tharp, R. G., Estrada, P., Dalton, S., and Yamauchi, L. A. (2000). *Teaching transformed: Achieving excellence, fairness, inclusion, and harmony*. Westview, Boulder, CO.

Trimble, S. B., and Miller, J. W. (1998). Principals' and teachers' perceptions of the work of teaming teachers in restructured middle schools. *Research in Middle Level Education Quarterly* 21:1–13.

University of Hawai`i Institutional Research Office (2002). Enrollment of Hawaiian Students, University of Hawai`i at Mānoa Fall 2001. Author, Honolulu, HI.

Vygotsky, L. S. (1978). *Mind in society: The development of higher psychological processes*. Harvard University Press, Cambridge, MA.

Yamauchi, L. A. (2003). Making school relevant for at-risk students: The Wai'anae High School Hawaiian Studies Program. *Journal of Education for Students Placed at Risk*. 8:379–390.

AUTHOR NOTE

We wish to thank the Hawaiian Studies Program teachers, Dan Forman, Linda Gallano, Mike Kurose, and Erich Smith, for their assistance and commitment to our study of their instruction. We also acknowledge the participation and support of HSP students and community partners. We are grateful to Barbara DeBaryshe, Ernestine Enomoto, and Tracy Trevorrow for feedback on earlier drafts of this paper and to Valerie Dutdut for technical assistance. This research was supported under the Education Research and Development Program, PR/Award R306A6001, the Center for Research on Education, Diversity & Excellence (CREDE), as administered by the Office of Education Research and Improvement (OERI), National Institute on the Education of At-Risk Students (NIEARS), U.S. Department of Education (USDoE). The contents, findings, and opinions expressed here are those of the author and do not necessarily represent the positions or policies of OERI, NIEARS, or the USDoE.

Correspondence concerning this chapter should be addressed to Lois A. Yamauchi, Department of Educational Psychology, University of Hawai`i, 1776 University Avenue, Honolulu, HI 96822. Phone: (808) 956-4294. Email may be sent via Internet to yamauchi@hawaii.edu.

Chapter 10

Aligning Practice to Theory
Attitudes of Students in Re-cultured and Comprehensive High Schools

Nina K. Buchanan

Charlie, Ryan, and Mike are busy building a rock wall at the agriculture nursery. Next to a row of fish tanks, a community resource specialist is showing Amy, Sarah, Parker, Willie, and Robbie how to make a siphon. Rhodell, Ron, and a community mentor are installing PVC pipe for a small pond that will be used to recycle water from the reef tank. Meanwhile, Jackie, Cat, Angela, Kathleen, and Ashton are patching the holes in a V tank in which they will grow exotic guppies to sell to local pet shops. Jenny and Nate build a framework for their greenhouse project.

Later that day, the configurations have changed. Toni, Ryan, Willie, Ashton, Ron, and Amy of the landscape module meet with their teacher/advisor while Ian and Parker, members of the Technology/Computer module, update the school web site. . Rhodell sits apart from the working groups on an electric vehicle and organizes his folder. Robbie and Jason leave campus to attend Student Senate at the local public high school. Other students sit quietly at the picnic table writing while Sara purchases popcorn at the student run store from Toni. Erin and Amanda are at the bone yard searching for material to use for their coldwater agriculture beds. Still at it, Jenny and Nate continue their work on their greenhouse. Kathleen talks with a teacher about a personal problem while Liz and Sarah chat nearby. David, Jeff, Josh, and Cat check out tools to other students and organize the tool room.

These adolescents are attending a re-cultured high school, the West Hawai`i Explorations Academy (WHEA). As students, they have an opportunity to learn through hands-on projects guided by teachers and community mentors in classrooms without walls, bells or traditional discipline-based 50-minute classes. Over the past six years teachers, students, community mentors and faculty members from the local university have developed and implemented an integrative curriculum in a non traditional context, organized by function, not academic subjects. In this chapter, I describe this unique learning context, discuss the theoretical background upon which the school is built, and compare school experiences and attitudes of WHEA students to those of students at the local traditional high school to which they would have gone had WHEA not been created.

THE WEST HAWAII EXPLORATIONS ACADEMY CONTEXT

WHEA began as a major re-culturing effort initiated by an award winning physics teacher in 1993 and partially funded by the National Science Foundation to create an alternative to the traditional high school curriculum and structure with particular emphasis on science. The school is located on the site of the Natural Energy Laboratory of Hawai`i (NELH), established in 1974 by the Hawai`i State legislature to promote alternative energy development. The Laboratory promotes scientific research and commercial operations by providing land, surface and deep cold seawater, scientific and technical staff, and machinery and infrastructure. The Academy is situated on 5 acres at NELH and utilizes the facilities and expertise of the scientists at the Lab.

The mission of WHEA is to provide an integrative curriculum that addresses individual, community, and global concerns. To pursue this mission, the staff is committed to creating an environment that will: motivate and challenge students, encourage participatory decision making, provide connections with the community by integrating knowledge and skills in real-life, hands-on experiences, maintain an effective learning environment for students from diverse backgrounds, foster life-long learning, and provide opportunities for personal growth.

WHEA was initially designed to be a school-within-a-school, part of a 1500 student, traditional comprehensive high school[1]. Tenth- through twelfth-grade students who were registered at the high school had an opportunity to apply to the Academy. If accepted, they attended full time for a minimum of one academic year. At the conclusion of their first year, students could apply to be part of a leadership team for a second and, in some

---

[1] After charter school enabling legislation was passed, WHEA in the 2000/2001 school year became one of the first New Century Charter Schools in Hawai`i and expanded to include students in grades 8–12.

cases a third year. If successful, students at WHEA received seven credits toward graduation for each year at WHEA. Because more students applied than could attend, attempts were made to select a heterogeneous mix of approximately 80–120 students per school year with preference given to 12th graders. The goal was to have an ethnically diverse population as well as students of various ability levels including special education and gifted/talented students.

Learning opportunities at the Academy are constructivistic. Students are not given a science textbook but, by engaging in self-selected projects, are able to construct knowledge inductively through active inquiry. Learning is also situative in nature as students experience science in the context of the Natural Energy Laboratory scientific community. Learning at WHEA is guided by the belief that powerful, personally meaningful learning occurs in an environment where integrative curriculum meets individual, community, and global concerns (Greeno, 1997; Lave & Wenger, 1991). Unlike interdisciplinary programs, the Academy curriculum strives to be fully integrative. According to Beane (1997), integrative curricula require that: projects are real or lead to real results, be significant as defined by the student, and transcend traditional academic disciplines; workplace/worksites are community based; and students are empowered to take risks, succeed or fail, and produce knowledge, not merely reproduce it. Students read, write, calculate and apply scientific, environmental and business concepts in context as they plan, construct and implement projects. The role of teachers and mentors is not to plan lessons and tell students what they should learn but, instead, to continually challenge students to develop their individual talents and grow personally through self-directed and cooperative learning activities as well as through small group and individual advice and council. Adults from the NELH and the local community are actively involved as mentors for specific projects; guest presenters share their work or research and challenge students to design projects in a variety of areas.

THEORETICAL FRAMEWORK

Comprehensive high schools, modeled after turn of the century factories, have changed little since the late 19th century (Wraga, 1998). However, they are becoming larger and larger as the school population grows and districts consolidate (Angus, 1999; McQuillan, 1997; Noddings, 1995; & Teeter, 1997). Consequently, more students are becoming less involved in school activities, are absent more, and experience alienation leading to increased probability of dropping out (Garbarino, 1978; Gregory & Smith,

1987; Lindsay, 1982; Oxley, 1994; Pittman & Haughwout, 1987). National reports such as "What Work Requires of Schools" (Secretary's Commission on Achieving Necessary Skills (SCANS), 1991), "High Schools of the Millennium" (American Youth Policy Forum (AYPF), 2000) and "The Lost Opportunity of Senior Year" (National Commission on the High School Senior Year (NCHSSY), 2001) decry the failure of American high schools to meet the needs of today's adolescents, businesses and American society. High schools have become places "that stifle creativity while fostering competition, conformity, intolerance, and mean spiritedness reflected in society" (Hardy, 1999, p. 31). Students leave high school unprepared for college or the workplace (SCANS, 1991; NCHSSY, 2001). Administrators advocate humanizing America's high schools while many policy makers continue to support oversized comprehensive high schools, in part because they believe them to be efficient (Garbarino, 1978; Raywid, 1999). It is easier to "beef up" schools with add-on programs (Kelly, 2000) or to make other changes that don't fundamentally alter the traditional high school culture (Lindsay, 1982; Pittman, 1987; & Raywid, 1999). However, many educational, business and community leaders have begun to question the relevance of this model in light of massive social change (Beane, 1997; Greeno, 1997; & McQuillan, 1997).

Emerging models of adolescent development challenge conceptions of the ideal secondary school learning environment. While adolescents physically mature earlier and are targeted by advertising media that proclaim their adulthood, they are segregated in high schools from the adult world, told what they should learn and consider important, and governed by forces outside their control (Gregory & Smith, 1987). Chang (1992) describes the adolescent ethos in high school as focused on relationships with friends and measured against hallmarks of independence such as getting a driver's license, having a job, demonstrating responsibility through participation in extracurricular activities. In her year of data collection in one high school, Chang found that students lacked interest in, and motivation for, academic work and learning. This is consistent with senior year report findings that "The extent to which students have turned their backs on the school by the senior year came through strikingly in focus groups conducted for the Commission" (NCHSSY, 2001, p. 16). Motivation to achieve academically in high school does not appear to be important in today's high schools. But why?

Current models of learning suggest that motivation and the learning context can be integrated to promote the conceptual change necessary to enhance student learning (Pintrich, Marx, & Boyle, 1993). Adolescents who are focused on mastery, that is becoming increasingly competent, skilled and knowledgeable, and not their performance, how they look when compared to peers, select moderately difficult tasks, persist when they encounter difficulties, and have positive attitudes toward learning (Ames, 1992; Ames & Archer, 1988; Dweck, 1988). However, students who are concerned with gaining high ratings from others and not being last tend to select easy tasks, focus on doing better than peers, give up when they encounter difficulty and in general, have a negative attitude toward learning (Ames, 1992; Ames & Archer, 1988; Dweck, 1988).

The learning environment makes goals salient and influences which goals students are more likely to adopt. Indeed, Carol Ames (1992) identified three structures in the learning environment that exert such influence: tasks, evaluation, and authority. Ben-Ari and Eliassy (2003), building on the work of Ames, examined the effects of two different teaching strategies in promoting mastery goals and adaptive motivation. The traditional instructional strategy focuses on the teacher who selects the skill or knowledge to be learned, designs the tasks, and promotes compliance. All students using the traditional strategy engage in the same tasks. Evaluation is standardized so that all students do the same assignment or take the same test. Students are judged by comparing them to their classmates. Grades and teacher recognition are incentives and the results form a system for sorting and rating students. The teacher is the authority in the class who is responsible for the tasks, evaluations and student motivation.

Ben-Ari and Eliassy (2003) contrast this traditional frontal instructional strategy with complex instruction. Tasks in complex instruction are performed in small groups, require the use of complex thinking and skills, promote inquiry and allow for multiple correct routes to a solution. Evaluation is individualistic and focuses on learning from mistakes, encouraging self-reflection and encouraging cooperation. The authority in the complex instruction is shared with students through group processes. In addition to promoting motivation, shared authority allows students to perceive control of the learning environment, increasing task persistence and leading to higher achievement (Schunk, 1996). In the Ben-Ari and Eliassy (2003) study of 6th graders the two learning environments promoted different goal orientation and motivation.

Motivation combines with ability to predict what, and how much, students will learn. At one time, intelligence or ability was thought to be a unitary construct that could be measured by a single score. One who had more intelligence would be expected to achieve more in school and continue to be successful in college. In school, students could be sorted into like-ability groups and prepared for the future. However, newer views

of intelligence challenge the concept of general intelligence by identifying multiple intelligences (Gardner, 1983; Guilford, 1950; Sternberg, 1983).
Multiple intelligence research also has implications for school learning environments. For example, in the *Unschooled Mind*, Gardner (1991) proposes
that schools become more like museums; rich in artifacts, providing information in different ways to attract people with varying interests, allowing
attendees to select or ignore exhibits and spend time in their areas of interest. After much exploration in a museum-like school, students would be
ready to enter apprenticeships where they would work with experts on the
job to learn and practice specific skills. Finally, they would enter a formal
study in the discipline.

While most research focuses on individual student learning and motivation, educators and researchers have begun to shift their focus to situative
cognition; the study of interaction systems that include individual students
as participants in the social and cultural context of school as well as with
available materials, instructional methods, and representational systems
(Greeno, 1997). Lave and Wenger (1991) present a convincing case "that
learning is an integral and inseparable aspect of social practice" (p. 31)
and, further, that "there is no activity that is not situated" (p. 33).

Integrating the knowledge from the research on motivation, learning,
intelligence, learning environments and contexts is a challenge for practi-
tioners. Public high school leaders are faced with competing philosophies
of education which lead to different approaches to reform. Some politicians and educators advocate curriculum and accountability reform from
the national level (top down), providing prototype high standards to be
measured by standardized tests (Clinchy, 1997a; Darling-Hammond, 1997;
Rivera, 1997). Others promote improvement by recognizing the diversity
of local schools, advocating decentralized decision-making, and providing
support for collaborative, inquiry-driven curriculum and assessment (bottom up) (Clinchy, 1997a; Darling-Hammond, 1997; Rivera, 1997; Wagner,
1995). Reform efforts nationwide apply competing philosophies to new
models for school improvement (Northwest Regional Educational Laboratory, 1998).

High schools have responded slowly to these efforts (Angus, 1999).
As Leslie Siskin (1997) summarized, "... the size of the faculties and student bodies, the complex mix of differentiated programs with multiple
and sometimes competing purposes, and the deep divisions of the subject
departments confound the problems and processes of reform" (p. 605). According to the American Youth Policy Forum (2000), high schools "often
have a culture that is risk-averse, hierarchical and that discourages communication, sharing of information, empowerment of workers and students,
and innovation" (p. v).

An increasing number of educators are adopting the bottom up, decentralized route to reform. Some have begun to apply holistic, situated learning and knowledge of social contexts to the task of re-culturing high schools. According to Hannay & Ross (1997), "re-culturing involves adapting the cultural norms in schools, including how individuals interact, how priorities are established in the school, and/or conceptions of what is deemed to be the essence of secondary school education" (p. 589). Instead of adding new structures to the traditional model of a comprehensive high school, re-cultured schools begin with a fundamentally different set of assumptions about the role of the school in adolescent development and learning and the local community.

If comprehensive high schools aren't meeting student needs, then what should replace them (Raywid, 1997)? National reports and research focused on adolescent development during the high school years consistently recommend re-culturing high schools by: creating small, personalized learning communities (Ancess, 1999; AYPF, 2000; Gregory & Smith, 1987; Lange, 1998; Raywid, 1999); acknowledging and planning for students with different intelligences and ways of learning (AYPF, 2000; Costa, 1987; Gardner, 1991; NCHSSY, 2001); understanding that learning occurs in many different settings, in and out of school (AYPF, 2000; Lave & Wenger, 1991); providing complex instruction (Ben-Ari & Eliassy, 2003); immersing adolescents in the adult world through authentic, real life tasks and activities (Beane, 1997; AYPF, 2000; Gardner, 1991; SCANS, 1991); connecting adolescents to their community through volunteerism, service and work (Beane, 1997; Meier, 1997); giving students some choice and control of tasks, performance appraisal and time (Ames & Archer, 1988; Ben-Ari & Eliassy, 2003; Gardner, 1991); assessing students using multiple performance-based measures (AYPF, 2000; Gardner, 1991); and making learning competency-based, not seat time or credit-based (AYPF, 2000; NCHSSY, 2001; NECTL, 1994).

The learning environment at WHEA is designed to align practice with theory to meet the social and personal, as well as academic, needs of today's adolescents. Students at WHEA assume the authority to control their time, select team members with whom to work on a variety of short term and long-term projects and build apprenticeship/mentor relationships with adults. They explore personal interests through in-depth projects that challenge them to develop skills that blur the distinctions between disciplines.

WHEA is a working model of a re-cultured high school and an integrative approach to adolescent learning. If the curriculum is no longer organized into classes by discipline, how then can it be organized? In the next section, I describe curricular structures that provide a framework for learning at WHEA.

THE WHEA INTEGRATIVE CURRICULUM MODEL

The curriculum unfolds through three overlapping entities: strands, structures, and specific skills designed to facilitate the development of self-regulation (Figure 1). In brief, the *strands* are underlying processes and personal/social skills that are necessary in order for students to become increasingly responsible for their own learning. The primary structures that provide an organizing curriculum framework at the Academy are: *projects* which are self-selected, organized undertakings to solve a problem or to find out what works; *modules,* comprised of small groups of students doing tasks that sustain the smooth functioning of the school; and *activities,* which are short-term, skill focused sessions or one time events.

In addition, students develop *specific skills* that enable them to be successful in projects, modules and activities and engage in volunteer and paid work in the community. No distinctions are made between grade levels in this multi-aged environment. Unlike the traditional comprehensive high school, WHEA has no formal athletic program. Students are encouraged to participate in sports such as soccer, football, etc. and to take advantage of art, music and drama in the community. The content emphasis is in-depth study of areas of personal interest.

Strands

The school year begins with the introduction of strands that provide a framework for personal, social, and academic growth. These strands are time management, teamwork, ownership, mentorships, and career exploration.

For example, during the school day at WHEA, students are involved in free flowing individual and small group work; there are no bells or fixed periods of study. In this setting it is important for students to learn to manage their time wisely. Beginning with the first day of school to assist students in managing their time, the teachers create an agenda for the day; a model for time management. Throughout the first weeks of school, students are reminded that eventually they will be managing their own time; planning major tasks to accomplish. During the first half of the first quarter, teachers plan the agenda, introduce students to methods of planning and managing their time, and help students record the teacher-created agendas. As students are given responsibility for planning some of their own time, the teachers provide partially completed time management sheets. By the end of first quarter, students are responsible for planning some (an hour or two) Student-Initiated Time (SIT) during which they decide on what to work. They may focus on a project, an experiment or

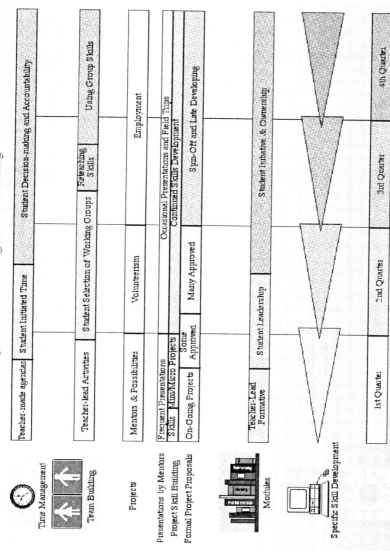

Figure 1. Schematic depiction of the interrelationship among levels of student development accross the academic year.

development of reading, writing or computer skills. Gradually, students plan more SIT time. As they become increasingly responsible for larger blocks of time, students are asked to assess the accuracy of their plan by recording what they plan to do and then what they actually accomplish. By the third quarter, time management is primarily student directed. The other strands are developed in much the same way starting with teacher modeling and progressing to student direction and control.

Structures

The integrative curriculum at the Academy is organized into three basic structures: activities, modules, and projects. At the beginning of the school year, teachers identify appropriate activities, introduce modules, and provide community mentors who challenge students to pursue a variety of projects. Students maintain flexibility and choice in the selection of and work on activities, modules, and projects.

Activities

Teachers, mentors or students can design short-term, single-focused activities. Activities support individual and group learning as well as school improvement. They might be thought of as a combination of electives and special interest clubs in a traditional high school. In general, activities are consistent with agreed upon skills and knowledge appropriate for 10th-through 12th-grade students as detailed by the *Hawai`i State Commission on Performance Standards* (1994). Initially, teachers plan the activities. For example, during one of the first weeks of school students rotate through three skill building centers in which they learn to: 1) assess water quality; 2) define chemistry terms and build scientific vocabulary; and 3) use metric measurement. These activities are designed to provide background information for upcoming projects or to enrich student experiences.

At times, as at the beginning of the year, specific activities are required. As the year progresses, students diagnose their own needs and interests. For example, students volunteer to help with short-term construction on the school site. Recently, students dug trenches and laid PVC pipe to provide sources of water for a variety of projects. Teachers offer workshops students have requested or on topics of personal interest or expertise such as electricity, astronomy and poetry writing.

Modules

In traditional high schools, there are clubs such as math, drama, and student council. In addition, students may take electives such as yearbook class that support the smooth functioning of the campus as a whole. The difference between activities and modules is that modules are ongoing for at least a year while activities are short term or one-time-only. Students at the Academy may choose to become involved in a variety of modules consistent with the WHEA context. Typical modules include: construction; fund raising; media/publications; tool room; field trips; vehicle/gold cart maintenance; landscaping; yearbook; leadership; and computers/technology.

Projects

Theoretically, projects are an ideal way to integrate content, practice teamwork, provide opportunities for students to use their learning strengths (intelligences), and make learning personally relevant. They are real inquiries, significant as defined by the student, and go beyond a single discipline to produce knowledge. Ideas for projects come from mentor presentations, Natural Energy Laboratory of Hawai`i (NELH) tenants, the community, and student initiated interest. After deciding on potential projects, students form teams and refine project ideas by conducting background research in order to decide upon a plan of action. Teams submit written plans to the staff for feedback. Preliminary plans provide the framework for discussion and include topics such as: the type of project; specific goals; team members; expected mentors and staff advisors; preliminary research conducted; parts of the project and who will be responsible for each; anticipated deadline; and how the project addresses each of the core subject areas. After a potential advisor critiques the written plan, the project team makes a formal oral presentation to the entire school and receives feedback and suggestions. Each Academy student is engaged in at least one project; most pursue two or three (simultaneously and/or sequentially) during the school year.

For example, students in the Aloha Kai Project decided to learn more about the NELH and provide tours for community groups. As they worked with their advisor and mentor, the tour was expanded to include several individual learning centers that focused on marine organisms through which local elementary and middle school students could rotate. In this project, WHEA students conducted research on marine organisms, child development and teaching. A marine biologist and several student teachers from the University mentored Aloha Kai members. During the school year, project students conducted tours and presented centers to more than 3,000 k-6th-grade students and their teachers from the Big Island, Maui, Kauai, and Oahu. Some projects such as mini-electric vehicles, solar car design and construction, reef monitoring, clown fish breeding, hydroponics and cold water agriculture are on-going. Special one-year student projects have included:

- Makaloa—The endemic Makaloa reed grows in anchialine ponds along the coast of the Hawaiian Islands. A WHEA student, with guidance from the National Biological Service, the Amy Greenwell Ethnobotanical Garden, and Bishop Museum, successfully completed phase one of a study to determine if additions of nutrients to Kailua-Kona tertiary wastewater would create variances in the length of the Makaloa reed grown.
- VOG—One student collected air quality measurements to help determine the concentrations of particulate matter in the air; these can be used to monitor VOG, or volcanic smog, emanating from the Kilauea summit. She discovered significant VOG vertical layering and was a state finalist for her presentation at the Pacific High School Science Symposium sponsored by the Hawai`i Academy of Science.
- SEMFISH—Four WHEA students initiated studies on runt fish as part of a larger effort of the Stock Enhancement of Marine Fishes in the State of Hawai`i program, a federally funded activity designed to promote aquaculture rearing, growout and release of significantly depleted near-shore fishes.

SPECIFIC SKILL DEVELOPMENT

In addition to using skills in the context of activities, modules and projects, students are expected to develop essential skills. To succeed in the workforce or at college, students need to be able to communicate effectively both orally and in writing. Each quarter students are required to complete journal entries, research papers and literary critiques designed to provide feedback to help improve their reading and writing skills. In addition, in order to promote leadership development, build self-confidence and improve oral communication, students make oral presentations to the school, their parents, and the community each quarter. These are self and teacher assessed according to agreed upon standards. While written and oral communication is important, computer literacy has also become essential. Each quarter students are asked to complete and document technology tasks that become increasingly more demanding as the year progresses. Because students are receiving credit for business education, they are responsible for specific job skills such as writing business letters, creating a resume, completing a job application and practicing job interviews.

Whenever possible, job skills are applied to obtaining paid and volunteer positions in the NELH and local businesses.

At WHEA, students have opportunities to learn basic skills while interacting closely with peers and adult mentors and teachers. The curriculum is designed to give adolescents choice and control over where to attend high school, what to study and how to use their time at school. Instead of moving from English class to Algebra and then on to Biology and American Government in response to a predetermined bell schedule, WHEA students, with teammates, plan and implement a variety of projects, participate in activities and contribute to the school by working on modules flexibly throughout a school day. Their learning is expanded into the community as they volunteer and work in the community for a minimum of 25 hours each quarter.

The theory and the practice appear to be aligned, but do students perceive the differences between what and how they learn at WHEA and what and how they learned at the traditional high school? Is there a difference between student attitudes about school and learning before and after attending WHEA? Are there differences in the way traditional comprehensive high school and WHEA students describe their school experiences? As part of systematic evaluation of WHEA, the staff designed a self-report survey to assess student attitudes.

Procedures

A 20-item survey was created to assess desired WHEA program outcomes that could not easily be measured by other means. Table 1 shows the outcomes we wanted to measure matched to the survey items created. On the first day of school at WHEA and again in May, each new and returning student completed a survey. In collaboration with the local traditional high school, we asked a sample of comparable students, who had not applied to WHEA to complete the survey at the end of the school year.

Data reported here are based upon the 1997/98 school year sample of 40 WHEA and 60 comprehensive high school (CHS) students. The openended responses were transcribed verbatim, printed and given to two independent coders who identified patterns and themes in the data. They placed each individual response into what they considered the appropriate category. The categorized data were given to two members of the WHEA staff, who made revisions where they deemed appropriate. Categories were arranged from most to least frequent for each group. Forced-choice and bipolar responses were analyzed using a chi square nonparametric test of significance.

Table 1. Survey Items Matched to Desired Program Outcomes

OUTCOME	Survey Item
Positive attitude toward school and learning	What three things did you like best about school this year? What three things did you like least about school this year? If you were trying to convince a friend that he or she should attend your school, what three important reasons would you give?
Important, powerful learning	List three things you learned in school this year that you consider VERY important.
Pride in school work	What are you most proud of doing in school this year?
Realistic self-appraisal	In school this year, as a student I am: excellent, good or fair.
Application of school skills to employment	Did you have a job during this school year? If Yes, where? Do you have prepared job resume? Do you have a job portfolio? During this year, have you had a job interview or practiced for a job interview?
Relevance/usability of knowledge learned in school	Circle the phrase that tells how frequently, outside of school, you are likely to use information and skills learned this year in school in the following subjects: math, science, English, social studies.
Choice and control of learning	Make an X on the line between TEACHER and ME that tells who has say in deciding each of the following: subjects studied, activities/projects, assignments and weekly schedule.
Ability to manage time wisely	My time management skills (how I organize my time to get things done) are: Not Good, OK, Pretty Good, Excellent.

Results

Students new to WHEA responded about the same as the comprehensive high school students on the pre survey that was administered in August and based on their experiences at the CHS. However, after attending WHEA for nine months, the new WHEA student responses matched the returning WHEA student pre and post survey results. In this section, only the responses to the WHEA post-survey (new and returning) and the CHS survey will be reported.

The first item asked students to list three things they liked about their high school this year. Table 2 compares WHEA and CHS student responses on the categories that emerged from the analysis, provides sample responses within each category, indicates the percent of responses in the

Table 2. What WHEA and CHS Students Liked Best about Their High School

Categories with Examples	CHS %	CHS Rank	WHEA %	WHEA Rank
Social/Relationships (e.g. people, meeting new friends, socializing, friendships, girls)	15	1st	10	2nd
Lunch/Recess (e.g. morning recess, lunch, recess)	13	2nd		
Specific Classes (e.g. English, Japanese, photography class, 6th period, my elective)	12	3rd		
Extra Curricular Activities/Events (e.g. senior prom, assemblies, clubs, winter ball, homecoming)	12	3rd		
Teachers (e.g. new teachers, Mrs. H., some teachers, Mr. M., cool teachers)	11	4th	5	5th
Leaving School (e.g. half days, short Wednesdays, the ending)	10	5th		
Learning Environment (e.g. education, lots of opportunities, making my own decisions, learning new things, independent learning)	6	6th	20	1st
Sports (e.g. going to state for volley ball, football)	5	7th		
School Structure/Schedule (e.g. block schedule, 4 classes a day, meetings, curriculum, starting school at 9am)	5	7th	10	2nd
Projects (e.g. Aloha Kai project, koi project, keeping my salt water tank up and running)	1	9th	20	1st
Hands-on Learning (e.g. lots of hand-on activities, hands-on work, it's all hands-on)	1	9th	20	1st
Field Trips (e.g. field trips, excursions)	2	8th	8	3rd
Physical Environment (e.g. fresh air, space, outside environment)			6	4th
Freedom (e.g. freedom, freedom from sitting down all day)	1	9th	5	5th
Other	6		4	

category and their rank order. The only category to appear among the top five on both the WHEA and CHS rank order list was Social/Relationships. Both groups liked school because it was an opportunity to socialize and interact with peers. Students used phrases such as "meeting new people," "working in groups with other people," "socializing and being with friends." CHS students (25%) cited lunch and recess, and extra curricular activities/events as things they liked best about school.

With the exception of social interaction, the other top categories for each group were quite different. WHEA students (20%) cited features of the learning environment such as "making my own decisions," "student initiated time," "actually accomplishing something," "real life learning," "independent learning," "pick what you want to learn" more often than any other feature. Only 5% of the CHS sample mentioned such things as

Table 3. What WHEA and CHS Students Liked Least bout Their High School

CHS Categories with Examples (N = 60)	CHS %	CHS Rank	WHEA %	WHEA Rank
School Structure/Schedule (e.g. schedule, having 7 classes, schedule changes, regular cleanup)	35	1st	17	3rd
Teachers/Staff General (e.g. teachers, advisors, administration, bad teachers)	11	2nd		
Specific Classes (e.g. math, guidance/health, 3rd period, Algebra, biology ll)	10	3rd		
Lunch/Recess (e.g. lunch, time for lunch)	9	4th		
Specific Assignments/Activities (e.g. tests, pep rally, yearbooks, evidence folder, research paper)	9	4th	26	1st
Physical Environment (e.g. the smoking at school, stink bathrooms, things breaking, the heat, the planes)	8	5th	21	2nd
Specific Teachers/Staff (e.g. Mr. B., Mr. M, the security person)	6	6th		
Social/Relationships (e.g. rudeness of other students, people complaining, some students' attitudes)	5	7th	15	4th
General Classes (e.g. classes, boring classes, no direct learning classes)	4	8th		
Fights (e.g. fights, people fighting)	3	9th		
Learning Environment (e.g. relaxed atmosphere, went by too fast, not able to use the computer when I need to, the opportunities)			5	5th
School Location (e.g. the drive to school, too far, long car rides from home)			5	5th
Personal (e.g. losing the electric car race)			3	6th
Nothing			3	6th

"learning," "lots of opportunity," "education." The second most numerous responses from WHEA students (20%) were descriptions of project related activities. They cited activities such as "Solar electric car," "Reef tank project," "doing tours," "clown fish project," "keeping salt water tank up and running." Only two students in the CHS group mentioned projects. While WHEA students mentioned hands-on learning and the school structure in 20% of the responses, only one CHS student mentioned hands-on activities and the only response about the school structure was about a new schedule.

There was more agreement among the WHEA and CHS students on things they liked least about their school experiences (see Table 3). Both cited the school structure/schedule and specific assignments/activities

Table 4. WHEA and CHS Students' Reasons for Attending High School

Categories with Examples	CHS %	CHS Rank	WHEA %	WHEA Rank
Social/Relationships (e.g. less fights, meet new people, racial diversity, hangout, plenty fights, like a family, not so many people)	33	1st	6	5th
Classes (e.g. easy classes, Japanese class, great band, options for classes, good classes)	21	2nd		
Teachers (e.g. better friendlier teachers, good teachers, certain teachers, Mr. M., caring teachers)	19	3rd	7	4th
Learning Environment (e.g. education, it's not as bad as people say, aloha spirit, having a say in my education, learning different things, the atmosphere)	11	4th	47	1st
Sports (e.g. good football team)	6	5th		
School Structure/Schedule (e.g. no enforcement of rules, block schedule, there are no classes, get to plan your own day, reasonable rules, projects)	5	6th	19	2nd
Personal (e.g. be self-motivated, responsibility, independence, you get out what you put in)	1	7th	11	3rd
Location (e.g. outside, it's outside on the beach)	1	7th	5	6th
Food (e.g. the food is good)	1	7th		
Freedom (e.g. more freedom)			2	7th
Hands-on (e.g. hands-on experiences)			2	7th

among their top four categories. However within the School Structure/ Schedule category, the CHS group more often referred to the schedule while the WHEA students focused on the specific aspects of their day like the opening and cleanup. WHEA students disliked specific assignments while the CHS students focused on general activities and assignments. WHEA students cited Social/Relationships as least liked in 15% of the responses while the CHS (21%) focused on their teachers and specific classes.

There was no overlap in top responses on the important reasons for attending WHEA or the CHS (see Table 4). Almost 50% of the WHEA students cited the learning environment using phrases like "I know that it works better for me than the traditional high school," "doing new things, I enjoy it," and "having a say in my education." Another 19% of the WHEA students said that the school structure was an important reason to attend. The CHS sample once again cited relationships and the social aspects of school (33%) as important reasons to attend. They also cited specific classes (21%) and teachers (19%).

Table 5. What WHEA and CHS Students Learned That was Important

Categories with Examples	CHS %	CHS Rank	WHEA %	WHEA Rank
Social/Relationships/Skills (e.g. to get along, my social skills, make plenty of friends, don't gossip, how to become a team, how to work together well)	39	1st	8	4th
Specific Subjects (e.g. Hawaiian language, lots in band, Spanish language, world history, English)	24	2nd		
Personal Skills/Understandings (e.g. Algebra is hard, apply to college early, have to attend, responsibility, maturity, independence)	22	3rd	26	2nd
Life Skills (e.g. how to use a computer, how to cook, how to find jobs, how to do business)	8	4th	2	6th
Time Management (e.g. don't do things at the last, be on time)	4	5th	4	5th
Extracurricular/Sports (e.g. weight training, the school store)	3	6th		
Project-Related Skills & Knowledge (e.g. constructing experiments, how to make a self-sustaining water tank)			35	1st
Communication Skills (e.g. how to write a paper/lab report, phone/office skills, good English)			17	3rd
Construction Skills (e.g. construction, plumbing, mechanical work, engineering skills, cement work)			8	4th

What did these high school students learn that they considered important? WHEA students reported a variety of specific skills and information learned through their projects (35%) like how to set up a hydroponics garden or do a scientific experiment; personal skills and understandings like responsibility, independence and creativeness (26%); communication (17%); and construction skills (8%) (see Table 5). While the CHS students also cited skills, the focus was once again on Social/Relationships (39%) specific subjects (15%) as well as personal (15%) and life (9%) skills in 2nd, 3rd and 4th rank.

When asked about what they were proud of doing at school, about half of the CHS students cited grades and graduating. They also mentioned extra-curricular activities (15%) and personal achievements (11%) (see Table 6). WHEA students also cite personal achievements (9%) but only mentioned grades 3 times. Instead they focused on what they did in their projects (70%) and social relationships (7%) that made them proud.

Table 6. What WHEA and CHS Students are Proud of Doing in School

Categories with Examples	CHS %	CHS Rank	WHEA %	WHEA Rank
Grades & Graduating (e.g. passing 11th grade, my grades, B+ on a U. S. history test, maintaining a 3.3 GPA, getting straight A's)	49	1st	5	4th
Extra Curricular/Sports (e.g. playing varsity football, being part of this years Volleyball team, being sophomore president)	15	2nd		
Personal (e.g. driving to school, being pretty good in band, getting into the National Honor Society, the responsibilities I have gained, accepted at the marine symposium, being the newsletter editor, having a pea named after me)	10	3rd	9	2nd
Learning (e.g. learning Japanese, learning new things, learning about science)	7	4th	5	4th
Projects (e.g. projects, making an ukulele, the Indonesia project, my ciguatera project, getting my greenhouse running, building and racing an electric car)	7	4th	70	1st
Going to School (e.g. going to classes, just going to school)	7	4th		
Social/Relationships (e.g. pulling together, making best friends, made lots of friends)	5	5th	7	3rd
Volunteer Work (e.g. making a difference in the community)			2	5th
Specific Assignments (e.g. research paper)			2	5th

Significantly more WHEA students ($\chi 2 = .609$, $p \leq .05$) report that they have jobs outside of school. But there were no significant differences in job related skills. About 60% of the WHEA students and 50% of the CHS students report that they have prepared resumes. About 20% of the students in each group reported having job portfolios. In the past year, 67% of WHEA and 58% of the CHS students report that they have had a job interview or practiced for one.

The teens in this study may have had opportunities to use the skills they learn in school outside of school, but do they make a connection between skills taught in school and those used outside of school? WHEA students report using math ($\chi 2 = 10.61$, $p \leq .05$), science ($\chi 2 = 46.4$, $p \leq .0001$) and social studies ($\chi 2 = 61.97$, $p \leq .001$) significantly more frequently did the CHS students. There were no differences in reported use of English information and skills.

Not only did WHEA students make more connections between school and work but they also reported having more say (autonomy) over the subjects they study in school ($\chi 2 = 61.97$, $p \leq .0001$), their activities/projects ($\chi 2 = 64.48$, $p \leq .0001$), assignments ($\chi 2 = 27.27$, $p \leq .0001$) and school schedule ($\chi 2 = 19.02$, $p \leq .001$) than did the comprehensive high school students. In addition, they rated themselves higher in time management skills ($\chi 2 = 12.08$, $p \leq .01$) than the CHS students. Overall when asked to rate themselves as excellent, good or fair students, there were no significant differences between the two groups.

DISCUSSION

Students at WHEA experience a re-cultured, non-traditional learning environment designed to facilitate an intrinsic motivation to learn and holistic development. They like the learning environment and school structure of WHEA and indicate that it better meets their needs than did the comprehensive high school from which they came. According to Schunk (1996), the learning environment affects students' perceptions of themselves and their place in the world, motivation to learning and what they actually learn. Key factors found to influence the learning environment are: activities and tasks; the extent to which students have choice and control over learning activities; the kinds of recognition, incentives and rewards available and attainable in the environment; social and academic groupings; methods of monitoring and assessing performance; and the way time is allocated in relationship to the workload (Epstein, 1989).

Teachers, according to CHS students, have the most say (control) over the activities and tasks in which students engage during the normal school day. They select the subjects, make the assignments, decide which projects students can do and determine the schedule for each period, quarter, and semester. CHS students mentioned learning activities and tasks in their academic classes much less frequently than they did social relationships, electives and extra curricular activities. At WHEA however, students select activities, modules and projects that match their interests and needs. Because the students make personal selections and decisions, they enter the activities and tasks with a sense of ownership and personal connection.

Adolescents are in transition, attempting to join the adult world. In order to transition successfully, they must have opportunities to be become increasingly more autonomous, make increasingly more complex choices and assume more control of their lives. It isn't surprising to discover that students at CHS like most the areas of comprehensive high school life that provide a sense of choice and control such as social time before and after class and at recess. They like best classes and activities they choose such as electives (photography, band, ceramics, etc.) and participation in extra-curricular activities and sports. In contrast, students at WHEA report that they have a great deal of say over all aspects of their school life. This is most evident in their affirmation of the WHEA learning environment, projects and hands-on activities. Students report the importance of "making my own decisions," "independent learning" and experience the satisfaction of initiating, maintaining and concluding projects. Students become empowered to control their time, activities and assignments as well as the subjects they study.

At the CHS recognition and incentives are primarily in the form of grades, external judgments of performance in relationship to others. Consequently, CHS students were most proud of grades and graduating. They did not seem to connect the academic subjects learned in school to work out of school perhaps because the reward for academic performance (grades) don't always translate easily into the world of work. WHEA students on the other hand were rewarded by the intrinsic, self-defined successes they experienced through their projects, not on external judgments of their performance. While some students at WHEA participated in the statewide Electric Car competition and the marine symposium that gave them opportunities for recognition beyond the school, the overall focus was on personal growth and the development of skills that they could use outside as well as inside school.

The social and academic groups in the CHS are often desperate. CHS students select their social groups according to mutual interest as a way to express their individuality within the safety of a group or clique. For example, many accounts of the culture of high schools identify cliques such as the jocks, brains, computer nerds, and weirdos (Katz, 2000; Tonso 2002). (See the adolescent ethos described by Chang, 1992.) In order to engage in social interaction at CHS, students use the only free time they have, lunch time, extra curricular activities and clubs. Academic classes often isolate students by grade level and discipline and control their time by the bell schedule. When teachers do use within class groups, they generally determined the group members. In contrast, academic work at WHEA is a social activity as students design and implement projects in small groups mentored by adults from the community and advised by teachers. During a typical school day, WHEA students flow into and out of modules, activities and projects often with different configurations of other students, mentors and teachers. In this context there is continual social interaction and opportunities to engage in what people in Hawai`i term "talk story" while working.

In today's educational climate of accountability and high stakes tests, assessment has become increasingly important in all schools. In the CHS, students are graded on assignments and tests. Assessment and evaluation are most often external to the students but may provide important benchmarks for students' self evaluation of their school competence. Perhaps, it is good that the CHS students don't connect what they do in school to their life out of school because students who are unsuccessful at school can still develop healthy self-concepts out of school in spite of poor grades. The emphasis at WHEA is on intrinsic motivation and a mastery goal orientation (Ames, 1992). In general, students at WHEA don't take tests but judge their own performance using agreed upon rubrics. Each WHEA student is responsible for providing evidence of what they have learned in each content area for which they ultimately receive credit. Only three of the 40 WHEA students mentioned grades. The vast majority was more proud of skills they had learned and projects in which they were involved than an external evaluation of their work.

Although school reform efforts have resulted in some variations of the traditional 6 classes of 50 minute each and of the school year, time in the CHS is mandated externally by the school board, school-community based councils or the teachers' union and then controlled internally by the bell schedule. This factory model designed for efficiency in the late 1800's continues in spite of massive societal change. At WHEA time is self-structured according to task, not allocated by subject and period. Students first learn about how agendas and daily schedules are made and then they are given increasingly more control of and accountability for planning and using time wisely.

Emphasis on external control is prevalent in large comprehensive high schools from THE bell schedule (block, year round or regular), security guards, teachers as hall monitors and additional security, lockout and attendance policies and required classes. One result of this learning environment is that students come to depend on external control and evaluation so that the CHS students in this sample were most proud of grades and graduating, not of internal, intrinsic rewards of managing their own time, completing a self-designed project or learning a new skill. The CHS students reported that the social skills they learned and the experiences they have had in extra curricular activities are really important and intrinsically satisfying. The question for educators might be, how can we re-culture high schools to promote a mastery goal orientation and use the adolescent ethos to promote academic learning?

Our society has few and ill-defined rites of passage that enable adolescents to move into adulthood. Chang (1992) cites getting a driver's license, having a job and taking responsibilities through extra curricular activities, clubs and other youth organizations. Over half of the students in this sample reported having jobs outside of school. One would expect these students who have made the transition from high school to work to be even less invested in high school academics that are disconnected from the real word. As educators engage in reforming, restructuring and re-culturing schools, it will be important to consider the total school context (Lave & Wenger, 1991) and how one becomes intelligent in a field (Gardner, 1991). Perhaps, it is time to make high schools fit today's students not vice versa.

Educational Significance, Importance, and Relevance

Survey results from WHEA and CHS students support the recommended practices from research. I believe with Gregory and Smith (1987) that, "The high school has become a fundamentally flawed institution" (p 4). Tinkering with the structure or the bell schedule or the class offerings are not enough to produce the changes needed to meet the challenges of a new millennium. At the macro level, WHEA represents a departure from traditional education toward a holistic view of adolescence and offers a curriculum model that is a viable alternative for any community. It re-connects adolescents with the community by providing hands-on experiences with support from skilled adults in the context of meaningful learning. Students become origins of their own educational goals and successes (deCharms, 1976) controlling their time, directing their talents, and acquiring skills that will enable them to enter college or the workplace prepared to work collaboratively with others, apply decision-making and problem-solving skills learned by doing, not by being told what to do.

At an individual level, WHEA has changed lives. Students formerly identified for special education services have been able to identify their strengths and be successful academically for the first time in their school career. Case studies of one special education and several at-risk students document the changes in attitude and academic achievement.

There are several limitations of this study. The sample is small and may not be representative of all levels of achievement and ability or ethnic groups. In the future, a sample matched by achievement, gender and ethnicity will be used. While the WHEA sample had an equal number of boys and girls, the gender composition of the CHS sample is unknown. WHEA may not be the optimum learning environment for every student. The staff is using information from case studies to better describe students who may benefit the most from attendance. Until more alternative models are available for study, theory should drive practice and research should continue to refine models that can work in a variety of settings.

At the Academy, students are placed in a rich environment, much like the museum type school advocated by Gardner (1991). They are gradually provided with the skills and autonomy to select areas for exploration, and assume responsibility and control of their own learning by tackling relevant challenges with the support of knowledgeable adults. Educators now have one working model upon which to build increasingly more effective re-cultured high schools.

REFERENCES

American Youth Policy Forum. (2000). *High schools of the millennium report*. Washington, DC. Available: http://www.aypf.org/subcats/erpubs.htm.

Ames, C. (1992). Classrooms: Goals, structures and student motivation. *Journal of Educational Psychology* 84, 261–271.

Ames, C. and Archer, J. (1988). Achievement goals in the classroom: Student learning strategies and motivation processes. *Journal of Educational Psychology* 80:260–267.

Ancess, J. (1999). *Organizing schools to be communities of commitment*. Paper presented at the annual meeting of the American Educational Research Association. Montreal, Canada.

Angus, D. L., and Mirel, J. E. (1999). *The failed promise of the American high school, 1890–1995*. Teachers College Press, New York.

Beane, J. A. (1997). *Curriculum integration: Designing the core of democratic education*. Teachers College Press, New York.

Ben-Ari, R. and Eliassy, L. (2003). The differential effects of learning environment on student achievement motivation: A comparison between frontal and complex instruction strategies. *Social Behavior and Personality* 31 (2):143–166.

Bernauer, J., and Cress, K. (1997). How school communities can redefine accountability assessment. *Phi Delta Kappan* 79(1):71–75.

Brice, L., and Lamb, P. (1999). Restructuring high school: Students' perceptions of CLUB. *The High School Journal* 83 (1):55–70.

Burke, D. (1996). Multi-year teacher/student relationships are a long-overdue arrangement. *Phi Delta Kappan* 77(5):360–361.

Clinchy, B. M. (1997a). The standardization of the student. In: Clinchy, E. (ed.), *Transforming public education, a new course for America's future*, Teachers College Press, New York, pp. 66–78.

Clinchy, E. (1997b). A new course charted? In: Clinchy, E. (ed.), *Transforming public education, a new course for America's future*, Teachers College Press, New York, pp. 182–189.

Chang, H. (1992). *Adolescent life and ethos: An ethnography of a US high school*. Falmer Press, Washington, DC.

Costa, A. (1987). What human beings do when they behave intelligently and how they become more so. *B.C. Journal of Special Education* 11 (3):239–49.

Darling-Hammond, L. (1997). Reframing the school reform agenda: Developing capacity for school transformation. In: Clinchy, E. (ed.), *Transforming public education, a new course for America's future*, Teachers College Press, New York, pp. 38–55.

deCharms, R. (1976). *Enhancing motivation: Changes in the classroom*. Irvington, New York.

Dweck, C. (1986). Motivational processes affecting learning. *American Psychologist* 41:1040–1048.

Epstein, J. L. (1989). Family structures and student motivation: A developmental perspective. In: Ames, C., and R. Ames, R. (eds.) *Research on motivation in education* Volume 3, Academic Press, San Diego, pp. 259–295.

Garbarino, J. (1978). The human ecology of crime: A case for small schools. In: Wenk, E. (ed.), *School crime*, National Council on Crime and Delinquency, Davis, CA, pp. 259–295.

Gardner, H. (1983). *Frames of mind: The theory of multiple intelligences*. Basic Books, New York.

Gardner, H. (1991). *The unschooled mind: How children think and how schools should teach.* Basic Books, New York.

Goals 2000: Educate America Act (H.R. 1804). (1994). Available at http://www.ed.gov/legislation/GOALS2000/TheAct/.

Greeno, J. G. (1997). On claims that answer the wrong questions. *Educational Researcher* 26 (1):5–17.

Gregory, T. B., and Smith, G. R. (1987). *High schools as communities: The small school reconsidered.* Phi Delta Kappa Educational Foundation, Bloomington, IN.

Guilford, J. P. (1950). Creativity. *American Psychologist* 5:444–454.

Hannay, L. M., and Ross, J. A. (1997). Initiating secondary school reform: The dynamic relationship between restructuring, reculturing, and retiming. *Educational Administrative Quarterly* 33 (Supplement):576–603.

Hardy, L. (1999). A cold climate. *American School Board Journal* 186 (3):31–34.

Katz, J. (2000). *Geeks: How two lost boys rode the internet out of Idaho.* Villard, New York.

Kelly, K. (2000). *Seeking a cure for senior-year slump,* Harvard Education Newsletter: Research Online. Available: http://www.edletter.org/research/senioryear.shtml.

Lange, C. M. (1998). Characteristics of alternative schools and programs serving at-risk students. *High School Journal* 81 (4):183–199.

Lave, J., and Wenger, E. (1991). *Situated learning, Legitimate peripheral participation.* Cambridge University Press, Cambridge, United Kingdom.

Lindsay, P. (1982). The effect of high school size on student participation, satisfaction and attendance. *Educational Evaluation and Policy Analysis* 4:57–65.

Liu, J. (1997). The emotional bond between teachers and students. *Phi Delta Kappan* 79 (2):156–157.

McQuillan, P. J. (1997). Humanizing the comprehensive high school: A proposal for reform. *Educational Administration Quarterly* 33(Supplement):644–682.

Meier, D. (1991). How our schools could be. In: Clinchy, E. (ed.), *Transforming public education, a new course for America's future,* Teachers College Press, New York, pp. 145–155.

National Commission on the High School Senior Year (NCHSSY) (2001) *The lost opportunity of senior year: Finding a better way. Preliminary Report.* Washington DC: U.S. Department of Education, the Carnegie Foundation of New York, the Charles Stewart Mott Foundation.

National Education Commission on Time and Learning (NCTL) (1994). *Report of the National Commission on Time and Learning.* Washington, DC: Author. Available: http://www.ed.gov/pubs/PrisonersOfTime/

Noddings, N. (1995). A morally defensible mission for schools in the 21st Century. *Phi Delta Kappan* 76 (5):365–368.

Northwest Regional Educational Laboratory and the Education Commission of the States (March, 1998). *Catalog of School Reform Models.* Available: http:www.nwrel.org/scpd/catalog/index.shtml

Oxley, D. (1994). Organizing schools into small units: Alternatives to homogeneous grouping. *Phi Delta Kappan,* 75 (7):521–530.

Oxley, D. (1997). Theory and practice of school communities. *Educational Administration Quarterly* 33 (Supplement):624–643.

Pintrich, P. R., Marx, R. W., and Boyle, R. A. (1993). Beyond cold conceptual change: The role of motivational beliefs and classroom contextual factors in the process of conceptual change. *Review of Educational Research* 63 (2):167–199.

Pittman, R., and Haughwout, P. (1987). Influence of high school size on drop out rate. *Educational Evaluation and Policy Analysis* 9:337–43.

Raywid, M. A. (1997). About replacing the comprehensive high school. *Educational Administrative Quarterly* 33 (Supplement, December):541–545.

Raywid, M. A. (1999). On the viabillity of the comprehensive high school: A reply to Professor Wraga. *Educational Administrative Quarterly* 35(2):303–310.

Rivera, J., and Poplin, M. (1997). Listening to voices on the inside: Beyond the conservative-liberal-radical debate to a common vision for schools in our multicultural society. In: Clinchy, E. (ed.), *Transforming public education, a new course for America's future*, Teachers College Press, New York, pp. 97–110.

Schunk, D. H. (1996). *Learning theories: An educational perspective* (2nd ed.) Prentice-Hall, Inc., Englewood Cliffs, NJ.

Secretary's Commission on Achieving Necessary Skills (1991). *What work requires of schools: A SCANS report for America 2000.* Department of Labor, Washington, D.C.

Siskin, L. S. (1997). The challenge of leadership in comprehensive high schools: School vision and departmental divisions. *Educational Administration Quarterly* 33(Supplement):604–623.

Sternberg, R. J. (1985). *Beyond IQ.* Cambridge University Press, New York.

Teeter, A. M. (1997). Bread and roses. In E. Clinchy (Ed.), *Transforming public education, a new course for America's future*, Teachers College Press, New York, pp. 156–169.

Tonso, K. L. (2002). Reflecting on Columbine High: Ideologies of privilege in "standardized" schools. *Educational Studies* 44 (4): 389–421.

Wagner, T. (1995). What's school really for, anyway? And who should decide? *Phi Delta Kappan* 76(5):393–398.

Wraga, W. G. (1998). The comprehensive high school and educational reform in the United States: Retrospect and prospect. *The High School Journal* 81 (3):121–134.

Zimmerman, B. J. (1998). Developing self-fulfilling cycles of academic regulation: An analysis of exemplary instructional models. In: Schunk, D. H., and Zimmerman, B. J. (eds.), *Self-regulated learning: From teaching to self-reflected practice*, The Guilford Press, New York, pp. 1–19.

Index